When a Loved One Dies

The Complete Guide to Preparing a Dignified & Meaningful Goodbye

Katherine Mariaca-Sullivan

Madaket Lane Publishers

Mariaca-Sullivan, Katherine
When a Loved One Dies: The Complete Guide to Preparing a Dignified & Meaningful Goodbye
1. Family & Relationships-Death, Grief, Bereavement
2. Self-Help
   ISBN 978-0-9832324-3-8

Printed in the United States

Cover design by Madaket Lane Publishers
Cover photograph copyright © Katherine Mariaca-Sullivan

This book is dedicated to my father, Peter Edward Mariaca,
who gave us laughter,

and to my niece, Jahmila Kyla Bertie-Mariaca,
who spread joy upon the world.

Contents

PART I:
Understanding Your Options

NOTE TO READERS

Death is not an easy subject to discuss. There are aspects of it that are unnerving, uncomfortable and even harsh. Unfortunately, death is real, and there are very real decisions that have to be made when a loved one dies. Decisions that will have lasting effects on your family, and ones that you will have to make when you are at your most vulnerable.

I have written this book to help you through a difficult time. That being said, I have chosen not to tiptoe around the difficult subjects (and there are a few). Why? Because in order to get through this time and to make the best decisions you can, you need to know what to expect. And you can only know what to expect if I am honest.

You should know – I am not a doctor, nor am I an attorney. I am not a religious counselor or a psychologist. The information I include, then, is not intended as medical, psychological, spiritual or legal advice. I am simply a person who has had to deal with the deaths of loved ones and I know how absolutely devastating that can be.

You should also know that each death is unique, families and friends have different preferences and manners of saying goodbye, and there are few "shoulds" and "should nots." At the back of the book, in the Resources section, I will include a number of checklists and worksheets that you may find helpful. Of course, they cannot contain every possible circumstance, but they should be a good starting point for you to begin your process of saying goodbye.

In this book, I will discuss the historical, practical, customary and legal (in the case of The Funeral Rule) aspects surrounding death. Some of the information may be too detailed for you at this time.

There are others, though, who feel the need to understand, no matter how grim the reality. Knowledge can help them feel that they are, in some respects, in control. At the very least, knowledge can help them make informed decisions.

I hope that this book helps you make the best decisions for your loved one, for you, for your family, and your friends.

INTRODUCTION

On Wednesday, March 30, 2011, at 12:34 a.m., a ringing phone woke me from a deep sleep. I fumbled the phone to my ear. "Hello?"

The voice on the other end of the line came across as a howl. While I'd never heard such a sound from her before, I could tell the noise came from my mother. My immediate thought was that something had happened to her husband, my step-father, Chris.

Somehow, I was standing beside the bed, the phone pressed to my ear. "Mom? Mom?"

"It's Jahmila," my mother wailed. "She's dead."

Jahmila Kyla Bertie-Mariaca was born August 16, 1992 in San Juan, Puerto Rico, just six months before my son, Derek, was born. She was a charming, lively baby, doted on by her two older sisters, Audrey and Nicole, and she would grow into a beautiful, vivacious, sweet-tempered young woman.

On March 29, at about 9 p.m., when she and her best friend were just eighteen years old and first-year college students, Jahmila and Mazelle Demeraski drove west on Southern Boulevard in West Palm Beach, Florida in Jahmila's new Toyota Camry.

That particular stretch of road is dark and lonely. It cuts, east to west, through miles of farmland and sugar cane fields. There are few stoplights, and, for miles on end, no streetlights.

The girls picked up a friend and, at about 9:25, headed back east, toward Wellington. They had the right of way. Their headlights were on. The road was straight and they could see, and be seen, for miles.

Just east of 20-Mile Bend, a 72-year-old trucker had just filled his rig with a load of lettuce and was beginning the long journey back to North Carolina. When he was finally tracked down, more than thirty miles from the crash site, he would say, "I saw the lights coming, but thought I had time."

The trucker, who had a stop sign, as well as a blinking red light, whose running lights, for whatever reason, were not turned on, pulled out in front of the Camry. The Camry skidded under the truck, behind its back left wheels. The two girls in the front seat did not make it. Their friend in the back seat did, albeit with injuries. Thus began the worst period of my and my family's lives.

DEATH IN AMERICA

Unlike other societies, Americans are not well-prepared for death, especially sudden, unexpected death. In other societies, death is accepted as the natural conclusion to life, as the completion of the cycle of life. As such, when it comes, the people that it affects naturally begin its rites and rituals. That is not to say they are not immensely saddened by their loss, but that they know what needs to be done.

Americans, on the other hand, seem forever surprised by death, even by death that comes after a long illness. We fight tooth and nail to avoid it, to prolong life, even by artificial means, even if it will bankrupt our children while adding only a day or so to our human existence.

Further, we avoid talking about death. We don't say, "So-and-so died." Instead, we gloss over death by saying that someone "passed away" or "went to heaven" or "moved on."

By not openly accepting the inevitability of death, we Americans are often shocked and confused when confronted with the death of a loved one. We don't know what needs to get done, much less how to get it done.

In 1997, when my father died of pancreatic cancer at the age of 58, I was first introduced to the process of planning a funeral and saying goodbye to a loved one. You would think that even though his illness was relatively long and the outcome inevitable, we would have been prepared. You would think that the viewing and funeral and cremation would flow gently, that we would have had music picked out and farewells written and an "in lieu of flowers" decided upon.

You would have been wrong.

Even knowing that those with Stage 4 pancreatic cancer rarely last months, we were in denial. Even when the doctors told us there was nothing else they could do for my father and he was admitted to hospice, we held out hope. Even when he slipped into his final coma, we waited for him to wake up.

To many Americans, it seems macabre to prepare for death while a loved one is still alive. I know that for me, in my father's case, accepting his death while he struggled to maintain life would have seemed sacrilegious. I would have felt as if my acceptance somehow hurried the process along. For that reason, I maintained a steady stance of denial.

When my grandfather died, years earlier, in Bolivia, my mother and aunt prepared his body for burial. They washed him and dressed him and laid him out for the viewing. It was more than a practical matter in a country where bodies are not whisked away by unknown funeral home employees, it was a loving gesture by two women who deeply cared about the man they were attending. The time with his body allowed them to express that love, and forced them to accept that yes, he really had died.

When my father died, on the other hand, in a Florida hospital on a muggy November day, his body was hurriedly covered with a sheet by the nursing staff and he was rushed away, and only returned to us days later, a cold, unnatural shell, coifed and made up and dressed in a suit, laid out in a rented casket.

While my father's "earthly remains" were attended to by people unknown to us, or to him, my mother, sister, brother and I were presented with a bewildering array of details that had to be addressed. Cremation or burial? Religious service or not? Open casket or closed?

Friends, relatives and business acquaintances had to be notified. Money had to be found (as my parent's bank accounts were frozen until all the details of his Will could be worked out). Clothes had to be picked out, music had to be chosen, a service had to be prepared. Meanwhile, friends and relatives were flying in and rooms had to be found for them, as well as food to feed so many.

The irony of losing a loved one is this: so much has to be done, so many details attended to, that even on our best days, important details can be overlooked. When a loved one dies, however, it is never our best days. It always happens on our worst days, when we are at our most vulnerable, when we are the least capable of making important, wise decisions.

This book is meant as a guide to help you through this terrible time. While it can never lessen your loss, it is meant to help you understand the decisions you will have to make, and to ensure that your goodbye is both meaningful and dignified.

END-OF-LIFE CARE

I **will** start out by recognizing that speaking about death with someone who is dying or who is likely to die sooner rather than later, as in the case of extreme illness or advanced age, is difficult. It may be the most difficult conversation you ever engage in. As difficult as it is, however, it may also be the most important.

There are a number of end-of-life decisions that can be made to ensure that the ill or aging person's wishes are followed. These include:

- Whether to resuscitate or not

- What, if any, life-prolonging measures should be taken

- Whether last rites or other religious services are desired

- Whether organ and/or tissue donation is desired

- Whether the body should be cremated or buried

- The type of funeral/memorial to be held

In the best case scenario, your loved one will have already thought through these issues and will have prepared Advance Directives.

Advance Directives are written instructions that indicate how a person wants to be cared for when he is unable to speak for himself, is dying, or is likely to die. Advance Directives include a Living Will and a Durable Power of Attorney for Health Care.

A Living Will sets out the care a dying person wants and does not want. For instance, it might indicate that life-prolonging measures are not to be taken, or that only pain medication is to be administered.

When a patient enters a hospital, and he or she is conscious, the hospital staff will often ask if she has a Living Will and, if possible, will request a copy of it.

A living will can also indicate who the patient would like to make decisions on her behalf if she is unable to do so. That person, called a health care surrogate, representative, agent, attorney-in-fact, or proxy, is entrusted to evaluate and make decisions on the patient's behalf. A major benefit of declaring a proxy is that the dying person can be sure that someone with the same or similar beliefs will be acting on her behalf. The other major benefit is that the end-of-life does not follow a steady journey. A proxy can make decisions and change plans as necessitated by unfolding events.

As a note of caution, if you have been asked to act as health care proxy or surrogate for a loved one, it is always a good idea for that person to have a Durable Power of Attorney for Health Care written, especially if you are not related.

A Durable Power of Attorney for Health Care is a legal document. End-of-life can be a very traumatic experience for family and friends, and not everyone may have the same ideas about how a dying person should be cared for. A notarized Health Care Power of Attorney makes it clear to the medical staff who should be making *health care* (not legal or financial) decisions on the patient's behalf.

If you have been asked to be a health care proxy, make sure you have a copy of the document with you when you go to the hospital or medical facility. Medical decisions often need to be made immediately and you may not have time to return home or to your office to look for the document.

Please know that rules and regulations differ from state to state. If there is time, what-if's should be discussed with an attorney before a Durable Power of Attorney for Health Care is ever needed. In the best case scenario, you and your loved one will have discussed the what-if's in depth and will have met with an attorney together to have the papers drawn up and executed.

There are instances when neither a Living Will nor a Durable Power of Attorney for Health Care has been created. There are also cases where the documents exist but no one knows about them or can find them. Again, regulations vary from state to state and you should familiarize yourself with your state's laws.

If you do not know your state's laws and are confronted with a situation in which a loved one is hospitalized, at the very least, take copies of important documents with you to the hospital. Documents that might come in handy include:

- A marriage certificate if it is your spouse who is injured or dying

- A birth certificate if your child is the patient

- Your own legal identification

The whole point in having proper documentation is to ensure that the patient is provided with the type of care that he/she would want. When she cannot speak for herself, the medical practitioners will have to do what they think is *medically* best unless or until someone can prove that he is legally entitled to make decisions on the patient's behalf.

There are some instances when it seems obvious who can speak on the patient's behalf. Parents, for instance, can usually make decisions on behalf of their underage children. Be sure that you understand when a child is considered of age in your state, however, as in some states, parents are no longer legally allowed to make medical decisions for a child who has reached the age of eighteen.

Marriage does not necessarily make you the legal health care representative for your spouse, either. Or being the child of an elderly parent.

If you have no legal documentation indicating the patient's wishes, you may be confronted with differences of opinion, either between family members, or between family members and medical staff.

End-of-life care disagreements between family members can cause long-lasting rifts. If the family cannot agree on care, it is possible that an outside source can help make the decisions easier.

A family friend who is familiar with the dying person's ideas and opinions may be able to help. A religious counselor who can give insight into the dying person's religion's point of view may offer a new/different perspective. Discussions with doctors may sway the conflict one way or another. In very severe debates, a mediator can be called in.

Mediators are impartial outside negotiators whose one objective is fair resolution of disputes. You can ask the health care facility where your loved one is being cared for if they have an on-site mediator, or if they can recommend one. You will find links to the <u>Association for Conflict Resolution</u> in the resource section of this book.

Disagreements between family members and medical caregivers can also cause problems, and can even have legal repercussions. Doctors are just as human as the rest of us and they can bring to the table opinions and ideas that are inconsistent with those you know your loved one to have had. A doctor may believe, for instance, that prolonging life through artificial means is not medically advantageous. You, on the other hand, may wish that all means be used.

While you may not be able to avoid disagreements about the best and proper care of your loved one, do not forget that you can always ask for a second, or even a third, medical opinion.

When my father was dying, for instance, he regularly had to have liquid removed from his lungs to keep him from drowning in his own fluids. My father was conscious at the time and I was with him on the day that his doctor told him that removing the liquid would do him no good. That made no sense, either to my father or to me. Keeping him from drowning was a pretty good reason to continue removing the fluid, as far as we were concerned. We asked for a second opinion.

It turned out that removing the fluid would not help my father *medically* as his disease had progressed so far that he only had days to live. So, in that case, the first doctor was correct. On the other hand, removing the liquid from his lungs would make my father more comfortable as he went through his last days. The liquid was removed.

In our case, getting a second opinion helped us understand what his first doctor was really trying to say – that my father would die soon regardless and that instead of fighting a losing battle, he might be better off accepting the inevitable and saying his goodbyes.

Whether it is simply to help you to better understand the medical ramifications of your decisions, or if there is a real disagreement over the type of care that should be given, or simply as a means to search for new options, ask for and insist upon a second medical opinion if it will help you.

Alternately, you can contact an organization such as the <u>Society for Critical Care Medicine</u>, which may be able to answer your questions. Their contact information can be found in the Resource section of this book.

When your loved one is ill and/or dying, his doctors may recommend palliative care. Palliative care is care that makes your loved one more comfortable and which seeks to improve his quality of life. It is a life-affirming, multi-disciplinary approach that can include medical, spiritual, physical and/or emotional care aspects. It is important to understand, however, that palliative care is meant to relieve the *symptoms* of a disease or condition without actually curing it. Palliative care is appropriate in all stages of illness, and it can include pain management, nutritional support, help with shortness of breath, nausea, and/or other symptoms. It can be offered in conjunction with medical treatment or along with hospice care.

Hospice care can include palliative measures, such as pain management, but generally refers to situations in which the patient is expected to live less than six months. If your loved one is dying from a terminal illness, which is an active and worsening condition that cannot be cured, and which will likely result in death, her doctors may recommend that your loved one enter hospice.

It is important to understand that there are different conditions under which hospice services are offered depending upon where your loved one lives. In Florida, for instance, my father entered an inpatient hospice facility located within a hospital. In New Hampshire, where I am certified as a hospice volunteer, the services are more likely to be provided at the patient's home by visiting nurses or in a freestanding hospice facility.

Generally speaking, hospice services include palliative care in the form of supplying, at the least, nutrition and pain management. Non-palliative, *medical* care ceases. If your loved one is dying from cancer, for instance, he will no longer receive chemotherapy or radiation treatment while in hospice. The point of hospice is to provide comfort to the patient. An ancillary benefit of hospice is that it allows the dying person and his loved ones to begin the process of acceptance and to say their goodbyes.

As part of the entering hospice process, your loved one (or you, if you are making decisions on his behalf), may be requested to sign a Do Not Resuscitate (DNR) order. This document informs all caregivers that, should your loved one's heart or lungs stop, CPR (cardiopulmonary resuscitation) is not to be given. While no laws govern or mandate the DNR provision as part of entering hospice, some facilities require it. If your loved one wants to be resuscitated should it be necessary to prolong life, then be sure this is not a requirement of the facility you are considering for him.

Again, whenever possible, have all the legal documents necessary for your state (or country) in place before they are needed. When that is not possible, take as many relevant documents with you as you can. You can find a list of End-of-Life Documents you may need at the back of this book.

THE DYING PROCESS

While each death is unique and we all die from different causes, there is a process that, when you know what to look for, will help you understand what your loved one is experiencing. Knowing the stage your loved one is in can help you to prepare yourself and your family, and to help your loved one gently through this sometimes difficult journey.

It should be understood, of course, that this process applies to those who die after a long life, whose life is winding down, and to those who are near the end stages after an illness. Accident victims, those who die suddenly from a traumatic event, and others whose deaths are abrupt, will not experience this "process." Further, not everyone will experience all of these milestones along the way, nor will everyone meet them in this order or at the estimated times.

In the last month to several months prior to death, your loved one will begin experiencing physical and emotional changes. Physically, she may begin to tire more easily and to want to sleep more. She won't want to participate in activities she once enjoyed and she may prefer to spend her time quietly and, often, alone. Her appetite may begin to decline and she won't want to eat as often or as much.

Generally, this is not a reason for concern, as her body is slowing down and so does not need as much nourishment. If you are worried, however, of course contact her physician.

If your loved one is aware that she is dying, this may be a time when she begins to grapple with her mortality. She may revisit times in her life, and question whether she lived her life well and to the fullest.

She may become irritable or even angry. While the anger is really directed against Fate, you may feel as if it is directed toward you or to others you know she cares about. Reprimanding her, arguing with her, or becoming angry yourself will not help the matter. Rather, this is a time for understanding, as difficult as it may be to supply in the moment.

In the last weeks of life, your loved one may begin to sleep most of the time. When awake, she may appear disoriented, or may converse with people who are not in the room. She may hallucinate and see friends and family members who have died before her.

Whether you believe that there is an afterlife and she is on its doorstep conversing with those who have already made the journey or not, do not worry at this seemingly odd behavior. Believing that she will soon be reunited with loved ones of her own can be a great comfort to the dying.

When she is awake, she may not care to participate in day-to-day events. Making decisions, attending to chores, and even participating in conversations begins to lose interest for her. She is turning inward as she realizes that the physical world will not be hers much longer and her wide world view is narrowing.

As her body begins to shut down, you may notice physical changes that can include:

- A lowering of blood pressure

- Her skin may feel cold as her blood pressure drops

- Likewise, she may become pale

- Her lips and nail beds may take on a bluish tinge (again as a result of lower blood pressure)

- The skin of her hands and feet may become mottled and look bruised

- Her breathing may become irregular and it may be difficult for her to take a full breath

- Her lungs may become congested and you may hear a rattling sound as she breathes

To help her through this time, you might attempt to adjust her position. Propping her up may help the fluids to drain and may make breathing easier. Adding a blanket or two may help keep her warn. Be careful not to put too many blankets on her, however, as this may weigh her down and make breathing even more difficult. Do not use an electric blanket as her skin is fragile and you can easily burn her.

During the last days, you may find that your loved one seems to recover her energy, albeit for a short amount of time. She may become hungry and thirsty after days of not eating. She may even want to talk with loved ones and, seemingly, to take an interest in life again. This last gathering of strength should not be mistaken as your loved one returning to life. Somehow, the body knows what is happening and often gifts people one with the opportunity to spend one last meaningful time with loved ones.

In the last hours of life, your loved one will most likely lose consciousness. Her brain will be receiving less oxygen and, physically, her system will be shutting down. You may hear her mumbling in her sleep and she may even sound agitated, but chances are that she is not in pain.

While she seems to be fully unconscious at this time, some of her senses may still be working. It is thought that the dying still have the ability to hear and to process meaning. Avoid speaking of anything in your loved one's presence which may agitate or upset her. Instead, speak to her in a calm and loving voice. She is dying now and your last message should be a comforting one.

While you may want her to stay, while you may desperately want her to spend more time in this life, please understand that one of the most important expressions of love you can give her at this time is to reassure her that those she is leaving behind will be fine and that it is OK for her to move on.

As I've said, I am not a doctor. I cannot give you medical or scientific facts to support my belief that it is important that you help your loved one to move on. Even when it is the very last thing you want for *you*, it is, perhaps, the ultimate gift you can give your loved one.

When my father was dying, he was in hospice in Broward County, Florida, about an hour's drive north of Miami. While he had originally wanted to die at home, he eventually asked to be moved to the hospice floor of a local hospital. He was dying of pancreatic cancer and the pain was terrible. Having to wait for a hospice nurse to go to the house to replenish his supply of morphine caused him too much pain and anxiety. He figured that being in the hospital would mean that his pain medication could be replenished as needed.

That last week, I practically lived in the hospital along with my mother, brother, sister, and other family members. He was unconscious his last couple of days and, while we knew he was dying, we had no idea which day would be his last. Because of that, I took a chance one day and drove down to Miami for a job interview.

About half an hour into the interview, I received a call that my father was about to die and that I needed to return to the hospital as quickly as possible.

The entire drive, I worried that I would not get to my father in time, that I would not be able to tell him one last time how very much I loved him. I arrived at the hospital, ran from the car and took the stairs to the hospice floor.

When I arrived, my family was gathered around my father's bed. My sister was lying next to him and, when she saw me, she got off the bed and allowed me to take her place. "We've all spoken with him," my brother said. "He's been waiting for you."

That was a strange statement because we had no idea whether my father really was "waiting" or not. But, it made perfect sense. He'd heard from my mother, sister and brother. The only person he had yet to hear from one last time was me.

"Hi, Daddy," I started, my hand entwined with his, "I'm here."

For the next thirty minutes, I spoke to my father. I told him how much I loved him and how much I appreciated that I had won the lottery and gotten him for my dad. I told him that we were all there with him and I reminded him that, because of how he and my mother had raised us, we three kids were inseparable. I assured him that we would stick together and that we would take care of our mother.

As I spoke, I sensed my father's body relaxing. Did he hear me? Did he understand me? I don't know. But, I believe so. "We love you, Daddy," I continued. "We understand. It's OK, you can move on now. We'll be fine here and it is OK for you to go. Go toward the light, Daddy. It's OK."

I don't know if you believe in "moving toward the light" or even if there is an afterlife. I don't know if I believe in it, quite frankly. What I do know, however, is that my father loved his family more than anything. If I can think of anything that would have caused him pain and agitation, it would have been the idea that we would be lost without him, or that we, as a family, would fall apart. The most loving message I could give him, therefore, was to assure him that we would stick together and that it was OK for him to let go.

Knowing your loved one and what was important to her, can you think of a final, loving message you can give her? Is there anything you can think of that would bring her peace? If so, tell her. Those last hours offer you the perfect opportunity.

PHYSICAL CHANGES AT TIME OF DEATH

There may come a time when you are with a loved one at the time of his death. Not only is that a painful time, emotionally, but it can be even more upsetting when confronted with the physical changes a body goes through as it passes from life to death.

At the moment of death, the heart stops beating and the lungs stop breathing, which means that the cells of the body, dependent upon the flow of blood and oxygen, will begin to die. Because the body is made up of different types of cells, not all cells stop functioning immediately, or even quickly.

One of the first changes you may notice when your loved one dies is that his muscles relax. This can mean that his bowels and bladder muscles will loosen and his digestive tract will empty. At the same time, there may be a discharge from his mouth and nose.

The discharge, which is called "purge", is not universal. It generally occurs when there is food or liquid in the stomach or digestive tract. If your loved one has been dying slowly, over days or even weeks, and has not been eating or drinking regularly, any discharge at the time of death will be minimal.

His jaw muscles will turn lax and his mouth may drop open.

Any gas that has built up in the body may also escape at this time and you may hear what sounds like a sigh, or even a burp or gurgling noise. The sounds can be disconcerting and the associated smells unpleasant.

Without the heart to keep blood flowing, it will begin to settle. Gravity will pull the blood to the lowest part of the body. As a result, the upper parts of the body, deprived of blood, will begin to pale, while the lower areas will darken.

As blood pools or collects in any part of the body, it may cause small capillaries to burst. Burst capillaries may appear as bruising in the area and can be as small as a pin head, or much larger in diameter.

Without the pressure of blood flow, your loved one's eyes may sink in. His eyelids may remain open, his pupils will dilate and his eyes will dull and turn cloudy.

As blood settles, you will notice that your loved one's skin begins to cool. It will generally cool to the surrounding temperature.

As the body's cells die, lactic acid begins to accumulate in the muscle tissue. In life, lactic acid buildup can cause stiffness and soreness. In death, the build-up of lactic acid causes an extreme form of stiffness called rigor mortis.

Rigor mortis begins to set in about three hours after death and will last approximately 36 hours, freezing the body during that time into whatever position it is in. For this reason, whenever possible, it is helpful to make sure your loved one is placed flat, preferably on his back, before rigor mortis sets in. This position will make transportation to a funeral home easier.

After about thirty-six hours, all the cells in the body will have died and the body will lose its stiffness. Throughout this time, however, bacteria will have already begun the decomposition process.

Weather will have an impact on the timing of these processes. Cold weather, or a cold ambient temperature, can slow the process down, while heat will speed it up.

WHAT YOU CAN DO AT TIME OF DEATH

When a person dies, her body will begin to undergo extreme physical changes. There are a few steps you can take within the first couple of hours after death which will help prepare your loved one's body for the next step on its journey.

If you can, do the following:

- Lay your loved one on her back, arms and hands at her sides. This position will make it easier to transport her body to a funeral home, or to the morgue. It will also make it easier to clean and dress her body.

- If possible, place a small pillow behind her head.

- Close her eyelids. Do not be surprised if they open again. This is normal. If they do, simply close them.

- If your loved one wore dentures in life, put them in her mouth for a more natural look should you choose an open casket service.

- Once her muscles go slack, her mouth will open. Gently wrap a scarf under her chin and around the top of her head and tie it. Alternately, roll up a hand towel and prop it under her chin. As rigor mortis sets in, this will ensure that her mouth is closed.

- Contact the appropriate authorities. If your loved one was in hospice or a medical facility setting, call a nurse or doctor. If at home or elsewhere, notify the appropriate authorities by calling your local law enforcement agency.

- If your loved one died at home or work (or anywhere not under medical care), a coroner (or other legally-qualified official) will be called in to determine if the death was natural or not. If there is a question about cause of death, an autopsy will be performed. If cause of death is obvious and not suspicious, your loved one's body may be released to the funeral home of your choice, or back to you if you will be holding a home funeral.

Before releasing your loved one's body to you or to a funeral home, a Death Certificate will be filled out, signed and registered.

First Steps After a Loved One Dies

After your loved one dies, take whatever time you need to spend with his body. Some people take comfort in prayer, others in sitting quietly, while still others are too upset to do anything other than cry. Some feel the need to walk away, while others manage their pain by becoming involved in funeral preparation and moving forward.

Please understand – grief takes many forms and until you are confronted by such an event, you will not know how you will react. And that is OK.

Take whatever time you need. If your loved one died in a hospital or hospice, where people know what to expect, chances are that you will be checked in on from time to time, but will be left alone for as much time as you need.

If your loved one died in an accident and the police or a rescue team is involved, you may not have the opportunity to spend as much time with your loved one as you would like.

If you are notified of the death of a loved one and you need transportation to get to him, please do not drive. Even though you may feel able, it is never a good idea to drive when you have received a shock or are upset. Call a family member, friend, co-worker or neighbor and ask that person to drive you. At the very least, call for a taxi.

There are many instances when you will not be able to be with your loved one's body. He may have died overseas, or away on a business trip. He may have died in an accident or there may be questions about cause of death and his body has been taken to the coroner's office. He may have been exposed to radiation or to a communicable disease prior to death and his body has been quarantined.

Not being able to see and care for his body may feel unnatural and, in reality, it is. Historically speaking, people cared for their loved one's bodies and prepared them for whichever funeral arrangements were practiced. That time with the body gave people the chance to recognize and accept that their loved one really had died and would not be returning. When you don't see your loved one's body, it can be difficult to accept that he really has died. That, however, is the reality of modern times.

Regardless of how and when and where your loved one died, you may feel shock and disbelief. You may feel anger or guilt. You may experience extreme sadness or abject denial. Whatever you feel, it is OK. Feelings are complicated and they are convoluted. Further, they are not necessarily pure. You may feel extreme sadness, yet be angry, angry even at your loved one for "leaving you alone."

The important thing to understand when confronted with the death of a loved one is that it is OK to experience your emotions and it is not immediately necessary to do anything. You may have to make decisions, but not immediately.

If you are notified of a loved one's death and you are the one who will have to make decisions on or for his behalf, it is always a good idea to reach out to a trusted friend or family member. Ask that person to be with you. Over the next days, you may find that you can just not understand what people are saying to you, or you may forget what has been said within minutes of a conversation. Having someone with you who is not in shock can be extremely helpful.

If you are extremely distraught and unable to handle or deal with all of the details that are to come, you many need to reach out to your physician and ask for medication to help you function. The important thing to understand and to remember is that everyone deals with death differently and there is no shame in asking for help.

Very soon after death, other people will have to be notified. Again, if you are able to make the phone calls yourself, fine. If not, ask someone to make the calls on your behalf.

If your loved one died at home, of apparent natural causes, without an attending physician who agrees to sign the death certificate, you will need to inform the authorities. These can vary according to your town, county, or state's particular regulations (a list of state agencies can be found in the <u>Funeral Law State-by-State Resources</u> section of this book). In general, though, the following calls should be made:

- First, contact your county coroner or local medical examiner. The coroner/medical examiner will be able to pronounce the death of your loved one. Her number can usually be found in your local phone book, online or by dialing 411 and giving your city/town and state.

- If it is after hours and you cannot contact the coroner, a simple call to your local police station can tell you what is required where you live. Please note, if your loved one has already died and there is no other emergency present, contact the police through their normal business phone number rather than through 911.

- If you have already decided to use a local funeral home, you can call their office next to arrange for transportation of your loved one's body. If you have not yet made that decision, you will have to make another call.

- That call will be to your area's Office of Vital Statistics to report the death. This number can be found in your local phone book, online, via 411, or through your local health department.

- The Office of Vital Statistics will inform you how to reach your area's Registrar. The registrar will provide the final death certificate. The Registrar can also provide you with a transportation permit, if you will be taking your loved one to a funeral home, burial ground, crematorium, etc., yourself (again, transportation laws vary from state to state), and can provide a cremation or burial permit.

- Once the legalities are covered, you should begin to make a list of other people who should be notified. These may include:

- Family members

- Friends

- Workplace associates

- Religious counselors

- Attorneys (if any legalities are involved, such as a Will)

- School administration (if your loved one attended school or your loved one had children who will be missing school for the duration)

- Any civic societies of which your loved one was a member

- Media, if your loved one held a personal or professional position that would make his death "news" (note that it is not necessary to write an obituary at this time – that will come later)

- Anyone with whom your loved one may have an upcoming appointment

- An organ and tissue bank if your loved one intended to donate (note, this call needs to be made quickly or donation may not be an option)

- A full-body donation procurement agency if your loved one planned to donate his or her body to science or to a medical school (again, this call should be made as soon as possible).

ORGAN & TISSUE DONATION

Every 11 minutes, on average, in the United States, a new person is added to the organ donor waiting list. Likewise, on average, 77 people in the United States receive some form of organ donation each day. Unfortunately, in that same time, about 19 people waiting for an organ match die.

While donation is often considered a life-saving operation, it is not always restricted to life-and-death situations. Some forms of donation can enhance, rather than save, the lives of other individuals. A cornea transplant, for instance, can mean that a blind person will see. A skin transplant can allow a burn victim to recover and go home. In fact, more than 800,000 people benefit from tissue donation each year.

In most cases of the death of a healthy individual, organ donation can save the lives of up to eight people while tissue donation can help up to one hundred people.

Currently in the United States, the following organs and tissues can be donated and transplanted:

- **Organs:** heart, kidneys, pancreas, lungs, liver, and intestines

- **Tissue:** cornea, skin, heart valves, bone, blood vessels, and connective tissue

Many states allow the living to indicate a desire to donate organs each time a driver's license is obtained or renewed. Additionally, most states have an online donor registration program where citizens can indicate, at any time, their desire to have their organs/tissues donated after death.

Unfortunately, too few people register for organ and tissue donation while they are alive and able and it is often left to their health care proxies to make donation decisions of their behalf.

There are restrictions on donation that you should be aware of. People with certain diseases, such as HIV/AIDS, Hepatitis B, Hepatitis C, Tuberculosis, Creutzfeldt-Jakob disease, and Meningitis may be restricted from donating their organs to help the living because the disease may transfer.

In other cases, restrictions may be limited to affected organs. My niece, Jahmila, for instance, had neurofibromatosis, a disease that causes noncancerous tumors to grow in the nervous system. Because of her disease, she could not donate her organs, but was able to donate her corneas.

There may be religious and/or cultural restrictions on donation that you should consider if you are ever in the position to make a donation decision on behalf of a loved one. While saving another's life may seem like the ultimate memorial you can arrange for your loved one, you would probably want the decision to be in alignment with his beliefs.

To avoid making a decision that would have gone against his beliefs, you can simply contact his place of worship, explain the situation, and ask if donation would contradict the beliefs of the faithful.

If your loved one is going to have his or her organs or tissue donated for transplantation, you should be aware that she may need to be connected to machines to keep her heart and lungs functioning until the medical staff is ready to recover the indicated tissue/organs.

This has at least two repercussions:

- If your loved one has indicated that she does not want to be resuscitated, but has indicated that she wants to donate organs, she may have to make a provision (or you may have to on her behalf) to indicate to the medical staff that her desire for donation supersedes her DNR order, and,

- The visible appearance that your loved one is alive may

cause you to believe that she has not yet died.

Having a loved one hooked up to supportive machinery can be an extremely stressful time for friends and family. The patient may have already been declared brain dead (more about this in a bit), but he feels warm to the touch and appears healthy, though asleep.

The fact that your loved one appears to be alive may cause you to re-consider donation. In fact, it may cause you to want to have him continue on the machines indefinitely.

I am not going to make a recommendation here, but I will share what I have learned from my research.

For tissue and organs to be viable for transplantation, they require the flow of blood and oxygen until they can be recovered. Recovery may not be immediately possible as the correct surgeons need to be located, or the recipients need to be located and moved to a medical facility. The machines, as I understand it, simply maintain the necessary blood and oxygen levels necessary to keep the organs and tissue in an animated state.

The fact that blood and oxygen are supplied to the body by mechanical means does not mean that your loved one himself is "alive" (again, this is from my research).

A person is considered "dead" when there is a total absence of brain and brain stem activity. Brain death is "the unequivocal and irreversible loss of total brain function."[3] From a medical standpoint, this means that the person's brain can no longer--and will never be able to again-- control necessary-to-life functions such as making the heart beat and the lungs breathe.

That being said, some religions and cultures have different definitions of death and, if you are in the position of having to make decisions for a loved one, you will have to familiarize yourself with the mandates and customs of your loved one's religion and/or culture.

Questions You May Have about Organ and Tissue Donation

Are there age limits as to who can donate?

Not really. Each potential donor is considered based upon the condition (health) of her organs and tissue. A young person with a long-standing or severe illness may not be able to donate, while a healthy 70-year-old may be a great candidate for donation. Parental consent may have to be obtained for a donor under the age of 18.

Does the donor's family have to pay for the removal and transplantation of donated organs and tissues?

No, the donor's family does not pay for the procedure. If you have doubts, ask prior to recovery. The family (or estate) will have to pay for medical procedures and care prior to recovery, as well as for the funeral, but the expenses directly related to donation will go to the procurement agency.

What is a procurement agency?

Procurement agencies act as the "middle men" between donors and recipients. They have access to the United Network for Organ Sharing (UNOS), the private, non-profit organization that manages the nation's organ transplant system under contract with the federal government. As such, procurement agencies can quickly determine the best match between donor and recipient, as well as coordinate the removal, or procurement, of organs/tissues and the transfer of these to the medical facility(ies) where the recipient(s) is/are waiting.

How are donors and recipients matched?

There are a number of factors taken into consideration when matching donors with recipients. These include blood and tissue type, size of the organ, medical urgency, length of time on the waiting list, and geographic distance between the donor and the potential recipient (for heart and lung transplants).

How long will my loved one's organs be viable after brain death?

A respirator (machine) can keep blood flowing, which will extend the viability of organs for a limited amount of time. However, "life" is more complicated than blood flow and simply providing blood/oxygen will not make the organs viable indefinitely. Which is why time is of the essence. Once removed from the body, each organ has a limited window of viability for transplantation. These are:

Heart	4 - 6 hours
Lungs	4 - 6 hours
Pancreas	12 - 24 hours
Liver	12 - 24 hours
Intestine	12 - 24 hours
Kidneys	48 - 72 hours

How can tissue donation help others?

While organ donation is mostly a one-on-one process, meaning one donor to one recipient for each organ (the kidneys, because there are two, can help two recipients), tissue donation can help many more people. Below are some of the ways tissue donation can improve the quality of life of the living:

- Skin grafts can save the lives of burn victims

- Skin can be used for hernia repair, pelvic floor reconstruction, and for breast reconstruction following mastectomy

- Long bones can be used to replace those destroyed by cancer

- Bones can be used to reconstruct shattered limbs to prevent amputation

- Bone can be used to straighten and strengthen backs distorted by scoliosis and other diseases

- Replacement of hip bones can restore mobility

- Damaged tendons and ligaments may be reconstructed, thus strengthening the joint and assisting the patient in walking or running

- Corneal transplants can prevent blindness

- Corneal transplants can restore sight

- Heart valves can be used to replace damaged heart valves

- Saphenous veins can be used in coronary artery by-pass operations

What happens to the parts of the body that are not donated?

They are returned to the family (or to the family's representative, which could be a funeral home), for either burial or cremation.

Will I be able to meet the recipient?

Truthfully, I don't know. There may be legal and/or privacy issues involved. If this is important to you, make sure you discuss it with the organ procurement organization your loved one is listed with.

Can I make the decision to donate my loved one's organs after he dies?

This is unlikely. There is a very slim window of time after brain death to recover organs and tissue while they are still viable. Without a constant supply of blood and oxygen, the cells that make up the organs and tissues will begin to change and, soon, to decompose.

If your loved one did not indicate that he wanted to be a donor, and you can show that you can legally make decisions on his behalf, and you believe that he would want to help others by donating, you need to tell the medical staff as soon as possible.

If your loved has not yet died and you have made the decision to donate his organs and tissues, the medical staff will make every attempt to keep his organs and tissues viable for as long as necessary through artificial means.

WHOLE BODY DONATION

Donation for transplantation is not the only form of donation available. Full or partial body donation to a medical college or to a research facility is also possible. If your loved one had a rare disease, he may want his body donated to a research facility that will help find a cure. Or, if he had a connection to a medical school, he may want to lend his body to the school to help future doctors learn.

Please understand that the best time to arrange whole body donation to a medical school or research facility is while the patient is still alive.

If no arrangements have been made prior to death, there is a possibility that the offer will be rejected. There are many reasons why this may occur including that fact that the institution may just not need bodies at that time, that too much time elapsed post mortem and decomposition has begun, or that the deceased suffered from a communicable disease that would put the researchers at risk.

There are companies in the United States that specialize in whole body donations. They act as middlemen between donors and the receiving institution or facility. By working directly with one of these companies, you can save yourself a great deal of time and stress as they take over all the necessary arrangements and, some weeks later, provide you with death certificates, as well as the cremated remains of your loved one.

Questions You May Have about Whole Body Donation:

What are these companies called?

One recognized industry term that applies is "non-transplant tissue bank." As some of these organizations do facilitate tissue donation for transplantation, this term may not apply to all. One woman I interviewed described her company as a "body donation organization for advanced medical and science facilities."

Will my loved one still be able to donate organs & tissues?

This will, of course, depend on a number of factors, including viability of your loved one's tissues and organs, as well as on the procurement agency you are working with.

In the best case scenario, your loved one will already be listed as an organ donor and every attempt will be made to retain the viability of his organs through artificial means (by connecting his body machines that will continue to supply oxygen and blood to the body). If he is not a registered donor, then you need to make your wishes known as soon as possible, preferably before death but certainly upon death.

The body donation organization you work with may or may not accept bodies that have already had organs or tissue removed for transplantation. In the Whole Body Donation Resources section of this book, I have included a number of procurement companies. Please visit their websites to find the best company to work with.

Who pays for full body donation?

This may differ from facility to facility, but the body donation companies that I have researched all indicate that they cover the full costs involved with full body donation, including retrieval of the body, transportation, eventual cremation and, in the cases of for-profit companies, any costs involved in the return of cremated remains to the family.

As a note, some of the non-profit procurement agencies will charge a fee for return of the cremated remains to the family. This is because, as a non-profit specializing in donation services, they are limited to only those services surrounding donation. The return of the remains is not part of the donation service itself and, therefore, they must pass the charge onto someone or risk losing their non-profit status. For the record, this charge, if any, is usually quite low, around $15.00.

Will they then sell my loved one's remains?

First, you should know that The Revised Uniform Anatomical Gift Act (2006) prohibits the sale of human organs or tissue in the United States. Of course, these companies procure full bodies so it may be stretching the Act a bit by indicating that they adhere to it.

I cannot speak for any specific company, but I can say that the body donation companies provide services similar to those of blood banks. Blood banks do not charge hospitals for the blood they provide. Rather, they charge a service fee to the hospitals for supplying the blood. Likewise, I have been told, body donation organizations do not charge for the bodies themselves. Rather, they charge medical schools and research facilities for the service of providing the bodies or body parts.

One agency put it this way: we are "compensated for costs incurred in recovering, processing and matching donors with medical researchers and educators."

The costs of this service can be quite high. They include collection of the body by a local funeral home, refrigeration, transportation to final destination, delivery of the body, cremation of the body, and any costs associated with filing and procurement of a death certificate.

Are there restrictions as to who can donate a full body?

Yes. Some procurement agencies will not accept a body if the person had a contagious disease. Diseases that may prohibit full body donation include: HIV/AIDS, Hepatitis B, Hepatitis C, Tuberculosis, Creutzfeldt-Jakob disease, and Meningitis.

Further to this, there are a few other restrictions that may be relevant depending upon the procurement agency you work with. These include:

- A donor must be at least 18 years of age,

- In some cases, a donor cannot weigh over 300 pounds at time of death. This last is because there are high and low limits to acceptable BMI (body mass index),

- A body cannot be in a state of decomposition,

- Bodies processed by a Medical Examiner may not be acceptable.

Again, please contact the agencies listed in the <u>Whole Body Donation Resources</u> section of this book (and any other that you may learn about) to discuss your loved one's individual case.

Are there location restrictions on who can donate a full body?

Possibly. Some of the agencies I contacted had location restrictions. At least one of the agencies cannot accept bodies from Hawaii or Alaska because the transportation charges are prohibitive. The state of Minnesota also places restrictions on donated bodies being shipped out of state to anything other than a medical school.

Are these companies regulated?

The non-transplant tissue bank industry is not nationally governed, as far as I can tell. Many individual states, however, do have their own oversight rules. The American Association of Tissue Banks (AATB) is a professional, non-profit, scientific and educational organization that is the only national tissue banking organization in the United States. While it offers accreditation to for-transplant tissue banks, it also recognizes four non-transplant tissue banks. These are:

- LifeLegacy Foundation

- Medical Education and Research Institute

- ScienceCare

- ScienceCare of Colorado

Will my loved one's body be segmented?

I don't know, but I recommend that you ask if it is important for you to know.

What, exactly, is segmentation?

Just like the term implies, segmentation is when a donated body is cut into one or more parts. It occurs because certain industries, medical schools or research labs may only require a certain body part, or parts. For instance, a research facility developing body armor for soldiers may only need torsos, while a helmet manufacturer may require heads. In cases like these, the non-tissue organ bank may elect to send only the required body part to the lab, while other parts may be sent to different labs. Or not.

While this may sound horrible to you, there is a bigger picture and that is that bodies donated to science and research help to save lives and to protect the living. It is not glamorous and may be considered undignified or even gruesome to some, but it is an essential method of testing that computer simulations and animal stand-ins cannot replicate.

If you are considering full-body donation, you should interview the various non-tissue organ banks to understand their policies. If you do not want your loved one's body to be segmented and possibly to be sent to a number of different facilities, you should contract with a bank that keeps the body intact.

On the other hand, if you feel that your loved one would have wanted his body to be used in a worthwhile way that can help the living, you may not mind if segmentation occurs. If you would like his ashes returned to you regardless of how your loved one's body is used, you should ask that this be done.

What are some of the ways my loved one's body might be used?

While we do not often hear about it, donated bodies are used in many ways. Some, of course, go to medical schools where students dissect them in order to learn, first hand, how a body is put together. Other bodies, or segmented parts, are used later on to allow doctors to update their skills or to learn new ones. The theory, of course, is that it is better to practice on a dead body than on a living one.

Science and technology often require the use of real human bodies to test products and theories. The so-called "Body Farm" of the University of Tennessee Medical School uses bodies to test forensic theory. There, bodies are placed in any number of environmental situations so that scientists can discover and understand how to pinpoint cause of death under various environmental circumstances. One body, for instance, might be submerged in river water and left to decompose naturally, while another might be left out in sub-freezing temperatures. By studying, among other things, rates of decay under different circumstances, scientists are better able to determine when and how a crime victim died.

These are just a few examples of how your loved one's remains might be used to further science and medicine. If you are truly interested in learning more on the subject, I highly recommend the book, *Stiff: The Curious Lives of Human Cadavers* by author Mary Roach.

Can I find out what research was performed formed on my loved one?

This varies from company to company, but I have been assured that a number of the companies do supply information regarding the research or medical facility that benefited from your loved one's donation.

If you are considering whole body donation for your loved one, and prior arrangements have not yet been made, contact the various donation companies listed in the Whole Body Donation Resources section of this book, or call your local medical schools, or speak with the hospice or hospital caring for your loved one. Each institution has its own policies about accepting donations and you may have to call (or have someone call) to ask about its particular policies.

Understand that it is best to do this while your loved one is alive, but if that is not possible, alert the hospital to your plans so that they can, if possible, arrange to have your loved one's body kept refrigerated until such plans can be made. If your loved one died at home, do your best to keep her body cool. You can accomplish this by placing bricks of dry ice under and around her body or, if that is not practical, by doing the same with ice packs.

THE DEATH CERTIFICATE

Knowing time of death and cause/manner of death is important, for both legal and practical reasons. Both will be noted on a Death Certificate.

The Death Certificate is the legal proof that someone has died. The government will use the information provided on a Death Certificate to stop social security payments, pensions and other benefits. The family will use it to settle a person's affairs, including obtaining a burial permit, making a life insurance claim, settling an estate and obtaining death benefits. If the decedent had life insurance or if her death was the result of an accident, the insurance company is going to need a copy of the Death Certificate in order to initiate a payout.

While each state can create its own Death Certificate, the majority of states use a form provided by the Centers for Disease Control & Prevention's National Center for Health Statistics, called the "U.S. Standard Certificate of Death." The CDC wants all states to use the form by 2013 because it complies with the World Health Organization's International Classification of Diseases, which is an attempt to unify global health reporting.

The Death Certificate will list both the immediate cause of death, as well as anything that led up to the death. This could be a long illness, something in the decedent's medical history, or a summary of the last few hours of her life.

Only certain trained individuals are allowed to sign a Death Certificate. While the laws vary from state to state, the following professionals are generally allowed to sign it:

- Coroner

- Medical Examiner

- Death Investigator

- Primary Physician

- Attending Physician

- Non-Attending Physician

- Nurse Practitioner

- Forensic Pathologist

In some states, elected officials can sign death certificates. A coroner, for instance, is an elected or appointed government official. This is important to note because a coroner does not have to have any sort of medical training. If there is any question about cause of death, the untrained (or even the trained) official may miss important information.

You should know that not all deaths require an autopsy. In some cases, a medical examiner can pinpoint cause of death by performing an exterior examination of a body. For instance, in the case of decapitation, the cause of death is obvious from an external viewpoint, and an autopsy may not be necessary. In other cases, adequate medical history might exist to document an illness that led to death, and an autopsy may not be necessary to determine cause of death. In those cases, a physician's signature on the death certificate is often all that is required.

Obtaining a death certificate is necessary before you can make final disposition arrangements for your loved one. The death certificate tells funeral homes and crematoriums that there are no further questions about cause and manner of death and so final disposition can go forward.

There are three sections on the U.S. Certificate of Death:

- The first supplies information about the decedent including full, legal name, place and date of birth, the full legal name of a surviving spouse, and means of final disposition. This must be filled out by a "Funeral Director."

- The second, which is signed by a "medical certifier", includes information about cause and manner of death.

- The third section, also filled out by a "Funeral Director", includes information about the decedent's race and education.

Because the death certificate requires that a "funeral director" fills out certain sections, many families wonder if this means that they HAVE to hire a funeral director. This is a very valid and significant question.

First of all, requiring the use of a Funeral Director is seen by many as an imposition on free choice. Many families want to care for their loved one's body themselves, including arranging a home funeral, and forcing them to hire a funeral director inserts a stranger into the process.

Second, the Funeral Rule (discussed in a later chapter) allows funeral homes to charge a "non-declinable fee" for basic services. In 2009, the average non-declinable fee in the United States was $1,817. By insisting that a funeral director be involved in the death certificate, it seems that the government is forcing families to pay, at the very minimum the non-declinable fee. So, just the fact that a family member has died would mean that the family could expect at least $1,817 in out-of-pocket death expenses.

While the U.S. government wants all states to use the uniform death certificate form, it does not require that a funeral director be involved in each death. However, some states DO require the hiring of a funeral director in the case of every death. Yes, as unfair as that it, this is because the funeral industry lobbyists are still quite strong in those states (which will be discussed in an upcoming chapter).

If you live in one of those states, you will have to hire a funeral director to fill out the death certificate and to oversee all or part of your service plans.

In states that do not mandate the hiring of a funeral director, the U.S. government offers some leeway in filling out the death certificate. In those states, the two sections that state "To Be Completed by:

Funeral Director" can be completed by:

a) A licensed funeral director, or,

b) A person acting as such.

Below are the instructions as supplied by the Centers for Disease Control & Prevention in its publication, *Funeral Directors Handbook on Death Registration and Fetal Death Reporting* (2003 Revision):

"Part 1- General Instructions for Completing Certificates and Reports

The funeral director or person acting as such is responsible for completing and filing the death certificate. He or she shall obtain the personal information from the best qualified person and shall obtain the medical certification from the person responsible therefor. In most cases, the best qualified person to obtain the personal information from, the informant, is a member or friend of the family.

The following individuals can be the informant and are listed in order of preference: spouse, a parent, a child of the decedent, another relative, or other person who has knowledge of the facts.

Whatever the source may be, the name, relationship to decedent, and mailing address of the informant must appear on the certificate in the space provided.

It is essential that certificates and reports be prepared as permanent durable records. Completing a death certificate involves the following guidelines:

Use the current form designated by the State.

Complete each item, following the specific instructions for that item.

Make the entry legible. Use a computer printer with high resolution, typewriter with good black ribbon and clean keys, or print legibly using permanent black ink.

Do not use abbreviations except those recommended in the specific item instructions.

Verify with the informant the spelling of names, especially those that have different spellings for the same sound (Smith or Smyth, Gail or Gayle, Wolf or Wolfe, etc.).

Refer problems not covered in these instructions to the State office of vital statistics or to the local registrar.

Obtain all signatures; rubber stamps or other facsimile signatures are not acceptable. If jurisdiction permits, authenticate electronically.

Do not make alterations or erasures.

File the original certificate or report with the registrar. Reproductions or duplicates are not acceptable."

While choosing to act as funeral director for your loved one will save you a great deal of money and may help you to feel as if you are accomplishing important tasks on your loved one's behalf, you should not take on this responsibility blindly. There is much to be done and having a support team to oversee the different tasks will be extremely helpful, especially if this is your first time doing so. To give you an idea of just some of your responsibilities, the CDC states that the following tasks are the responsibility of the funeral director (or person acting as such) with regards to the death certificate alone:

"Complete, or have completed, all items on the death certificate.

Obtain the cause-of-death information and certification statement from the attending physician or medical examiner or coroner.

Secure the signature of the person pronouncing death on the certificate, and review the certificate for completeness and accuracy.

File the certificate with the proper State or local official within the time specified in the vital statistics laws of the State.

Notify the medical examiner or coroner of any death that is believed to have been due to an accident, suicide, or homicide or to have occurred without medical attendance, unless this has already been done by the pronouncing or certifying physician or the police.

Obtain and use all necessary permits and other forms associated with the death registration system.

Cooperate with State or local registrars concerning queries on certificate entries.

Cooperate with pathologists in cases involving postmortem examinations.

Be thoroughly familiar with all laws, rules, and regulations governing the vital statistics system.

Call on the local or State office of vital statistics for advice and assistance when necessary."

SPECIAL CIRCUMSTANCES: STILLBIRTH

A **stillbirth,** or miscarriage, can feel as equally painful as losing someone with whom you've spent years. I myself have lost five babies to miscarriage. While they were in different stages of development, the love and hope I had for each was great and losing them was devastating.

The grief of stillbirth can be compounded by insensitive people who dismiss the event with comments such as, "Well, you can always have another," and, "It wasn't as if the baby had actually been born." Even with the most loving caregivers supporting you, however, understand that you have experienced a real and meaningful loss and that you will go through a grieving process.

As for practical matters, as usual, different states have different laws regarding stillbirth. In the past, stillbirths were not recognized as viable people and so the bodies were treated more as medical waste than with the dignity and respect that we show "live births."

In most states, there is a clear delineation between fetuses who have not yet reached 20 weeks of gestation, and those who have. The latter often require fetal death certificates when they are delivered stillborn and, in some states in some cases, their deaths must be reported to the medical examiner.

For grieving parents, it can feel, at best, ironic, and at worst hateful, to be issued a death certificate without ever having received a birth certificate. To remedy this, states have begun to issue documents called a "birth certificate resulting in stillbirth" to parents who request the formal recognition. While this may be merely symbolic, it is some form of validation.

To date, at least 20 states offer birth certificates of stillbirth. If you experience a stillbirth, please contact your state's Office of Vital Statistics or your local health department to ask if your state issues them.

Regardless of which state you live in, if your fetus reached at least 20 weeks of gestation, a fetal death certificate may be necessary. Again, the rules differ according to the state where the event occurred, as well as to the circumstances that resulted in the fetal death. According to the Centers for Disease Control and Prevention (CDC), "In the United States, State laws require the reporting of fetal deaths, and Federal law mandates national collection and publication of fetal death data. Most states report fetal deaths of 20 weeks of gestation or more and/or 350 grams birth weight. However, a few states report fetal deaths for all periods of gestation."

In a handbook for funeral directors, the CDC states that:

> "The responsibility for completing and filing fetal death reports varies from State to State. In some States, the responsibility is placed on the hospital or other institution if the fetal death occurred there and on the attending physician if the fetal death occurred somewhere else. In other States, the funeral director is responsible for completing and filing the fetal death report. If the fetal death was the result of an accident, suicide, or homicide, the medical examiner or coroner must be notified, and he or she must complete the cause of fetal death."

In addition to a fetal death certificate, family members who wish to bury, cremate or otherwise memorialize the fetus, must obtain (or have obtained for them by a funeral director) some form of authorization that releases the fetal remains.

In states requiring authorization, it must be obtained prior to:

- Removal of the fetus from the state,

- Burial or entombment of the fetus in a grave, crypt, mausoleum, or tomb,

- Cremation,

- Release of the fetus for scientific or educational study,

- Final disposal of the fetus in any other manner.

Once the proper authorization has been obtained, it can be given to the funeral director. This allows him/her to carry on with final disposition.

For families who want to act as their own funeral director in the case of obtaining a death certificate for fetal remains, please refer to the preceding chapter as the rules for filling out the form are the same as for those filling out a death certificate for someone who died post-birth (though, in the case of fetal death, the form "U.S. Standard Report of Fetal Death" is used).

AUTOPSY

Autopsy is a specialized form of surgery that is performed after a person has died. While this may sound strange, its purpose is to determine the cause of death, the manner of death, and to discover if any disease or injury was present prior to death. Autopsies are performed for medical, academic, and/or legal purposes. They are performed by a pathologist, who is a specially trained medical doctor.

Medical, or clinical, autopsies are performed when cause of death is in question, but foul play is not suspected. Academic autopsies are performed by medical students on bodies which have been donated to medical schools or by clinicians studying specific diseases. Forensic autopsies are those required when a crime may have been committed.

In the past, autopsies were regularly performed but now, in an attempt to cut back on rising costs, autopsies have become optional in the majority of cases when there are no suspicious circumstances surrounding the death. At the time this book was written, autopsies were being performed less than 10% of the time in the United States.

There are critics to the declining rates of autopsies in the U.S. Some believe that the lack of autopsy can cover medical mistakes and, by extension, negatively impact the care given to patients. In short, they believe that if mistakes are not uncovered, doctors, hospitals and other care facilities cannot learn and therefore cannot improve.

There are many reasons why an autopsy would be beneficial. Just some of the reasons to have an autopsy performed include:

- When the death was suspicious

- If the death was unexpected – a genetic cause of death could help relatives to avoid a similar death

- To rule out drugs or other contributing factors

- When a young, seemingly healthy, person dies suddenly

- If there is likely to be a legal battle between heirs

- If there is a life insurance policy on the decedent

- In the case of an accident when blame can become a factor

- If you suspect poor care by a hospital, nursing home or other facility

Pulitzer.org, the organization that recognizes excellence in journalism and the arts (among other specialties), cites a federal government report that found that in at least 8% of people who were autopsied, medical mistreatment and care contributed to their deaths.

Extrapolating from that, for every 100,000 who die, at least 800 had received improper medical treatment prior to death (100,000 x 10% of patients who were autopsied x 8% found to have had inappropriate care).

In the United States, cause of death is categorized as either natural, accidental, as a result of homicide, as a result of suicide, or undetermined.

A medical examiner may request an autopsy when cause-of-death questions arise. In those cases, the costs of performing the autopsy will fall to the taxpayers. Cases in which the medical examiner might request an autopsy include when a person dies:

- Of criminal violence

- By accident

- By suicide

- Suddenly, when in apparent good health

- Unattended by a licensed physician

- In any prison or penal institution

- In police custody

- In any suspicious or unusual circumstances

- By criminal abortion

- By poison

- By disease constituting a threat to public health

- By disease, injury or toxic agent resulting from employment

When a medical examiner does not require an autopsy, then the request falls to the next-of-kin. You can request that one be performed by the hospital where your loved one died, for free. The hospital may be unwilling to take on that cost, but you can argue that establishing a definitive cause-of-death is their legal, moral and ethical obligation.

If the hospital still refuses, you should ask for a quotation to have an autopsy performed. If the price is above your means, or if the hospital cannot have one performed, you can always reach out to a local funeral home and ask for references for a forensic pathologist.

In some instances, you may need two autopsies performed by independent medical examiners, which would the equivalent of receiving a second medical opinion for a living person. These cases can include those when fault may become a factor in potential litigation, or if there is a question about time or cause of death.

While you may not want to think about it, as a last resort, if cause of death may be in question, or some sort of litigation may become a factor, you can opt to have your loved one buried rather than cremated. Burial leaves open the possibility of exhuming a body for further testing, should that become necessary.

The purpose of an autopsy is to establish definitive cause of death. The pathologist will collect any fibers found in or on the body, will remove bullets and other foreign objects from the body, will take fingerprints and will test the blood and tissue for toxins, pathogens, drugs and anything else that can help establish cause of or contributory factors to death.

The pathologist will begin by examining the exterior of the body. Oftentimes, he will record his observations, using either audio or video, as he makes them. Prior to an internal examination, he will have the body x-rayed and will take a great number of photographs.

Once the exterior of the body has been thoroughly examined, the pathologist will make an incision in the chest in order to perform an internal examination. He will then remove the major organs, including the heart, lungs, liver and stomach. These will be independently weighed and examined. Tissue samples may be taken from the various organs for later examination.

During the internal examination, the pathologist will note any signs of disease, such as enlarged liver or scar tissue present on the heart. He will examine the contents of the stomach as these can help to establish time of death and, sometimes, cause of death. Additionally, the pathologist will take samples of all bodily fluids.

After the internal organs have all been inspected and samples have been taken, the organs will be returned to the body and it will be sewn up.

As a part of the autopsy, the pathologist will likely open the skull to remove, weigh and photograph the brain. Again, tissue samples are likely to be taken for further or future study. After study and sampling, the brain is returned to the skull and it is closed.

While unpleasant to think about, an autopsy is often necessary, as in the case of a murder investigation, or helpful, as when a young, outwardly healthy person suddenly dies. The information in the later instance may help family members avoid the same illness.

If an autopsy is required for your loved one, or if you choose to have one performed, you may worry that an open-casket funeral will not be possible. Actually, most signs that an autopsy has been performed can be concealed and you can go ahead with your plans for an open-casket funeral. You can, of course, let the pathologist (or whoever has requested or required that an autopsy be performed) know that it is your intention to hold an open-casket viewing.

If you are in the position to request an autopsy, you should first familiarize yourself with your loved one's religion's beliefs and practices. Some religions forbid (to the best of their abilities) autopsy. If your loved one's religion forbids or discourages an autopsy, but the coroner requires one, you can at least make your concerns known. Some states will consider next-of-kin's desires on a case-by-case basis. In cases where an autopsy is required regardless of religious beliefs, a religious leader may be allowed to supervise the procedure.

When an autopsy is performed on a loved one, you will want copies of two reports – the preliminary report, which is issued soon after death and lists (preliminary) cause of death, and the final report, which is issued by the Medical Examiner and which can take up to a month, or even much longer in complex cases, to prepare.

These documents can benefit you in a number of ways, including:

- They can answer any lingering questions you may have about cause-of-death,

- If your loved one was outwardly healthy, knowing the exact reason he died can alert other family members to genetic illnesses that may one day affect them,

- If your loved one died as a result of an accident and lawsuits are likely, they can complete the picture of events that led up to the accident (for instance, were drugs or alcohol involved? Was your loved one taking prescription medications? Did your loved one have a stroke? Was your loved one perfectly healthy?),

- Alerting you to an unknown health condition that, while it cannot take away your grief, may offer you the comfort of explanation.

Once an autopsy report is released by the Medical Examiner, it becomes public record. That means that any person may request and obtain a copy of the report.

THE FUNERAL RULE

The Federal Trade Commission (FTC) is the arm of the U.S. government that oversees consumer affairs. Because family and friends are under tremendous strain when a loved one dies and oftentimes least able to make rational, quality decisions, they can be easy prey for unscrupulous service providers and even scammers. Add to this the fact that most Americans are unaware of all the details that go into arranging a funeral until they are confronted with the death of a loved one, and they become double vulnerable.

To protect consumers and to minimize the financial toll a funeral can place on next of kin, the FTC created the Funeral Rule in 1984 (and amended it in 1994). Prior to that, consumers were often confronted with massive bills for unspecified or tacked-on "services", were required to purchase "packages" from specific vendors, and were left with few, if any, choices.

The Funeral Rule requires funeral providers to give detailed, written quotations to consumers in person, or, if requested, detailed quotations over the phone. It allows consumers to compare goods and services from different funeral homes and requires that disclosures of and references to any local or state law that obligates the purchase of a particular product be given to consumers. Further, it gives consumers the option to purchase goods and services à la carte, and from a variety of vendors, instead of in bundled packages.

The problem with "packages" is that they can include products or services that you do not want or need. For instance, you could end up paying for a high-end casket when you would prefer something simpler. Or, the package might include a photo montage to be shown during a viewing when you do not want that.

The Funeral Rule is also meant to keep funeral homes from steering you toward pricier goods and services. Some funeral homes, for instance, have rooms where their more expensive caskets are displayed. Without The Funeral Rule, the funeral home could leave you to think your only choice would be to choose from the caskets on display. The Rule requires that the funeral home give you a list of all their caskets, including the simple, less expensive ones that might not be displayed in the showroom.

The Funeral Rule gives you, the consumer, the right to:

1. Purchase only the goods and services you want,

2. Purchase separate goods (such as caskets and grave markers) and services (such as embalming or viewing),

3. Get a detailed quotation over the telephone – without having to provide your name, address or other information. You may also request that a price list or quotation be mailed to you. Because of this requirement of transparency, some funeral homes now post their price lists online,

4. Get a detailed, written quotation in person that you can take with you. This General Price List (GPL) must list all the goods and services the funeral home offers, as well as the price of each one,

5. Request a written Casket Price List before you are shown the caskets themselves. The reason for this is because funeral homes do not necessarily always have lower priced caskets on display and seeing the price list first allows you to inquire about lower priced items without feeling pressured when confronted with the higher priced items,

6. See an Outer Burial Container Price List. Outer burial containers, sometimes referred to as grave liners, are required by some cemeteries. They are meant to keep a gravesite from caving in as the ground settles over time. If the funeral home sells outer burial containers and they are not listed on the GPL, they may be listed on a separate price list and you have the right to ask for that list and to ask about lower priced options,

7. Receive a full, detailed and itemized quotation for the goods and services you want prior to paying for them,

8. Receive a written explanation in the quotation/ statement that identifies and describes any legal, cemetery or crematory requirement that compels the purchase of any funeral good or service for which you are being charged. If, for instance, you want an open casket viewing and the funeral home requires that a body be embalmed prior to such a service, then this should be identified and described in writing,

9. Use an alternative container to a casket in the case of cremation. No state law requires that a casket be used during cremation. You may choose, and the funeral home must make you aware of, an alternative container, such as one made of cardboard, pressed wood, fiber board, or unfinished wood. The funeral home must also make such a container available to you should you request one,

10. Provide the funeral home with a casket or urn you have purchased elsewhere. You are not required to choose from the caskets or urns the funeral home carries. You may purchase one online, from a different funeral home, from a store, or even make one yourself (or have one made). The funeral home cannot deny you this right, cannot charge you a "handling fee", or require that you be present when it is delivered to them,

11. Make arrangements without embalming. No state law (at the time of this writing) requires that embalming take place in every circumstance. Some states do mandate that preservation, either through embalming or refrigeration or another acceptable means, takes place if the funeral is not held within a certain amount of time, but they do not mandate embalming. You can, and should, ask if refrigeration is available should you not want embalming to take place. You should note, however, that some funeral homes do require embalming if there is to be a public viewing of the body. You can, however, ask about direct cremation and immediate burial (see below) if you do not want embalming, or about a private family viewing without embalming,

12. Receive a list and explanation (in writing) of any embalming services to be provided. You cannot be charged for any embalming that you did not authorize, unless that service is required by state law.

In addition to these consumer rights, the Funeral Rule requires funeral homes to supply potential customers with the prices for the following sixteen services (note, each item must be listed and priced separately):

1. The price for forwarding of remains to another funeral home,

2. The price for receiving remains from another funeral home,

3. The price for "direct cremation" (cremation without a service),

4. The price for "immediate burial" (burial without a service),

5. The charge for the basic services of funeral director and staff, and overhead,

6. The price of transferring the remains to the funeral home,

7. The price of embalming the body,

8. The price for "other preparation of the body" (restoration, grooming, washing, dressing, etc.),

9. The price for use of facilities and staff for a viewing,

10. The price for use of facilities and staff for a funeral ceremony,

11. The price for use of facilities and staff for a memorial service,

12. The price for the use of equipment and staff for a graveside service,

13. The price for the use of a hearse,

14. The price for the use of a limousine,

15. A Casket Price List listing the individual casket prices or range of casket prices,

16. An Outer Burial Container price list listing the individual container prices or range of outer burial container prices.

There are several things you should be aware of. For instance, any fees for the professional services of the funeral director and staff must be included in the individual prices (see numbers 1, 2, 3, and 4, above) for each of these services. The funeral home, for instance, cannot charge $400 for forwarding the remains of your loved one to another funeral home and then tack on additional fees to cover the cost of funeral home personnel having done so.

As for number 5, above, this charge may be a "non-declinable fee", meaning that the funeral home can charge it and you cannot refuse to pay it. It is here that the funeral home bundles all the unallocated overhead of its business, including facility maintenance expenses, utilities, advertising, etc.

According to the National Funeral Directors Association, in 2009, the average "basic" fee for funeral homes in the United States was $1,817. AARP places this fee between $695 and $3,000. Everything else chosen, then, was above and beyond that starting price. If you wanted to hold a viewing at the funeral home, for instance, you would add that cost to the $1,817 basic fee.

Please note that each funeral home decides individually whether it will make the basic fee non-declinable or not. If it chooses to do so, the funeral home must provide a disclosure to consumers (see the Non-Declinable Services Disclosure section of this book for more information on this disclosure) explaining what the basic fee covers. Further, it is important to understand that the basic service fee cannot include any of the other fifteen items that must be separately itemized.

A funeral home that makes this fee non-declinable must include a disclosure such as,

> *"This fee for our basic services and overhead will be added to the total cost of the funeral arrangements you select. (This fee is already included in our charges for direct cremations, immediate burials and forwarding or receiving remains.)"*

Do not make the mistake of choosing between funeral homes that make this fee mandatory and those that do not. As an alternative to number 5, above, funeral homes are allowed to bundle their overhead expenses into their casket prices. And, should you decide to purchase a casket elsewhere, they can still charge you a "casket fee", but must provide you with a disclosure that states something along the lines of:

> *"Please note that a fee of [specify dollar amount] for the use of our basic services and overhead is included in the price of our caskets. This same fee shall be added to the total cost of your funeral arrangements if you provide the casket. Our services include..."*

Please be sure to fully discuss and understand what is included in "other preparations of the body" (number 8, above). This can be as simple as washing and dressing the body, or, it can include restoration, grooming and other services. If you do not understand what is included, you may be disappointed, you may be paying for a number of services you did not want, or you may be charged individually for additional services you thought were included but that were not.

If you have chosen direct cremation, you may provide the cremation container yourself. You do not have to purchase one from the funeral home. As such, the funeral home must break down direct cremation pricing into a scenario in which you provide the container and one in which it provides the container. Additionally, it must provide individual pricing for containers they provide (i.e., the price for a cardboard container, for a pressboard container, for a simple pine cremation container, etc.). The same goes for immediate burial.

When visiting funeral homes, make sure you leave with three price lists: The General Price List, the Casket Price List, and the Outer Burial Container Price List. The Funeral Rule allows funeral homes to combine these price lists together (to attach them to each other), but pricing for all must be supplied to you prior to you seeing merchandise or discussing services.

The General Price List (GPL)

The GPL itemizes every service and product that the funeral home offers. It may include:

1. The Funeral Director's fee – this can consist of charges for consultations, paperwork, overhead, conferences, etc.,

2. Preparation, care and transportation of the body,

3. Facility and staff fees for the any services (viewing, wake, visitation, funeral and/or memorial),

4. Other, which may include flowers, music, video, funeral notices, cars, guestbook, etc.,

5. And, if offered, alternative services. For instance, if immediate burial and/or direct cremation is available, these should be itemized on the GPL.

The Casket Price List

This list must include details and pricing of all caskets offered by the funeral home, including those that are not on display.

You should know that caskets are often the most expensive part of a funeral. Casket prices are, more often than not, in the thousands of dollars, with some "specialty" models reaching well over $10,000.

You should not feel pressured into purchasing a top-end model. A casket can be as simple as a home-made pine box. In fact, depending upon the arrangements you make, a casket may not even be necessary. Should you choose a green burial, for instance, a burial shroud may be all that you require. For cremation, a simple cardboard box may make the most sense.

Regardless, shop around. Casket sales are no longer limited to funeral homes. Cemeteries often sell them and there is a growing online business in casket sales.

The Outer Burial Container Price List

Some cemeteries require casket liners or vaults. These are generally made of concrete, metal or plastic and either surround the casket on three sides or enclose it completely. Their purpose, according to the cemeteries that require them, is to keep the ground from caving in as the casket decomposes.

If you are going to bury your loved one in a cemetery that requires a liner or vault, you should ask the funeral home for its Outer Burial Container Price List, which is sometimes called the "Vault Price List." Use this to compare to pricing offered by the cemetery. If you are going to purchase one or the other, make sure that the one you purchase is sized to fit around the casket you purchase.

Special Circumstances

There are special circumstances that allow funeral homes to provide alternative price lists to consumers. These include pricing for children and infants, pricing for government agencies, and pricing for religious groups and memorial societies. Regardless of special pricing, the funeral home must comply with Funeral Rule regulations.

Bereaved Consumer's Bill of Rights

In March of 2011, Representative Bobby Rush (D-IL) introduced the Bereaved Consumer's Bill of Rights. The bill seeks to impose regulations on cemeteries, as well as on those companies that are not funeral directors/homes, but which provide funeral products (caskets, urns, etc.) directly to the public. Because the Funeral Rule does not extend to cemeteries and funeral product vendors, this bill would further protect consumers' rights.

A summary of the bill, written by the Congressional Research Service, a well-respected nonpartisan arm of the Library of Congress, follows:

"3/3/2011--Introduced.

Bereaved Consumer's Bill of Rights Act of 2011 - Directs the Federal Trade Commission (FTC) to prescribe rules prohibiting unfair or deceptive acts or practices in the provision of funeral goods or services. Includes among such rules: (1) a requirement that price information be disclosed clearly and conspicuously; (2) a prohibition on misrepresentations or conditioning the provision of goods or services upon the purchase of other goods or services from the provider; (3) a requirement that any presale disclosures and contracts are written clearly, stating the merchandise, services, and prices and disclosing any penalties for canceling or transferring a contract; (4) a requirement that cemeteries provide to consumers all written rules and regulations of the cemetery and all material terms and conditions of purchase; and (5) a requirement that cemeteries retain all records in existence on the date of enactment of this Act and accurately record and retain records of interments, inurnments, or entombments. Applies such rules to states or political subdivisions and tax-exempt organizations. Excludes cemeteries organized, operated, managed, and owned by a religious organization and that are not affiliated with a for-profit provider offering funeral goods and services for sale to the public. Gives standing to states to bring a civil action for violations of this Act."

As of this writing, the bill is in committee and has not yet been put to vote. Until such a time as the bill is enacted, please use, at the minimum, the Questions for Cemeteries/Mausoleums located at the back of this book when discussing arrangements with cemetery personnel.

TYPES OF SERVICE

One of the first decisions you will have to make is whether you want to hold a service (of any sort, not necessarily a religious one) for your loved one. If you establish that you would like a service, your next task is to decide upon the type of service you feel would best honor the decedent. Traditionally, there are a number of services you can hold and you may choose from among them, or can create your own.

Choosing the type of service you want can be confusing as different people have different ideas about what each service includes. Some, for instance, give the term "funeral" to those services during which either a body or cremated remains is present. Others reserve the term "funeral" for only those services conducted when a body (non-cremated remains) is present. To help clarify these terms, and to help you choose the best service(s) for your loved one, I've attempted to identify some of the more popular services below (note, these are in alphabetical order, not in the order they are performed):

Committal Liturgy

This is the third step of a Catholic funeral. It is the service that takes place when the body is interred (whether buried or as cremated remains).

Funeral

A funeral is a service that is held when the body of the deceased is present, whether the casket is open or closed. Because of the presence of the body, a funeral generally must take place soon after death, usually within one to four days after death.

Funeral Liturgy

The Funeral Liturgy, or funeral mass, is the second service provided for Catholic decedents. It takes place in a church and is led by a Catholic priest. The format for a Catholic funeral mass is quite standard, though a short eulogy may be given after communion. Please note: the Catholic Church has only recently (1963) allowed for the cremation of remains. In every possible circumstance, however, the Church prefers that the body of the decedent be present for the funeral liturgy. For that reason, the church prefers that cremation, if requested, not take place until after the funeral liturgy.

Graveside Service

A graveside service is a commemorative service that takes place just before a body is laid to rest (whether in an in-ground burial, in a mausoleum, columbarium, or other place of rest). It can take place beside the open grave itself or in a cemetery chapel. If the decedent was religious, the service may be led by a minister or other religious leader. Prayers are generally spoken, Taps may be played if the decedent served in the military, and a eulogy may be given.

Memorial Service

A memorial service takes place after the disposition of the body, whether through interment, cremation or some other means. Because the body is not present, there is more flexibility in planning a memorial service. It can take place anywhere and anytime, even months or years after the death occurred.

Non-Traditional Funeral

This is a funeral that follows the desires and wishes of the decedent (or the decedent's family) rather than the rituals of those performing the service. For example, a Catholic funeral celebrates the beliefs of the Catholic faith rather than the decedent's life and, as such, is a formally structured event. A civil funeral, or non-traditional funeral, on the other hand, is a created event that may be religious, semi-religious or non-religious. It might include a eulogy, songs, videos, prayer, poetry, or anything else that is meaningful.

State Funeral

This is a public funeral ceremony that follows the rules of protocol and that is generally reserved for heads of state or other important people of national significance.

Viewing

Oftentimes, loved ones will request an open casket funeral. A viewing takes place before, or in conjunction with, a funeral. It is a time when family members and/or friends can approach the open casket for one last look at the decedent.

Vigil Service

Similar to the traditional meaning of a "wake", a vigil service takes place the day or evening before a Catholic Funeral Mass, or Funeral Liturgy. It is the first of three services offered for a Catholic or traditional Christian (the Funeral Liturgy and Rite of Committal are the other two). The Vigil can be held at the decedent's home, a funeral home, or in the church, and is presided over by a priest, deacon or lay person. In the Catholic tradition, the vigil service is the preferred time for family and friends to offer stories, reflections, and eulogies on the life of the deceased.

Visitation

Visitation is often confused with viewing, and they can be the same. A viewing, though, always refers to an open casket, while a visitation can take place when the casket is closed.

Wake

The term "wake" has evolved over time. It used to be used to describe an overnight period when a body was laid out (usually at home) and watched over through the night by a family member or friend. Today, it often refers to a service held after the funeral or memorial service to celebrate the decedent's life.

Please note that this list is not exhaustive. Some religions, for instance, may have services that are not listed here. Further, certain organizations have unique ceremonies and rites for members when they die. These organizations include:

- Free and Accepted Masons

- Veterans of Foreign Wars

- The American Legion

- The Elks Club

- The Moose Club

- The Eagles Club

- The Knights of Columbus

HOME FUNERAL OR FUNERAL HOME?

While it may seem otherwise, in most states, you do not have to hire a funeral home or a funeral director. You can, and many choose to, conduct most, if not all, of the services at your home or at another location, such as on a beach, or in a park. Further, in most states, you can even prepare your loved one's body yourself.

When deciding between organizing and conducting your loved one's funeral/services yourself or hiring a funeral director, there are a number of questions you should consider. These include:

- How organized are you – especially at this time? Will you be able to do everything yourself, or do you have people who can help you with the organization and preparation?

- How much time do you have? Some religions/customs require the body to be buried or cremated within a specified amount of time. Can you accomplish everything you need to do within that time frame?

- Do you have a venue where the services can be held? The size of the needed venue, of course, will depend upon the number of mourners you expect. If only family and close friends are expected, then it is likely you can hold the services at your home. If many are expected, you will have to find another location (note, if you are thinking of holding the service on public land, be sure to contact the town/city to ask if there are any congregation limitations, hours of operation, etc.).

- Will there be a religious element to any of the services? If so, you may be required to hold some, if not all, of the services in a church, temple, mosque or other religious venue.

- What is your budget? While you may not be thinking of money at this time, knowing your budget is crucial. A funeral can cost tens of thousands of dollars and you may unwittingly purchase services you do not want or need if you are not careful. Each additional service that you hire out is going to add to your costs. If you are on a very tight budget, you may decide to conduct the services yourself.

- Will you be allowed to hold the kind of service you want in a funeral home? For instance, if you want a band to play, will this be allowed?

- Do you want an open casket service? Many funeral homes require embalming if there will be an open casket.

- Do you want the body embalmed? If so, you will have to hire an embalmer (who generally works for a funeral home).

- Will the body need to be transported? Perhaps from your home to the cemetery? If so, are there restrictions in your state against transporting a body?

- Funeral directors can be extremely helpful. That, in fact, is what they are paid to be. Further, funeral homes generally add an element of dignity to the service(s). They can also be quite expensive, however. When thinking about the amount of work you want to do yourself (or have a friend or family member do), you need to weigh what you can realistically accomplish against your budget.

- If you decide to hire a funeral home for some or all of the services, you should cover the following in an in-person or telephone conversation (in-person is best, of course, but not always practical):

- By law, the funeral home must supply you with a General Price List. This describes the goods and services being offered, as well as the price of each. The GPL must be provided to you prior to you making any decisions about what to purchase.

- You may make inquiries by phone. When you do, the funeral home must tell you about the goods and services offered, as well as their prices.

- The funeral home must provide you with separate (if not attached to their GPL) prices for caskets, urns, and vaults. They must provide the prices even for lower-end products that may not be displayed in their showroom.

- If there are "packages" or "mandatory fees", ask for a full listing of each product and service. Some funeral homes include services and products you may not want or need in their packages and mandatory fees, such as placing death notices in the local newspapers. If you do not want all the products and services included in a package or mandatory fee, then insist that the total be reduced by the value of that product or service.

- The Federal Trade Commission allows funeral homes to charge a non-declinable fee for "basic services and staff." In most cases, the consumer gets nothing for this fee as all goods and services must be listed and detailed separately on the GPL. This fee, then, covers such things as parking lot maintenance and the "cost" for having a staff member available to answer a phone. Unfortunately, as a concession to industry lobbyists who fought long and hard against requiring an itemized price list, the FTC allowed this fee to be included. While you cannot decline to pay the fee, it does vary from funeral home to funeral home. Make sure you review the fee with the homes you are interviewing. According to the National Funeral Directors' Association of North America, the average cost of this "basic fee" in 2009 was $1,817.

- Be aware that embalming is often included in mandatory fees and packages. If you do not want your loved one to be embalmed, make sure this is known and insist that the fee be reduced by the price of embalming. Also, if the funeral home says that embalming is "required", make sure you are provided a valid reason why (for more on embalming, please see the chapter "To Embalm or Not?").

- Make sure you are provided a written quotation for all the goods and services you require. Make sure the products are described in detail ("This casket has a 32 oz. solid copper sealer with a natural brush finish on top and sides with bronze rails. It has a beige velvet interior with swing bar hardware. Price: $3,895.00 delivered" for instance, rather than simply "Metal Casket"). Ask for a photo of everything you are quoted and, if they do not have one available, take a photo yourself with your cell phone camera and make sure you type in the name, style, item number and price in the photo's description.

- If you are going to rent a room in a funeral home for a service, or for a number of services, make sure you view the room first. Discuss the number of people the room can hold, ask about any time restrictions, and find out if they have any audio and/or video services available. Make sure you receive a detailed quotation for everything. If you will be using their audio or video services, make sure you find out what formats their equipment takes (CD, MP3, etc.).

Unfortunately, there are a few states that require the participation of a funeral director or funeral home and, if you live in one of those states, your options become limited. The states that have prohibitive requirements are Connecticut, Illinois, Indiana, Louisiana, Michigan, Nebraska and New York.

Connecticut

Connecticut has conflicting statutes on its books which make it difficult or impossible for families to handle the arrangements for loved ones. The first problem is with the death certificate.

According to the statute below, even if a family does not want to hire a funeral director, they must, at least for filling out and filing the death certificate. Because the Funeral Rule allows funeral homes to charge non-declinable basic fees, this means that families can be charged thousands of dollars for even this simple service.

> *Sec. 7-62b.* (b) mandates that only a licensed funeral director or licensed embalmer can "complete (fill out) and file the death certificate. He/She must get the medical information from a medical professional and the personal data from next of kin or "the best qualified person available."

Strangely, this conflicts with the following:

> "*Sec. 7-64.* The person **to whom the custody and control** of the remains of any deceased person are granted by law shall see that the certificate of death required by law has been completed and filed in accordance with section 7-62b prior to final disposition of the body."

The reason for this conflict is that Connecticut allows anyone over the age of eighteen to designate who will have "custody and control" of his or her body after death:

> "*Sec. 45a-318.* (a) Any person eighteen years of age or older, and of sound mind, may execute in advance of such person's death a written document, subscribed by such person and attested by two witnesses, either: (1) Directing the disposition of such person's body upon the death of such person, which document **may also designate an individual to have custody and control of such person's body** and to act as agent to carry out

such directions…"

When a person is not designated as having custody and control, then the state appoints control, in the following order, to a) the surviving spouse, b) surviving adult children, c) surviving parents, etc.

So, if you take Sec. 7-64 and Sec. 45a-318 together, the law states that the person given "custody and control" shall be in charge of filling out and filing the death certificate. That person is not likely a funeral director.

This conflict opens the door to an argument that a family does not have to hire a funeral director or embalmer for filling out and filing the death certificate. Unfortunately, a second statute mandates that only a licensed funeral director or embalmer can transport an *un-embalmed* body. So, unless your loved one died on the exact spot where he/she is to be buried, transportation will be necessary and you will have to hire a funeral home.

In researching this book, I had the good fortune of meeting Shawn M. Smith, Funeral Director of Connecticut Funeral Home. Mr. Smith explained to me that many funeral homes, understanding a family's desire to care for their loved one themselves, will make every effort to include family members. He also pointed out that, while the law does place restrictions on the transportation of un-embalmed bodies, once the body has been embalmed, there is no law that states that a funeral director is needed for transportation.

Illinois

Illinois statutes indicate that you must hire a funeral director for both the overseeing of the funeral, as well as for transportation purposes. As I am neither an attorney nor a funeral director licensed in Illinois, I am providing the statutes for your consideration.

"only qualified persons be authorized to practice funeral directing and embalming in the State of Illinois."

Funeral directing is defined as:

"the practice of preparing, otherwise than by embalming, for the burial, cremation, or disposal and directing and supervising the burial or disposal of deceased human remains or performing any act or service in connection with the preparing of dead human bodies."

"The removal of a deceased human body from its place of death, institution, or other location...The licensed funeral director may engage others ... if the funeral director directs and instructs them in handling and precautionary procedures and accompanies them on all calls. The transportation of deceased human remains to a cemetery, crematory or other place of final disposition shall be under the immediate direct supervision of a licensee unless otherwise permitted by this Section. The transportation of deceased human remains that are embalmed or otherwise prepared and enclosed in an appropriate container to some other place that is not the place of final disposition, such as another funeral home or common carrier, or to a facility that shares common ownership with the transporting funeral home may be performed under the general supervision of a licensee, but the supervision need not be immediate or direct."

Indiana

Indiana law requires that a funeral director "initiates" all death records. Under the Indiana Death Registration System (IDRS), a funeral director's staff may fill out the form, but the Director, him or herself, must enter an electronic pin certifying to its correctness (the forms are all electronic as of January 2011).

Further, a funeral director is needed to get authorization for final disposition from the local health department.

Louisiana

Louisiana has several statutes that make it difficult or even unlawful for a family to care for its own dead. These include statutes that state that:

- Only a licensed funeral director or "other person required by law" can initiate a death certificate.

- "Every dead human body shall be disposed of and prepared through a funeral establishment and under the supervision of a licensed funeral home or embalmer."

- Only a licensed funeral director can transport remains and must do so in "a container that eliminates direct contact by those not licensed to handle the dead and to offer protection to those who might accidentally come in contact with said body."

- Burial must occur in a "duly authorized cemetery." Which means that if you want to bury your loved one on private land, you will have to find a way to have that land re-zoned as a cemetery.

Further, it is unlawful for any person who is not certified and registered under the statutes to "conduct the business of funeral directing" which is:

"Funeral directing" means the operation of a funeral home, or, by way of illustration and not limitation, any service whatsoever connected with the management of funerals, or the supervision of hearses or funeral cars, the purchase of caskets or other funeral merchandise, and retail sale and display thereof, the cleaning or dressing of dead human bodies for burial, and the performance or supervision of any service or act connected with the management of funerals from time of death until the body or bodies are delivered to the cemetery, crematory, or other agent for the purpose of disposition."

It should be noted that, while this last prohibits the sale of caskets, urns and other funeral merchandise by people who are not licensed funeral directors, a case heard in U.S. District Court recently overturned this rule. The suit, brought on by an abbey that was trying to maintain itself through the construction and sale of caskets, was settled on July 21, 2011 when the court found that it conflicted with the Funeral Rule which allows consumers to purchase caskets and urns from anyone.

Michigan

Michigan requires that a licensed funeral director be included when a death takes place. Its laws include provisions that state:

- "The handling, disposition, or disinterment of a body shall be under the supervision of a person licensed to practice mortuary science in this state." -Estates and Protected Individuals Code, 700.3206

- A death certificate must be signed by **both** a physician/ Medical Examiner and also by a licensed funeral director (so you must hire one for at least this).

- Bodies must reach final disposition or be embalmed within 48 hours of death.

I read an insightful document authored by Erika Nelson, MSW and Michigan Mortuary Science Licensee. In the paper, Ms. Nelson argues,

> "Unfortunately, families that choose not to embalm are often required by funeral directors to choose services that do not permit viewing and must occur within a very brief time frame after the death. This limits the options available to families and constrains their ability to choose the services that are most appropriate for their circumstances.

> In order to assert the business policies that they have created, many funeral directors make reference to an Administrative Code rule known as the 48 Hour Rule. This rule, R 325.1141-325.1142, does NOT say that all bodies must be embalmed within 48 hours of death. This rule was created in a time when the shipment of biological materials

was considered unsafe, due to the inability to properly refrigerate or contain them. The use of dry ice or other forms of refrigeration has been shown to be a viable alternative to embalming when the body needs to be temporarily preserved."[10]

If your loved one died in Michigan and you do not want her body embalmed, but you are unable to arrange for final disposition of her body within the 48-hour period, please make sure you discuss refrigeration as an alternative to embalming with your funeral director.

Nebraska

Nebraska has some of the most restrictive laws of any state concerning caring for the dead. According to Nebraska statutes:

"The funeral director and embalmer in charge of the funeral of any person dying in the State of Nebraska shall cause a certificate of death to be filled out with all the particulars contained in the standard form adopted and promulgated by the department."

"No dead human body shall be removed from the state for final disposition without a transit permit issued by the funeral director and embalmer having charge of the body in Nebraska."

"All transit permits issued in accordance with the law of the place where the death occurred in a state other than Nebraska shall be signed by the funeral director and embalmer in charge of burial and forwarded to the department within five business days after the interment takes place."

"Except in those instances in which such removals are performed by public authorities in emergency situations, first calls or removals of dead human bodies shall be conducted only by persons licensed as embalmers or funeral directors in the State of Nebraska or pursuant to the direction of a licensed embalmer or funeral director."

"A licensed funeral director shall be in charge of each funeral service, in person, whenever a dead human body is present."

"Persons who are not licensed as either embalmers or funeral directors may assist in implementing arrangements made by a licensed funeral director as long as they are under his direct supervision and responsibility..."

"Dead human bodies which have not been embalmed shall not be transported by common carrier. Transportation may be made by privately owned conveyance under the direct supervision and responsibility of a licensed Funeral Director.'

"Exception. In the event the body is placed in a metal or metal lined hermetically sealed container immediately after death it may be considered for the purpose of transporting the same as an embalmed body."

"There shall be no additional restrictions to the transportation of embalmed bodies...provided the body is embalmed by arterial and cavity injection with not less than 10% of the body weight of a disinfectant embalming fluid containing not less than 5% formaldehyde gas. All body orifices shall be effectively plugged with absorbent cotton, and the body thoroughly bathed with a solution of 1/1000 bichloride of mercury, or other disinfectant of equal strength."

"Bodies dead of communicable diseases shall be thoroughly and promptly embalmed as previously outlined and shall be held in isolation from the public for a period of twenty-four (24) hours following the embalming.

"All bodies dead of any of the foregoing special list of communicable diseases and which are not promptly and completely embalmed shall be encased immediately after death in a metal or metal lined and hermetically sealed container, and under no condition shall the body be removed from the container."[11]

What does this mean for you when making final arrangements for your loved one in Nebraska?

- You must hire a funeral director or embalmer to initiate a death certificate,

- When a "dead human body" is present at a funeral, a funeral director must also be present (presumably, you do not need to hire a funeral director when cremated remains are present),

- If your loved one's body will be transported within the state, you will need a funeral director to sign a transit permit,

- "First calls" or removal of a body from place of death must be made by or under the direction of a funeral director or embalmer,

- If your loved one is not embalmed, only a funeral director or embalmer may provide transportation of the body (at least, the body cannot be transported by "common carrier"),

- An exception is made for un-embalmed bodies that have been hermetically sealed immediately after death within a metal or metal-lined casket. Those bodies are then considered embalmed for transportation purposes (and can be sent by common carrier),

- If your loved one's body is to be transported and you do not want to purchase a metal or metal-lined casket, her body must be embalmed using formaldehyde,

- If your loved one died of a communicable disease (as categorized by the Centers for Disease Control and Prevention), her body will have to be embalmed.

Unfortunately, this provision is quite broad. The CDC divides communicable diseases into "Quarantinable Communicable Diseases" and "Nonquarantinable Communicative Diseases." Nebraska's statutes do not make it clear which diseases (from one list or the other, or from both) require embalming. Without a more narrow definition, the decision may be left up to a funeral director or embalmer.

All this being said, please remember that I am not an attorney. There may be statutes that I have not discovered, or my interpretation may be off. If you have a loved one who died in Nebraska, please consult a funeral director and, if you still have questions, consult an attorney.

New York

New York is another state that requires you to hire a funeral director. According to NYC's Office of Chief Medical Examiner,

"By law, the medical examiner may release a body only to a New York State licensed funeral director."[12]

At the very minimum, then, a funeral director is needed to receive the body. This means that the funeral director can charge both his non-declinable fee (which averaged $1,817 in the U.S. in 2009) as well as the associated costs for receiving the body.

But, do not count on just these fees. In New York, a licensed funeral director is needed to:

- "accept the released body and paperwork,"

- "be present and personally supervise the conduct of each funeral service" (even those conducted in your home),

- "be present and personally supervise the internment or cremation (even when internment is on your own private land).

To find links to your state's funeral rules and board, please see the Funeral Laws – State-by-State resource section at the back of this book.

An excellent resource for families who want to make their own funeral arrangements is Lisa Carlson's book, *Caring for the Dead*. Updated and re-released in 2011, this book offers state-by-state information on "funeral law for the consumer."

Odds & Ends - Eric Jackson, a student of Mortuary Sciences in Ohio, explained to me why he chose that field of study: "Job security. I grew up in a blue-collar family where my dad was always worrying about losing his job. I knew I wanted to help people, but I also wanted job security."

PRE-PAID VS. AT-NEED FUNERAL SERVICES

Funerals are often referred to as "pre-paid" or "at-need." A pre-paid funeral is one which your loved one arranged and paid for prior to his death. An at-need funeral, on the other hand, is one that is arranged upon someone's death and for which no provisions have been made.

Being realistic, you should know that you may find elements of both types of funerals when handling your loved one's affairs. For instance, he may have purchased a cemetery plot (pre-paid) but may not have arranged for a casket (at-need). For the purposes of this chapter, I'll discuss pre-paid and at-need as separate possibilities.

Pre-paid Funeral Services

For so many and for so long, it seemed like a considerate and loving thing for people to do, to arrange for and pay for their own funeral service long before their death. By doing so, they were assured that their survivors would not have the financial and emotional burden associated with assuming these responsibilities.

In a perfect world, pre-paid funerals make perfect sense. You know you will one day die. You know that at that time someone will have to make all the arrangements for your funeral, burial, and/or memorial service. You know someone will have to pay the bills. So, you determine to take on all the decisions and arrangements yourself and to save your loved ones from having to do so. As additional benefits, you structure the services to fit your own beliefs, to respect your individuality, to reflect your personality. And, as prices rise, you have the comfort of knowing you locked in prices when they were low.

While pre-paid funeral services have helped a great number of people, there have been and continue to be instances when even the best laid plans have fallen apart.

Unfortunately, not all pre-paid funerals took into or take into consideration that change is inevitable. You may purchase a plot and arrange for a service in Delaware, and then move all the way across the country to Oregon. You may make arrangements with a certain funeral home, only to have it go out of business years from now. You may purchase a casket that, by the time you die, is no longer in production.

Or, the prices of items and services not provided by the funeral home may rise so much that there is no way they can deliver as promised. For instance, you may purchase five floral arrangements for your funeral service. The funeral home contracts out for those arrangements, but they do not control the future price of those arrangements and so must pay the going rate at the time of your death. Or, the price of locally-placed obituary notices may rise.

In an attempt to regulate the multi-billion-dollar per year pre-paid funeral business, many states have implemented regulations that would cover these and other eventualities. Many states insist that the funds for pre-paid funerals be held in escrow and that provisions be written into contracts allowing buyers to opt-out should their plans change.

But not all states. Even today, some states have lax rules and lax oversight. Some states allow funeral homes to refund only a portion of the monies paid to them in the event the buyer decides to cancel the contract. Texas, for instance, allows the funeral director to pocket 10% of all funds paid and half of all earnings (interest) should the contract be cancelled.

In the best case scenario, your loved one will have reviewed his plans with you prior to his death. He will have a contract that lists the products and services that he desires and he will have laid out instructions as to the services he wants held. Further, in a best case scenario, you will work with a professional funeral director whose every intention is to help you prepare the funeral as your loved one indicated. The casket your loved one ordered will still be in stock, the prices that your loved one locked in will still cover all the costs in the current market, and all will run smoothly.

Unfortunately, "best case" does not always happen and you will have to adapt.

If your loved one pre-paid for his funeral, one of your first tasks should be to meet with the funeral home that was hired. When you do, bring any written instructions that your loved one may have left with you.

Discuss the funeral with the funeral director. Ask her to walk you through the contract step-by-step. If some of the products or services your loved one requested are no longer available, ask the funeral director how she thinks you can best fulfill your loved one's desires, while incorporating whatever changes have to be made.

Understand that funeral homes build their reputations, and therefore their businesses, by serving their communities. They recognize that their standing in the community depends on honorably fulfilling their business agreements. That means that you will more than likely encounter a funeral director who will do whatever it takes to ensure your loved one's funeral goes according to plan.

If the funeral director indicates that she will be unable to fulfill the funeral as planned, you will have to decide if the new proposal is so far from the original that it is unacceptable to you. If it is, and you can find another funeral home that can better serve your needs, then ask for a full refund. As mentioned above, some states allow funeral homes to pocket a percentage of the original contract when a contract is cancelled.

You may find yourself in a position where it is understandable that the funeral home cannot fulfill the contract as written. For instance, if the casket your loved one ordered is no longer in production, you will have to choose a similar one, of equal quality and price. Or, if your loved one ordered a regularly sized casket and put on a great deal of weight in the intervening years, a wider casket may be necessary and there may be a justifiable additional fee.

Occasionally, family members find that their loved one made arrangements many years before and did not update his or her plans.

For instance, if a family member made arrangements to be buried next to his wife and then later divorced and remarried and you are certain he would not want to spend all of eternity next to his first wife (if she would even allow it, that is), then you may have to discuss changes with the funeral director or cemetery manager.

If you find yourself in a position in which you feel the funeral home has not fulfilled its agreement and is not acting in good faith to resolve the differences, you may have to contact your state's board of funeral directors. While different states have different rules and not all states have boards that govern funeral homes, you will find a state-by-state list of offices that can help, or at least direct you to the office that can, in the Funeral Law State-by-State resources section. Additionally, if you feel that the funeral home acted criminally, you may have to contact your state's Attorney General. There is a link to state Attorneys General in the Resources section at the back of this book.

At-Need Funeral Services

An at-need funeral is one for which no prior planning was done. What this means, is that you will have to make all the arrangements at a time when you are least able to make important decisions. For that reason, I highly recommend asking a friend or family member to help you. Choose someone who is level-headed and rational and who can guide you from making wholly emotional decisions.

Knowing ahead of time whether you want a "traditional" funeral, a home funeral, or a green funeral can save you a lot of time and confusion. Likewise, knowing if direct cremation or immediate burial are your choices can greatly cut down on the amount of "shopping around" that you will have to do.

"Traditional" Funeral – Nowadays, when people think of a funeral, they are probably thinking of a "traditional" funeral, one that includes a viewing (or visitation, if the casket is closed), a church or other religious service, and either burial in a cemetery or cremation. A funeral home is generally hired to handle some, if not all, of the details.

Home Funeral – A home funeral is one in which the family takes care of all, or many, of the details themselves and a wake/viewing/visitation occurs at the home of a family member or friend. A funeral home may handle the transportation of the body, especially in those states where transportation of the dead is limited to funeral directors or embalmers. Because the family takes care of many of the details, this type of funeral is sometimes referred to as a do-it-yourself funeral.

Green Funeral – A green funeral is one in which every attempt is made to limit harm to the environment. Green funerals usually do not include formaldehyde-based embalming, or the use of non-sustainable burial containers. The green funeral business is a growing one and a "green funeral home" can be contracted in some states to handle the particulars.

Direct Cremation – In direct cremation, a service is not held, at least not one that involves the crematory or funeral home, though the crematory staff may arrange transportation from place of death to the crematory. Further, in direct cremation, the body is not embalmed, nor is it "prepared" in any way. Once cremation authorization is received by the crematory, cremation occurs and, at a later date, the ashes are returned to the family. Depending upon the crematory used, a short visit by family members with the body of their loved one may be arranged. Direct cremation is one way to save money on the funeral. A memorial service, perhaps held when planning to scatter the ashes, may be arranged and conducted by the family at a later date.

Immediate Burial – Similar to direct cremation, immediate burial is one in which no service is held prior to the burial. The body is not embalmed or otherwise prepared (by a funeral home) and is buried soon after death. A memorial service, without the body present, may be arranged later by the family, or a short, graveside service might be arranged during burial.

There is a lot of overlap between the types of funerals you can choose from. That being said, having a general understanding of the services you want is helpful. For instance, if you know you want a green burial, taking the time to visit a funeral home that only handles "traditional" services would be a waste of time. Likewise, if you prefer the idea of holding a memorial service at a later date, direct cremation or immediate burial might make the most sense.

When preparing an at-need funeral, you should understand that the Funeral Rule protects consumers from having to purchase products and services that they do not want.

BURIAL, CREMATION OR NON-TRADITIONAL FINAL DISPOSITION?

Your loved one may have been very explicit about what he wanted done with his physical remains. He may have chosen burial in a cemetery or on personal property, cremation, burial at sea, or another form of final disposition. Ideally, he will have made these arrangements prior to death or will have left instructions in his Will or other document. Unfortunately, many of us do not like to think about death, about our own death in particular, and we leave the details to others to figure out.

If you are left to make the arrangements for the disposition of your loved one's body, you may be able to figure out the best course of action by asking yourself (and others) these questions:

- Was your loved one religious and, if so, does his religion indicate a preference for burial or cremation? If you are unsure, contact his place of worship and ask.

- Is there a question about cause of death? If so, you may want to consider burial on the very slim chance that his remains will have to be exhumed.

- Did he purchase a funeral plot? If you do not know, search his files, his credit card statements and checkbook to see if you can find any records. If members of his family were buried in a certain cemetery, call the cemetery's office and ask if he had purchased a plot there. If you are still unsure, contact other family members and friends to ask if they have any knowledge of a funeral plot.

- Was your loved one married, or in another long-term relationship? Has his wife or significant other already died and is she interred somewhere? Would he have wanted his remains to be near hers?

- Has he ever indicated a preference for how he would want his remains handled? If not to you, then to another family member, or perhaps to a friend?

- Did your loved one leave a Will? If so, his preference for burial versus cremation may be indicated therein.

- Did your loved one have an attorney he regularly consulted? If so, the attorney may have a copy of a Will.

- Did your loved one have a computer? He may have left a Will on his computer, or may have left a document there that indicates his preferences.

- Will you and/or his other loved ones find comfort in visiting a grave? If so, then burial may be best.

- If his remains are cremated, what would you do with his ashes? Would you scatter them at a favorite spot, keep them in an urn at home, or have them placed in a columbarium at a cemetery or place of worship?

- Was your loved one the kind of person who would have wanted a non-traditional memorial? Maybe having his remains become part of an artificial reef or sent into orbit would have appealed to him. Or, maybe the idea of having his ashes, or a part of his ashes, made into a piece of jewelry you can wear appeals to you.

- Cost. If you have exhausted all avenues of inquiry as to whether he would have preferred to be buried or cremated, cost may become a factor in your decision-making process. Both burial and cremation can be quite expensive. Unfortunately, if your loved one did not make prior arrangements, you will have to contact the various funeral homes, cemeteries and crematoria in your area to ask for quotations.

In the next few chapters we'll examine some of the traditional forms of memorializing a loved one (through burial or cremation), as well as some of the non-traditional means.

Understanding the Funeral Rule and knowing your rights as a consumer may help you to make decisions as to how to memorialize your loved one and will help keep you from being preyed upon by those who would take advantage of you at a time when you may be least able to make rational decisions.

To Embalm or Not?

For some reason, embalming has almost become synonymous with death in the United States. Someone dies, she is embalmed, and then a funeral is held. In reality, embalming is not required, and in some cases, may not even be desired. The Funeral Rule, which was discussed in a previous chapter, makes it illegal for funeral homes to tell you that embalming is required by law.

That being said, you may choose to have your loved one embalmed, and there are many valid reasons to do so. The point of this chapter is to familiarize you with the history of and current practice of embalming, to inform you about when it is and is not necessary, and to help you to make a decision as to whether it is what you want for your loved one.

Embalming has a long and varied history. The ancient Egyptians practiced a form of embalming called mummification because it was believed that the soul would at some point return to its physical body. Ancient Incans also practiced a form of mummification, as did the Chinese during the Han dynasty. During the Crusades, embalming was used to preserve the bodies of traveling noblemen so that their remains could be returned home for burial.

In addition to spiritual reasons, embalming has been practiced purely for practical reasons. In some instances, the embalming process can destroy pathogens that may remain viable even in dead tissues. Sanitation and disinfection, then, may help to halt the spread of disease.

It should be noted that, on this point at least, there are differing opinions. Many scientists and experts, including the Centers for Disease Control & Prevention, the World Health Organization, and the Pan-American Health Organization, conclude that disease is rarely spread through the handling of dead human bodies and so claims that embalming prevents the spread of disease are unwarranted and only further line the pockets of funeral homes. Furthermore, studies have shown, formaldehyde embalming may not actually kill all pathogens, including the prion that causes Creutzfeldt-Jakob disease, the human version of "Mad-Cow Disease."

In modern times, in the United States at least, embalming is essentially practiced for three reasons: Sanitation, Preservation, and Restoration. The combination of fluids injected into the body of the deceased both kill bacteria and other pathogens, and "fix" or preserve the tissue. By temporarily halting decomposition, embalmers can then "restore" the remains through the use of putties, sutures, glues, cosmetics, mastics, colorants, tints, etc., thereby making the deceased look as lifelike and peaceful as possible.

The time that a body will remain preserved varies and is dependent upon many factors. While internal bacteria are killed by the process, airborne bacteria and molds can still cause decomposition. High humidity and time will also have an impact on preservation. This is important to note because one of the dictates of The Funeral Rule is that funeral homes cannot promise you that their embalming methods will preserve your loved one forever.

Preserving your loved one "forever" is not, nor should it be, the reason for embalming. It is meant, rather, to preserve your loved one's body from natural decomposition for a short period of time so that you can offer an open-casket viewing, or so that any religious, customary or practical services can be carried out. More to the point, it is done more for the family and friends than for the deceased. As a practical matter, it ensures that their last memories of their loved one are somewhat protected.

Of course, this may only be because we, in the United States, have been conditioned over the last century to believe that an embalmed body is "natural." In the majority of other countries, embalming is rarely practiced.

If you are considering whether to have your loved one's body embalmed or not, there are considerations to make. These include whether your loved one's faith allows embalming, whether embalming is in line with or contrary to your loved one's beliefs, the type of embalming to be done, and the chemicals to be used.

Religion is a major factor in deciding whether to embalm or not. Some religions allow the practice, while others absolutely forbid it. While this list does not include all of the world's religions, following are the general positions taken by some of the more prevalent religions in the United States.

Christianity – Most of the Christian faiths, including Catholicism, allow embalming. An exception is Eastern Orthodoxy, which permits embalming only if required by law or other necessity.

Judaism – Traditional Jewish law forbids embalming. In general, the body is to be buried as soon as possible, within 24 hours after death is the ideal. Of course, there are instances when that cannot be accomplished, for instance when a body is held for autopsy after a crime is thought to have been committed. Another exception may be when a body is to be sent to Israel for burial. If you have questions about the appropriateness of embalming, contact your local Jewish Burial Society, or *chevra kadisha*, or contact a local Rabbi.

Mormonism - Mormonism does not prohibit embalming. The religion does have specific funeral/burial practices, however. These include washing and dressing of the body in funeral clothing by endowed Church members.

Hinduism – Generally, embalming is not allowed in the Hindu faith; however, it has been done, especially when the body is going to be repatriated to India or to the South Pacific.

Islam – Embalming (and cremation, for that matter) is forbidden for Muslims. It is believed that the spirit remains with the body until burial takes place. For that reason, burial is, when possible, supposed to take place within 24 hours of death, and the body is to be positioned with the feet pointing toward Mecca. There are provisions that allow for other methods of final disposition, but usually only in extreme circumstances. Consulting a religious leader can help you determine the best course of action.

Baha'i – The Baha'i funeral instructions do not preclude embalming, though this may simply be that it is understood that embalming should not take place. Rather, the instructions are that the dead are to be buried within 24 hours and within one hour's transportation (whether by land, air or sea) from where the death took place. The body is to be washed and dressed in white and to be buried with feet pointing toward 'Akká (the Qiblih).

Buddhism – Buddhists believe in reincarnation. As such, once death has taken place, a body is considered an empty vessel and the spirit is considered to have moved on to a new life. Buddhists allow the body, then, to be donated to science or for organ donation and they allow either cremation or burial of remains. Embalming is permitted, though overt attachment to the body (now an empty vessel) is considered detrimental to the living.

<u>Funeral Law</u>

Besides faith, there are other points to consider when deciding whether to embalm or not. These include whether any laws require embalming.

Currently, there are no federal laws that require embalming under usual circumstances. Usual circumstances being that there are no health risks involved and that the body will not be transported out of state. Below is a list of some of the rules currently on the books:

- Alabama, Alaska and New Jersey do require embalming when a body is to be transported out of state.

- Hawaii forbids embalming when the deceased died of certain communicable disease.

- California, Idaho, Kansas, and Minnesota require embalming when a body is to be transported via common carrier.

Funeral Home Regulations

While some states do require embalming under certain conditions, like those listed above, you should know that some funeral homes require it when an open-casket service is going to be held. Reasons given for this self-imposed rule include:

- To prevent the spread of disease (even though the CDC and WHO, among others, state that this is usually not a relevant reason to choose embalming),

- Seeing an unembalmed body would be too traumatic for visitors,

- The funeral home does not have the necessary refrigeration available on site to combat decomposition.

Federal law does not require that bodies be embalmed, though some states have statutes that make it easy for funeral homes themselves to implement rules forcing families to choose embalming if they wish to hold an open casket funeral.

Some states, including West Virginia, allow people to view unembalmed bodies – so long as the visitor is first provided with a written disclosure containing information about the potential spread of contagious disease or "other possible hazards." As you can imagine, this type of disclosure is alarming, yet it is required, even when the person died of old age and the viewing is held relatively soon after death.

To "protect" the funeral home, a signed waiver releasing the business from liability may be required before a person is allowed to view an unembalmed body.

In truth, this waiver is more an impetus for families to select embalming when they want an open casket viewing, than it is a protection against lawsuit for the funeral home. Imagine, if you will, holding a viewing in which hundreds of visitors are expected. Would you, as the person arranging the viewing, want the funeral home to provide visitors with disclosures about "contagious disease and other possible hazards" and then require each and every visitor to sign a waiver? Not likely. Not only would that incite unnecessary fear among your guests, but it would lessen the dignity of the service itself.

As you can imagine, it is more likely that you would choose between a) a closed casket visitation, and b) having your loved one embalmed so that you can hold an open casket service. The first does not add to the funeral home's profits as the charge is generally the same whether the casket is open or closed, but the second does increase the bottom line. In short, by imposing these rules, funeral home doesn't lose anything should you choose option a, but makes a great deal when you choose option b.

Other Considerations

Federal Trade Commission requirements state that if a funeral home does not first get permission to embalm from the authorized representative (usually the surviving spouse), then it cannot charge for the service. This follows the FTC's mandate that only agreed-upon services can be charged for. Like most things, of course, there are a couple of caveats to this obligation.

West Virginia, one such state that requires that funeral homes obtain permission from an authorized representative prior to embalming a body, offers two exceptions to this rule, exceptions that take the choice away from families. The exceptions are for a) unclaimed bodies, and, b) bodies with contagious disease.

The W.V. law states:

- "If you have made legitimate attempts to contact the next of kin or authorized representative without success within twelve (12) hours after the body was placed in your care, you are allowed to embalm the body AFTER this twelve (12) hour period has elapsed. You are required to document your attempts in detail."

- "If you have made legitimate attempts to contact the next of kin or authorized representative without success and have reasonable belief that the body could be infected with a contagious or communicable disease, you are allowed to embalm the body immediately upon receipt of certification by a public health officer that the body is infected with a contagious or communicable disease. You are allowed to embalm the body prior to the end of twelve (12) hour period as described in #1. Again, you are required to document your attempts in detail."

Pricing

Embalming contributes nicely to the bottom lines of funeral homes. That being said, it is a job that not many can handle and, in some cases, a job for which embalmers are clearly underpaid.

Remember that while funeral homes are required to obtain approval from authorized representatives prior to beginning the process, they do not always do so. Unfortunately, I know this from first-hand experience. My sister agreed to a package for her daughter's funeral, without realizing that embalming was included.

When negotiating with funeral homes, please make sure that you are given a full, detailed breakdown of any "packages" or "mandatory fees" charged by the funeral home. One of these may include embalming – a service you may not want. If you are told that embalming is required by law, ask for proof. The only reason that it may be required would be if your loved one died of one of a (small) number of communicable diseases. Even still, ask for proof that the law requires embalming for that particular disease.

If you decide upon embalming, ask for a full breakdown of services included. Does it include only arterial embalming, or is cavity embalming included? Is restoration a part of the embalming process, or will you be charged separately for restorative work? Are grooming services included, or will you be billed for hairstyling and makeup?

The National Funeral Directors Association lists the average price of embalming in 2009 as $628. The price for "other preparation of the body" services for that same year was $200. In researching this book, I found that some funeral homes charge an additional fee for "washing and/or disinfecting an unembalmed body." Be aware that all bodies are washed (or rinsed off) prior to embalming, or prior to dressing if embalming is not chosen, so you can be fairly certain you will be charged for this service regardless of whether you have chosen embalming or not.

You should be aware that there may be additional charges for preparing bodies that have been autopsied or that were accident victims. Funeral homes explain these fees by pointing out that those bodies may require a greater amount of restoration.

When discussing embalming with a funeral home, be sure to inquire about the fluid they use. If it is formaldehyde-based and you are OK with that, fine. If, however, you would prefer a "natural" embalming fluid such as the essential oil-based Enigma line (see the chapter, "Embalming: Alternatives to Formaldehyde-based Embalming Fluids" for more info), you must say so up front. Be sure to ask if choice of embalming fluid affects the price for the service.

THE EMBALMING PROCESS

Generally speaking, embalming is practiced by a mortician. That title is quickly falling out of favor, however. More often, the person carrying out the service is referred to as the embalmer, though "derma-surgeon" and "restorative artist" have lately been catching on. In some cases, your funeral director may also be an embalmer. Some states and counties require embalmers to be licensed or certified. Some require would-be embalmers to work first as apprentices under licensed embalmers. Others do not. Some embalmers undertake only the embalming process and hire a beautician to apply make-up and to fix your loved one's hair. In short, there are no steadfast rules.

The embalming process is carried out in several steps. The first step, of course, is to receive authorization. Authorization to embalm is usually granted by the family of the deceased. You should know that there are no laws that require embalming. In fact, the funeral home is prohibited from telling you that there are. Some funeral homes DO require embalming if you opt for an open casket service, however. If you do not want your loved one embalmed, you may have to shop around for a funeral home that does not mandate the service.

For your reference, here is the Federal Trade Commission's view on embalming from The Funeral Rule:

> "Except in certain special cases, embalming is not required by law. Embalming may be necessary, however, if you select certain funeral arrangements, such as a funeral with viewing. If you do not want embalming, you usually have the right to choose an arrangement that does not require you

to pay for it, such as direct cremation or immediate burial."

Should you want your loved one's body to be embalmed, and the necessary authorization has been given and the body released, the funeral home of your choice will pick up your loved one's body and take it back to their offices. There, they will fill out a detailed report. The report will include an inventory of any items that came with the body including clothing, jewelry, glasses, dentures, etc. It will also include details about any marks on your loved one's body, including injuries, bruises, discolorations, etc.

All clothing, bandages, catheters, etc. will be removed. If your loved one used a pacemaker, this will likely be removed as it can explode during cremation, if that is what you have chosen. Likewise, artificial limbs and joints may be removed. The metals, when cremated, can clump together with your loved one's cremated remains. If your loved one had silicone breast implants, these too may be removed as the silicone can adhere to and damage the retort, or cremator furnace.

If rigor mortis has set in, the limbs will be massaged to break the stiffness and make them pliable.

The embalmer will place spurred eye caps under the eyelids because, after death, eyes tend to sink into their sockets. The caps have a raised-spur outer curve that keeps the eyelids from opening. He may also apply a small amount of "stay cream" to each eyeball to keep the eye caps in place. Once the lids are closed and in position, he will tamp down on the lids to fix them to the eye caps. Finally, another dab of stay cream or super glue may be applied to each eyelid rim to ensure that the eyes remain closed.

After the eyes, it is important for the mouth to be fixed in a "pleasant" position. Because cheeks tend to sink in, the embalmer may fill the mouth and lip area with a non-absorbent mastic, after disinfecting the area. Likewise, he will seal the jaw with wire or sutures to keep it closed. He may position the lips in a slightly up-curled position and then line them with super glue so that they become "fixed."

To prevent, or inhibit, leakage from the body, the embalmer may pack the anus and vagina with cotton. Alternately, an A/V closure (screwed plastic plug) may be used for this purpose.

Because large breasts tend to droop when lying down, the

embalmer may bind them together with tape, a binding band, or sutures until the embalming fluid "sets" them in a more pleasing position.

If your loved one was injured in an accident, the embalmer may rebuild "limbs" using plaster. He will use mastic to rebuild tissue and mask trauma, and will inject fluids into dehydrated skin, such as into the fingertips and lips to plump them up.

The next step in the embalming process is to remove all the blood and gases from the body and apply embalming fluids that will preserve the body from major decomposition, at least through the funeral (as long as that is held fairly soon).

Historically, embalming fluids were combinations of oils, herbs and spices. In more recent times (the mid-1800's), arsenic was used as a preservative. It took the death of President Lincoln's 11-year-old son, Willie, for most Americans to learn about embalming, and the Civil War itself for it to become fashionable.

Upon Willie's death from (presumably) Typhoid Fever, the President and Mrs. Lincoln asked an early-days embalmer, Dr. Charles Brown, to care for their son's body. The parents were so impressed with the results (stories abound that the President twice had his son dug up to view his body again) that Mr. Lincoln approved embalming for Union soldiers whose families wanted their loved ones returned north for burial. According to estimates, some 40,000 soldiers were embalmed by the close of the War.

When President Lincoln was killed in 1865, Mrs. Lincoln asked Doctor Brown to embalm her husband's body. He did so and the President was returned, via train, to his hometown in Illinois. Along the way, more than one million people viewed Lincoln's well-preserved body and that viewing convinced many of those, as well as the reporters who wrote about it, that embalming was the best way to care for the dead.

Eventually, it became apparent that arsenic was too toxic a substance to handle and newer preservatives were sought (to this day, Civil War era graveyards show high levels of the toxin). In 1867, formaldehyde was discovered and it quickly became the chemical of choice for embalmers.

According to James Farrell in his book "Inventing the American Way of Death, 1830-1920", "by 1920, almost all dead bodies were embalmed." A comical 1920 advertisement in Boston offered the following rates for embalming:

> "For composing the features, $1.
> For giving the features a look of quiet resignation, $2.
> For giving the features the appearance of
> Christian hope and contentment, $5."

Contrary to common belief, formaldehyde is not the only chemical applied during the embalming process. The embalmer has a number of chemicals available for use including chemicals to break up clots, others to condition vessels, humectants to rehydrate dehydrated tissue, cell conditioners to prepare cells to absorb the arterial fluid, and others to remove fluid from tissue that has edema (too much fluid in it). Cauterants may be used to dry out, seal off and preserve open wounds. Additionally, dyes are often added to give skin a "healthier" hue. In general, about one gallon of fluid is needed for each 50 pounds of body weight.

"Arterial fluid" is the general term given to the chemicals that are injected into the body as blood is drained away. Arterial fluid contains a combination of preservatives, germicides, anticoagulants, dyes, and perfume. Formaldehyde (generally) is the main constituent in arterial fluid, though some embalmers may choose to use the less toxic chemical, glutaraldehyde.

Blood is drained from the body at the same time that arterial fluid is pumped through the vascular system using an embalming machine as a pump. To begin the process, the embalmer makes a small incision in an artery, often in the carotid artery, and another in a vein. As the arterial fluid is pumped into the artery, blood drains out the vein.

The fluid will reach all parts of the body via the circulatory system. This, however, may not be enough to combat decomposition, even for the short term. The majority of bacteria that cause decomposition are located in the digestive system and in the abdominal cavity. To kill them and thus delay decomposition, the embalmer will often use a special tool called a "trocar." This two-foot-long, large-bore needle has a sharp point on its end that is used to puncture the internal organs so that arterial fluid can be directly injected into them. The trocar is also used to aspirate the organs in order to remove pockets of bacteria and the gases they create.

It is important to treat the internal organs separately because they can bloat and, if left untreated, will eventually rupture. The stomach, for instance, may contain partially digested food. Even after the death of the host, the bacteria will continue to break down undigested food.

As the embalming fluid runs through the arterial system, it displaces blood. A tube, connected to a vein, allows the blood, and some embalming fluid, to drain from the body. It is then collected in a basin before being flushed into the sewage system to be treated by the local sewage treatment plant.

While this may sound unhealthy to the living, the process is nationally approved by the Environmental Protection Agency because the arterial fluid that mixes with the blood is said to disinfect it. It should be noted, though, that some counties in some states do require additional treatment of the waste. Regardless of county regulations, some embalmers, as an extra precaution, take it upon themselves to further treat the blood before it is disposed of.

If you do choose to have your loved one's body embalmed, there are several things you should be aware of regarding formaldehyde. First of all, a formaldehyde-based embalming fluid will not only "fix" the individual cells, but will "fix" your loved one's entire body. This means that his entire body will remain rigid in whatever position he has been placed. You will not be able to make adjustments to the body once it has set. If you have specific requests, therefore, about your loved one's body placement, be sure to discuss these with the embalmer prior to the process (for instance, if you want your loved one to hold a Bible, or to have his hands down by his sides, rather than in the traditional crossed-arms-over-stomach position).

Another thing you should be aware of is that his skin, too, will become rigid. It will no longer be soft and pliable, but will become hard, not unlike a hard, wax candle. Many people consider this "normal," but it can be disconcerting to those who are unprepared.

Formaldehyde embalming fluid has a very strong, noxious odor. Unfortunately, it is very hard to mask. It does, however, mask the odors of natural decomposition.

The entire point of "restoration" in the embalming process is to create an illusion of restful slumber by making the body appear as lifelike as possible. To this end, the embalmer, or cosmetologist/ beautician, will use makeup to enhance your loved one's appearance and grooming tools to style his/her hair.

THE CASE AGAINST EMBALMING

As mentioned, people have been attempting to preserve their loved one's bodies for millennia. There is something terrible and final about closing the lid on a casket and walking away. The opportunity to spend time with our loved ones, if only with their physical bodies, for a few more hours or days, is all-too-often impossible to pass up.

There are several arguments against embalming that you should consider, if only to reject them. The first has to do with how and why embalming has become so pervasive in the United States, the second with nature, and the third with embalming's effect the environment.

Embalming itself, or its cousin mummification, has been attempted for as long as there have been people who love or care about other people. Whether to give loved ones a body for their spirit to return to, or to deny the need to say a final goodbye for a few more days, there is nothing unnatural about the urge to preserve a loved one's body.

While the Ancient Egyptians were masters of mummification and certain dynasties in China had developed effective preservation techniques, embalming did not become fashionable in the United Sates until the Civil War.

Before the Civil War, family members generally lived within a short distance of one another. News of a death would spread quickly from farm to farm or house to house, the family would gather en masse and the person would be buried in a family plot. During the Civil War, however, two events conspired together to keep families from burying their loved ones nearby.

First, their loved ones, usually the men of the family, were leaving the homestead and travelling miles, sometimes thousands of miles, away from home. Second, they were fighting a war. Which meant that they were being shot at, when they weren't freezing or starving or falling dead of exhaustion.

Regardless of the distance and the increased likelihood of death, people still wanted their loved ones returned to them for a proper family burial. So, during those years, numerous attempts were made to discover or invent a way to preserve the dead long enough for their bodies to be sent home and buried. The results of most of these attempts were less than spectacular. Around that time, however, Dr. Thomas Holmes of New York perfected a solution that actually delivered positive results. The solution, which contained arsenic, was injected into the bodies of the dead using a hand pump.

Dr. Holmes was given a commission in the Army Medical Corps and was assigned to Washington D.C. There, over the course of the War, he claimed to have embalmed "4,028 soldiers and officers, field and staff." Eventually, Dr. Holmes recognized the commercial potential of his discovery and method and resigned his commission in order to offer embalming to the public for $100. He also patented his embalming fluid and sold it to other "embalming surgeons" for $3.00 per gallon.

Arsenic, of course, is a highly toxic chemical that as often as not harmed the embalmer. Today, Civil War era cemeteries continue to pose a health threat because of the high levels of arsenic given off.

In 1867, the German chemist August Wilhelm von Hoffmann discovered formaldehyde, a colorless, gaseous chemical compound that is highly reactive (which is why it is most often mixed with other chemicals). It was discovered that formaldehyde offered exceptional preservative benefits.

Formaldehyde works by "fixing" proteins (like those found in tissue and muscle). Once fixed, bacteria can no longer use the protein as a nutrition source. Additionally, the formaldehyde kills whatever bacteria are present, and thus acts as a disinfectant as well.

There have long been battles between chemical companies and environmentalists and the health conscious over the use of formaldehyde. Those concerned about the environment and human health have argued that formaldehyde is highly toxic. They claim that it not only causes damage to those working with it, but also to the environment when it escapes into the ground and/or air. The chemical companies that supply formaldehyde (and the many embalmers who use it) argue otherwise and have hired lobbyists to support their message that formaldehyde is safe under certain conditions.

All the while the arguments pro/con formaldehyde have been raging on, Americans have become accustomed to and dependent on the embalming process. In fact, we are so accepting of it, that when visiting a funeral home, "traditional funerals" are most often those that include the process.

The question, of course, is why funeral homes continue to promote embalming when their own staff members face an increased risk of developing cancer from long-term exposure to formaldehyde?

The answer is this: without embalming, the public has no reason to need funeral homes. Think of it. Because of the Funeral Rule, we are no longer limited to purchasing caskets and other funeral merchandise from funeral homes. Except in those states that, by law, require citizens to hire funeral directors, we can certainly plan our own funerals. We don't need funeral homes to help us purchase cemetery plots. Nor do we need funeral homes to help us arrange for cremation (though we do need a crematorium).

The only reason we need funeral homes is because they provide embalming.

The funeral industry has long recognized this. In fact, the entire business model for the industry is based on convincing Americans that embalming is necessary. Originally, it was necessary in order to return soldiers' bodies home for a "good Christian funeral." After the War, marketing efforts shifted to convincing the public that embalming was necessary to prevent the spread of disease. When that was disproven, marketing shifted to convincing people that seeing their loved one's unembalmed body would be traumatic and that embalming allows for a better "memory picture" (yes, that is what it is called in the industry).

In short, over the past one hundred years or so, any number of marketing tactics have been used to convince Americans that embalming is, if not necessary, then highly desirable. Today, we consider it "traditional."

While Americans as a whole do tend to choose embalming for their loved ones – even for those who are going to be cremated – it is important to recognize that no matter how much a body looks like it is sleeping, it is not. Embalmers work very hard to portray the image of restful repose, and, some claim, by accepting the "restored" image as our loved one, we are actually denying death and harming ourselves by doing so.

Quite a few religions mandate against embalming for the simple reason that so much damage has to be done to a body to make it look "natural" and "lifelike." Wounds are sewn together, plugged and glued, mastics and packing compounds are injected into body cavities (even into the cranium) to "plump" them up and to stop them from leaking. Dyes are injected into the circulatory system to lend skin a "rosy hue." Nair is applied to the inside of the nose and ears (yes, even of women) to get rid of any hairs that might mar a perfect appearance. Faces are shaved (yes, women and children, too) so that pancake makeup can be evenly applied. Plugs are inserted into orifices so that liquids won't leak and gases can be let off. Jaws may be broken so that they sit in a more pleasing position, before they are sewn or wired back together (to keep the mouth shut), eye caps are glued to eyeballs to correctly position the lids in a semblance of sleep. Tissue builder is injected into the face and hands to plump up emaciated skin. Breasts are hobbled (or sewn) together to keep them from drooping and the body is posed into the appearance of sleep. Finally, when all is ready and in place, embalming fluid is pumped throughout the body.

For those opposed to embalming, all this prepping and posturing does nothing to lend dignity to the death of their loved ones. Rather, they see the end effect as a sad mockery of life, rather than a respectable facsimile of sleep.

Besides the fact that embalming is not "natural" some are against the practice because of its effects on the environment. Formaldehyde is, of course, highly toxic as evidenced by the increased rate of some cancers among those who work with it. While some claim that it undergoes a chemical change when mixed with bodily fluids, thereby making it less toxic to the environment, that argument is not fully convincing to many. Science aside, there is a decided yuck factor when considering that as a body is prepared and embalming fluid is pumped into it, about 120 gallons of water, blood and embalming fluid is released into the sewage system to be treated and, often, returned as drinking water. Further, environmentalists argue, embalming prevents the natural breakdown of organic matter that should, by rights, return "dust to dust." In other words, it disrupts the life cycle.

Mark Harris, author of *Grave Matters*, said in an ABC interview, "I see the cemetery less as a bucolic resting ground for the dead... (than as) a landfill of largely non bio-degradable and in some instances hazardous materials."

According to Harris, "Over time, the typical ten-acre swatch of cemetery ground, for example, contains enough coffin wood to construct more than 40 houses, nearly 1,000 tons of casket steel and another twenty thousand tons of vault concrete. Add to that a volume of toxic formalin nearly sufficient to fill a small backyard swimming pool and untold gallons of pesticide and weed killer used to keep the cemetery grounds preternaturally green."

Hurricane Katrina brought the formaldehyde argument to a head when formaldehyde-infused wall-boards began making those who lived in government-supplied temporary trailers extremely ill.

Formaldehyde has long been a "suspected" carcinogen. Because of strong lobbying efforts, however, it has been kept off the US Department of Health and Human Services Report on Carcinogens, which is a science-based report that identifies chemicals and biological agents that increase an individual's likelihood of developing cancer. In an ironic circumstantial twist, less than an hour before I write this paragraph (June 14, 2011), formaldehyde and seven other chemicals were officially added to that list.

The National Institutes of Health released this statement:

"Formaldehyde was first listed in the 2nd Report on Carcinogens as a substance that was reasonably anticipated to be a human carcinogen, after laboratory studies showed it caused nasal cancer in rats. There is now sufficient evidence from studies in humans to show that individuals with higher measures of exposure to formaldehyde are at increased risk for certain types of rare cancers, including nasopharyngeal (the nasopharynx is the upper part of the throat behind the nose), sinonasal, as well as a specific cancer of the white blood cells known as myeloid leukemia. Formaldehyde is a colorless, flammable, strong-smelling chemical that is widely used to make resins for household items, such as composite wood products, paper product coatings, plastics, synthetic fibers, and textile finishes. Formaldehyde is also commonly used as a preservative in medical laboratories, mortuaries, and some consumer products, including some hair straightening products."

According to Robin Griggs Lawrence, writing today for *The Huffington Post,* "By January 1, 2013, all products sold in the United States will have formaldehyde emissions of 0.09 parts per million or less -- the most stringent standard for formaldehyde emissions in the world."

What will this mean for formaldehyde-based embalming? I don't know. What I do know, however, is that formaldehyde, as it is currently used, is a danger to the living and to the earth. You will have to make your own mind up as to whether it is important for you to have your loved one embalmed.

If so, you do have non-formaldehyde-based chemical options you can choose, and there is at least one other way to preserve your loved one's body for up to a few days without embalming of any sort. That method is not as well-established or as available as formaldehyde-based embalming formulas, but it is a "natural" alternative.

For the record, both my father and my niece were embalmed using formaldehyde-based embalming fluids. If it were up to me, knowing what I have learned while researching this book, I may have counseled differently. But, maybe not. As my husband pointed out, "We want everyone else to do the right thing, but we ourselves want to do whatever makes us feel best."

ALTERNATIVES TO
FORMALDEHYDE-BASED
EMBALMING FLUIDS

You might be interested to know that embalming is rarely practiced in other countries. Yes, there are some famous exceptions, including Eva Peron, Joseph Stalin, and several other heads of state. For the most part, however, embalming (with formaldehyde) is considered at the very least to be yet another American quirk, and at the most to be outright dangerous.

According to the London Hazards Centre, "The International Agency for Research on Cancer (IARC), which is part of the World Health Organisation, has designated formaldehyde as a known cause of several types of throat and nasal cancer."

There are, of course, exceptions. Australia and many European countries require embalming if the body is to be transported across borders. New South Wales, in Australia, requires embalming for above ground burials (in mausoleums), when a body is to be kept unrefrigerated for five hours or more, or when it is not to be buried for eight days or more.

Option 1: Glutaraldehyde

Some embalmers prefer to use glutaraldehyde as a replacement to formaldehyde as it is considered by some to be less toxic. While that may be so, my research does not convince me that it can be used without risk.

Glutaraldehyde is a colorless, oily, liquid chemical with a pungent odor. According to the Centers for Disease Control & Prevention (CDC), glutaraldehyde is used in a number of applications including:

- As a cold sterilant in the health care industry

- As a cross-linking and tanning agent

- As a biocide in metalworking fluids and in oil and gas pipelines

- As an antimicrobial in water-treatment systems

- As a slimicide in paper manufacturing

- As a preservative in cosmetics

- As a disinfectant in animal housing

- As a tissue fixative in histology and pathology labs

- As a hardening agent in the development of X-rays

- In embalming solutions

- In the preparation of grafts and bioprostheses

- In various clinical applications

Unfortunately, the chemical does pose health hazards (for the living). Again, according to the CDC, it can be absorbed into the body through inhalation, ingestion, and skin contact, and can cause side-effects, including:

- Throat and lung irritation

- Asthma and difficulty breathing

- Contact and/or allergic dermatitis

- Nasal irritation

- Sneezing

- Wheezing

- Burning eyes and conjunctivitis

Glutaraldehyde may not be as toxic to the environment as formaldehyde is. While I could find no definitive information regarding the United States' stance on how the chemical affects the environment, the Australian government seems to consider it at low risk for causing environmental damage.

According to the Australian Government's Department of Sustainability, Environment, Water, Population and Communities, "Glutaraldehyde is moderately toxic to aquatic animals and moderately to highly toxic to algae. Due to its short life in the environment, (however,) glutaraldehyde has minimal impact on the environment."[23]

Option 2: NatureEarth®

As a response to growing concern about the environment and calls for "green" burials, chemical companies are increasingly searching for non-toxic, but effective, chemicals to use in the embalming process. The company NatureEarth® by LDI, with its AARDBalm line, claims to have created just such products (please note that I provide this information as a service, not as an endorsement).

According to the company's marketing material, their formaldehyde-free embalming product:

- Uses all-natural, non-toxic ingredients,

- Is nearly odorless; no need for prolonged use of ventilation system,

- Offers broad efficacy to kill bacteria and viruses,

- Eliminates ground water contamination from leaching formaldehyde after burials,

- Is suitable for use in green burial grounds,

- Eliminates exposure to formaldehyde during embalming,

- Offers no threat of contamination if spillage accidentally occurs during treatment of the deceased or transportation,

- Offers containers that can be recycled. Do not require delivery charge premiums or special storage cabinets,

- Is not alcohol based, so it doesn't dehydrate and discolor the body,

- Alleviates hard leathery lips, scarring and pre-inflicted razor burns due to its re-hydrating quality,

- Does not firm the tissue of the deceased and therefore produces a more natural appearance,

- Provides no threat of contamination if spillage accidentally occurs during treatment of the deceased or transportation,

- Offers a more lifelike feel. During viewing families can hold the hand or caress their loved one as the body remains completely natural as in life.

The AARDBalm line is iodine based. Like formaldehyde, it kills the bacteria and microbes that naturally break down a body. Because of this, it stalls the decomposition process for "up to 7 days in an ideal environment, and longer when refrigerated."

Option 3: Enigma

Enigma was introduced to me by Joe Sehee, the founder and Executive Director and President of the Green Burial Council (GBC). The GBC is an independent, tax-exempt, nonprofit organization that works to encourage environmentally sustainable death care. The organization encourages green burial (discussed in an upcoming chapter), and offers its stamp of approval to providers of green burial services and products.

Enigma, produced by The Champion Company, is a natural, biodegradable, essential oil-based alternative to toxic and noxious embalming chemicals. At the time of this writing, Enigma is a four-product line that progresses from a topically-applied deodorizing product for minimal disruption of the natural cycle to an arterial embalming fluid that is injected into the body just as a formaldehyde-based product would be.

The benefit of the Enigma line, of course, is that the ingredients used harm neither the environment nor those who come in contact with them, while preserving the body for up to 3 – 5 days, or up to a week when using supplemental refrigeration. An additional benefit to the use of these products is that, while the arterial fluid may be prohibited by religions that do not approve defiling the body (which embalming can be considered), the topically-applied product may be acceptable.

The Champion Company markets their Enigma line as "ecobalming" products and reports that they can be used in either green burial or when cremation is desired. The Green Burial Council, which is extremely selective in issuing its stamp of approval, lends great credence to the company's claims. What does all this mean? It means that there are alternatives to formaldehyde-based embalming products and, depending upon your beliefs, customs and wishes, you can make choices that will best reflect your loved one's values and wishes.

If you would like your loved one's remains to be embalmed and are concerned about the chemicals used, be sure to discuss the matter with the funeral home you have chosen.

Dry Ice: An Alternative to Embalming

Quite a few religions forbid or frown upon embalming and other methods that interfere with the natural decomposition of the body. Others dislike the idea of embalming because of the harm toxic chemical exposure can do to those who spend time with the embalmed body, as well as to the environment.

Refrigeration is an effective method for preserving a body that does not require the use of embalming fluids. Of course, the refrigeration-only method is best when transportation is not necessary (or is very limited) as some states require embalming if a body is to be transported. According to Mortuary Response Solutions in its report on good ideas for the storage of human remains, the best temperature for body preservation is between 38 and 42 degrees Fahrenheit. At those temperatures, a body can be preserved for up to three months.

Dry ice is an alternative to the refrigeration method. While effective, caution should be used when handling dry ice.

Dry ice is carbon dioxide that has been cooled to -78.5 degrees Celsius (-109.3 degrees Fahrenheit). It offers superior cooling benefits, BUT can burn living skin and damage the remains of your loved one if applied directly to the body.

To avoid burning, the person handling dry ice should wear a leather apron and leather gloves. To avoid damaging your loved one's remains, the ice should not be applied directly to the body. Instead, make sure that a sheet or thin blanket is placed between the ice and body.

When using dry ice, it is best if the ice is cut into brick-sized blocks. These, then, can be packed around and under the body for maximal cooling.

Jerrigrace Lyons, a home funeral educator, explains, "For three-day wakes, we generally use dry ice. It is extremely cold (minus 110 degrees Fahrenheit). We place it under the torso of the body and a small piece on top so it freezes the fluids in the lungs and stomach. We have rarely seen any fluids coming from the mouth or nose because of this. Even when the deceased has purged a little brownish fluid from the mouth (again rare) it has not upset anyone. Families often deal with far more fluids and other matter released from the body when their loved one is in the dying process. We also use therapeutic-grade essential oils that are antibacterial and smell wonderful."

The dry ice will have to be replenished daily. Approximately 30 pounds will be needed to preserve a body for a 24 hour period, depending upon the ambient temperature. Because it can be difficult to find dry ice in such large quantities, you may have to call a number of suppliers in order to find the quantities you will need.

Some people who choose to use dry ice as a preservative also choose to use essential oils to mask any smells emitted by the body. Essential oils are very concentrated oils extracted from different flowers, seeds, leaves and other plant parts. Because of their concentration, they are highly fragrant. An additional benefit of using essential oils to anoint the body is that most have strong antiseptic qualities that can help to slow decay. A favorite is Lavender Essential Oil as its soothing properties can calm the living.

Pricing

Dry ice often sells for about $1 - $2 per pound. Because it sublimates (evaporates) at a rate of about 10 pounds per day in a typical ice chest, you will have to replenish it periodically. At 30 pounds needed per 24 hour period, you are looking at about $30 - $60 per day.

As a note of caution, do not store dry ice in your freezer. It will continue to sublimate there (meaning that you will not be "preserving" it by placing it in the freezer) and its extremely low temperature can affect your freezer's controls.

The price of Lavender Essential Oil varies. Make sure that you purchase pure, or therapeutic grade, essential oil as those that are "cut" with other oils will not offer the same benefits. If you cannot readily find Lavender Essential Oil, try contacting a health food store or a local spa or chiropractor's office, as it is often used in massage.

OTHER PREPARATIONS OF THE BODY

Embalming is not the only body preparation that is usually conducted when someone dies. If there is to be an open-casket service, the body must also be prepared for viewing. This can be as minimal as cleansing and dressing the body, or can be as extensive as repairing damage, applying makeup and styling the hair.

If you have requested any sort of preparation, other than the washing of the body, which is standard, you will most likely be asked to provide a photograph, or photographs, of your loved one. If your loved one wore dentures or eyeglasses, you may be asked to provide those as well.

If your loved one is to be embalmed using a fixative such as formaldehyde, his body will be posed before the embalming fluid is injected. Most people are posed with their hands either crossed at the stomach or with their arms and hands placed straight at their sides. Some embalmers will curl the hands around a wad of cotton to give them a naturally graceful appearance when the cotton is later removed, or to allow the embalmer to later place something between them (a bible or stuffed animal, for instance). The embalmer will also pose the legs, laying them straight out from the torso. Tape may be used to bind feet pointing up (instead of splayed out) as the embalming fluid "fixes" the body.

Many coffins have floor inserts that can be raised so that the decedent's face is closer to the casket opening during viewing.

Regardless, the head will be placed on a pillow to give the appearance of comfort and the face will be turned about 15 degrees to the right, thereby affording visitors an easier view.

Whether embalming is conducted or not, restoration may be necessary, especially if there are any signs of trauma to the body. Restoration includes repairing any tears, hiding injuries and, generally, making the decedent look as "natural" as possible, an effect the industry refers to as a "memory picture."

After embalming and/or restorative work, your loved one's body will be thoroughly washed, dressed and made up using either special mortuary makeup or, when it supplies enough coverage, store-bought makeup. If there is any hair on the face (other than a mustache or beard your loved one may have worn in life), that will be shaved and his nails and any shaggy hair will be trimmed. His hair will be washed and styled as well.

You should know that, even working with photographs, the person preparing your loved one's body may not be able make your loved one look "normal." He may apply too much makeup, or not enough. He may angle the eye-shadow in a way that your loved one never did, or choose the wrong shade of lipstick.

You can be very helpful at this point and, if you have the desire to do so, might even help with the preparations. I'll give you an example.

We have a large family and we are very protective of our own. When it came time to prepare my niece's body for an open-casket service, we spontaneously took over. At that time, my sister, Jahmila's three sisters, her half-sister, assorted cousins, another aunt, and I were at the funeral home simply to spend time with her body.

The Funeral Director who embalmed her, Kyle Smith, met us because he wanted to ask about the clothing we would like her dressed in, about how she styled her hair and about the makeup she wore. He had also asked us to bring her makeup so that he would know the colors she had liked to use.

Jahmila's nail polish was chipped. It so happened that I had a bottle of lime-green nail polish in my purse (it was her favorite color and we had all just had pedicures done with it as a tribute to her). I asked Kyle if he had any nail polish remover and asked my sister if I could paint Jahmila's nails. They both said yes.

What began as painting her nails, ended with us applying her makeup and styling her hair. Who better than those who loved her knew how she liked to look?

I will tell you that this was not an easy task to undertake. It was, in fact, extremely painful. But, it turned into a very meaningful event as it allowed us to perform one last service for our beloved daughter/sister/niece/cousin.

I encourage you, if you feel you can, to take part, however small, in whatever preparations you are able.

Pricing

Pricing of other preparations will vary, and sometimes greatly, from funeral home to funeral home. Price is also affected by the services you request. The National Funeral Directors Association lists the average price for "other preparations" in 2009 as $200. In researching this book, however, I have noted that washing the body and some grooming services may be charged over and above "other preparations."

As a general rule of thumb, make sure you are supplied a full, detailed list of the services included under "other preparations of the body" before agreeing to anything.

CONSIDERATIONS FOR AN IN-GROUND CEMETERY BURIAL

The history of burials dates back to before written time. While many ancient societies had their own rites and rituals to accompany burials, the fact remains that we have been burying our dead for eons.

Burial was often a wholly practical matter. It kept the unpleasant effects of decomposition away from the clan, protected bodies from scavenging animals and, in some circumstances, halted the spread of disease.

While today's burials afford us the same advantages they did our ancestors, there is an additional benefit to this arrangement that cannot be over-valued. Burial gives survivors a physical place to "visit" a loved one. Cemeteries, burial plots and gardens, and mausoleums are designed to instill a sense of peace and the feeling of continuity in the living. Through visiting and tending a burial plot, the grieving often feel a closeness to the departed and feel as if they are keeping their loved one's memory alive.

If your loved one indicated, or you have chosen, that burial would be preferred, there are choices to consider, products to purchase, and services to select.

One of the first decisions to make is where you want your loved one to be buried. If he owns a burial plot or indicated that he would like to be buried in a family plot, then the answer is obvious. If, on the other hand, burial has been decided upon but a plot has not been selected, you will have to start at the beginning.

When choosing a burial plot, things to consider include:

- Would your loved one have preferred to be buried in a cemetery affiliated with her religion? If she was a member (even if she only attended occasionally) of a church, synagogue, mosque or other house of worship, contact its office and ask if it has, or can refer you to, an affiliated cemetery.

- If your loved one lived in another state, should you choose a burial site close to where he lived, or close to where you or his closest kin live?

- Was your loved one a veteran or a direct family member of a veteran (spouse or dependent child), or did he hold a position that would allow him to be buried in a national cemetery? If so, this becomes a consideration as funeral expenses drop significantly for qualified veterans and their family members. National cemeteries do not charge families for opening or closing a grave, for vault liners or for marker placement (for more information on Veterans funeral entitlements, please refer to the chapter, "Military Funeral Honors").

- Is it a municipal site, or privately held? Is the management reputable? Is it owned by one of the three big cemetery conglomerates (which often charge more than smaller companies for the same services)?

- Is the management a member of either the National Cemetery Association or the American Cemetery Association, two groups that uphold high standards among their members?

- Does the cemetery have rules and regulations regarding grave markers, monuments, and/or restrictions on adornments (flowers, flags, etc.)? Some memorial park cemeteries, for instance, mandate that only small flush-to-the-ground bronze plaques be used, while others allow gravestones but not monuments.

- Can you purchase a grave marker from the vendor of your choice, or do you have to purchase it from the cemetery?

- Are they convenient to you, other family members and friends?

- Will you be given a deed to the site, meaning that it is sold as a piece of real estate, though with usage restrictions on it?

- If you are not deeded the site, what rights to use are transferred to you upon purchase? For instance, if your loved one purchased a plot and later decided to will his body to science, can the burial rights be transferred or sold?

- Are there fees besides the purchase price? For instance, are there perpetual care and maintenance fees? If so, how much are they and how are they billed (one time, monthly, yearly, etc.)?

- What happens if at some point you (or other family members) can no longer afford the maintenance fees?

- Can you choose to tend the grave yourself? If so, are there rules as to how the space must be maintained?

- Does the plot purchase price include opening and closing of the grave (which can be quite expensive - and, note, grave diggers expect to be tipped)?

- Is a grave liner mandated? Many cemeteries require these liners because they keep the ground from sinking or settling as, over time, the coffin itself settles or disintegrates. The liners are three-sided (placed on the sides and above the casket) and are usually constructed of reinforced concrete slabs that are assembled at the site. These are most often sold by the cemetery.

- Alternately, is a coffin vault, also called a burial vault, required? A coffin vault is more substantial than a grave liner. It is a one-piece unit that surrounds the entire casket and is constructed of concrete, fiberglass, plastic, or metal. Coffin vaults, when they are required, are usually chosen when a casket is purchased (so the sizing will be correct). If you purchase a casket from an outside vendor or even online, remember to ask for its outside dimensions so that you can be sure it will fit within the coffin vault supplied by the cemetery.

- Note: State laws do not require either a coffin vault or a grave liner. Cemeteries, however, can make the one or the other a requirement as they make long-term maintenance easier. You should be aware that The Funeral Rule covers funeral homes – and not cemeteries. Be doubly cautious when dealing with a cemetery and ask that any requirements, fees, restrictions and rules be provided in writing. Make sure you have a signed quotation prior to purchasing a plot.

- Can you purchase side-by-side gravesites (because you know that at some point you will want to be buried next to your loved one)?

- Do not purchase a burial plot sight unseen. Photos can be deceptive and, besides, you want to know the exact location of the plot prior to purchase. If you are unhappy with the plot shown to you, you can always ask if there are premium sites, maybe on a hill or under a tree. As in any real estate transaction, location matters and premium sites command higher prices. When you purchase a site, insist that he cemetery provide you with a plot map with your loved one's site clearly marked.

- Will you be burying your loved one on private ground? If so, are there any state laws or community rules that forbid you to do so? Please note that if you later sell the land, you should probably disclose the grave's location to any potential buyers.

- Are you limited to burying your loved one in a casket, or can you use some other sort of burial container? Caskets, especially "sealed" caskets, generally slow down decomposition because they place a barrier between your loved one's body and the microbes and bacteria in soil that will eventually turn it into the organic matter that can re-enter the life cycle. If returning to the lifecycle was important to your loved one, you may want to consider burial in an organic shroud instead of in a casket.

- Does the cemetery offer "green" burial sites? Green burial is becoming ever more popular as people are paying more attention to the environment. Some cemeteries offer "green" areas where embalmed bodies are prohibited and maintenance is more environmentally friendly than in traditional cemeteries.

Pricing

With more and more cemeteries being managed by a few large corporations, pricing for in-ground burial on cemetery land is becoming standardized. This does not help the consumer. By squeezing out smaller management companies, the larger corporations are losing competition and so are able to set higher prices.

Because the Funeral Rule applies only to funeral homes and not to cemeteries, cemetery management is allowed to tack on any additional charges it wants. Cost can vary greatly from cemetery to cemetery and it is important that you research your options.

Some factors that affect pricing include:

- Whether the cemetery is located in a metropolitan or rural setting, with metropolitan sites generally being more expensive,

- Whether the cemetery is public or private,

- Plot location, with "premium" plots (those on top of hills, those with better views, those with gardens nearby) costing more,

- Opening and closing fees (this is the polite term for digging the grave and filling the hole),

- Time of day and day of week grave is opened and closed. The cemetery has to hire/schedule grave diggers and on holidays and weekends, their fees can go up,

- Time of day and day of week for burial. Because of demand for weekend funerals, burials on Saturdays and Sundays (and on holidays) usually carry a "premium" fee, which can be as much as 50% over or even double weekday rates,

- Whether the deceased was a resident of a township or not. Some public cemeteries charge non-residents an additional fee,

- Time of year. If a snow plow is required to clear the grave or a hydraulic hammer is needed to break up the ground, there will be additional charges,

- Whether a grave liner or vault is mandatory, and, if so, whether you are required to purchase it from the cemetery or if you can shop around (a National Funeral Directors' Association survey found that the cost of a vault alone in 2009, increased total funeral costs by about $1,195.00),

- Whether plots are single, or "multiple-depth" (one on top of the other),

- Whether the cemetery management includes "set-up fees" in their pricing – this is usually preparing the site for a service (i.e., placing Astro Turf around the open grave, setting up chairs or awnings, etc.),

- Whether you can purchase your own marker or are required to purchase one from the cemetery,

- Whether the cemetery requires that you purchase a temporary marker to be put in place until the permanent marker can be prepared and delivered,

- Whether there are perpetual care fees.

Odds & Ends - In some states, burial plots are sold as real estate and the cemetery must be or must hire a licensed real estate agent to oversee the transaction.

Odds & Ends - Cemetery plots are considered assets and should be handled as such.

Odds & Ends – Burial vaults and liners are not required by many, if any, cemeteries outside of the United States. They were developed in the U.S. in the late 1800's by L.G. Haase Manufacturing Company. The Haase family owned a cemetery in Forest Park, Illinois and they dreamed up the vaults as a complementary product to their plot sales. Until that time, graves were often lined with bricks, which would hold some of the weight of the soil placed on top of a casket, and, hopefully, would keep the soil from crushing the casket itself. Several decades later, in 1930, after then-owner Wilbert Haase became interested in Egyptian mummification, the company began promoting "waterproof" vaults. The company eventually purchased a number of plastics companies and began to incorporate that material into its vaults. Today, the company's "premier" casket vault is the Wilbert Bronze, marketed as, "Precise engineering and more than 40 hours of hand-crafted detail produce Wilbert's supreme and only triple-reinforced burial vault." The Wilbert Bronze retails for about $9,850.00.

Odds & Ends - Service Corporation International, or SCI, is the largest death-care service company in the United States, owning and/or managing some 12% of the funeral and cemetery market. According to its 2nd Quarter 2011 published results, as of "June 30, 2011, we owned and operated 1,429 funeral homes and 379 cemeteries (of which 215 are combination locations) in 43 states, eight Canadian provinces, the District of Columbia and Puerto Rico."

While information on per burial fees is difficult to find, SCI reported cemetery revenues of $190.9 Million in its last quarter results (2nd Quarter 2011) with a gross profit of $39.6 Million.

In-Ground Burial on Private Land

Do you own enough land where an in-ground burial becomes a possibility? If not you, does a family member of yours? Or, perhaps a friend owns a large enough plot?

Burial on private land opens the door to more possibilities than on cemetery grounds. There are no "rules" and "restrictions" that keep you from burying your loved one in a way that is meaningful to you and that would have been meaningful to her. You are not limited to bronze plaques embedded on the ground, or to a restriction on floral arrangements. You do not need a multi-ton coffin liner, or even a coffin. And, you do not have to buy a plot or pay maintenance fees.

Burying your loved one on private land can feel more personal than burying her among strangers in a cemetery that holds thousands. It allows you to plant a tree or flowering bush above her grave and, perhaps, to install a park bench where you can sit and remember all that she meant to you.

It is not always practical, of course, to bury a loved one on private property. Some counties may place restrictions on private land burials. There may be acreage requirements, or laws that mandate how far from the border of your property you can bury someone, or that instruct on whether you can bury your loved one near a lake, creek or pond.

While burying your loved one in a cemetery can often seem "easiest" as the land has already been zoned for burial, the "rules" are already in place and, pretty much, all you have to do is show up and pay the bill, many people find more meaning in laying their loved ones to rest on privately held ground.

You should be aware that some states place restrictions on burial anywhere other than in a "duly authorized cemetery." States with such restrictions include Louisiana, Indiana, California and Washington State. If you want to bury your loved one on private land, then, you will have to contact the local zoning board and petition that the land be re-zoned. You may also be required to contact your local Board of Health.

Land designated for cemetery use contains certain perpetuity clauses that restrict future use as anything other than as a cemetery. This both protects your loved one's grave from being disturbed, but also ensures that, as land changes hands, future owners are informed that a grave exists on their land. Further, perpetuity clauses may require that a plan be in place for land maintenance in future years.

You should know that if you decide to bury on private land, there are statutes in some states that may stipulate that private cemeteries have an "implied easement in gross." This allows family members and the descendants of the decedent perpetual access to the burial site. Texas, South Carolina and Virginia are three such states.

So, what does this mean for you and burying your loved one on private land?

If you own the land, right of access is a good thing because, even if you sell the land at some future date, it is more than likely that you will have access to your loved one's grave. If you are burying your loved one on another's property, you are still in luck as you and your family should have access to the grave, even if you and the land owner have a falling out.

If, on the other hand, you are a landowner and a friend wants to bury his loved one on your land, you must understand that, even if you do have a falling out at some future date, the family members of the deceased can reasonably expect access to the gravesite, forever going forward.

If the idea of burying your loved one on private property appeals to you, below are a few things to consider. They are not meant to sway you in any direction, but to help you to make the decision that is best and most meaningful for you, your family and your friends.

- If you do decide to bury on private land, choose the location wisely. Is the area prone to flooding, earthquakes or other natural events that could possibly disrupt the gravesite? Is it near a river, or are there any plans to dam or widen the river in the works (the area may be dry today, but are there any plans that could turn it into a flood zone in the future)?

- Are you required by town, county or state ordinance to disclose the location of a grave located on private property to officials so that it will be entered into a record of any sort? The answer to this, by the way, is most likely, *yes*.

- Are there restrictions on lot size? For instance, does your town, county or state allow burials on private land that are at least two (or six or fifty) acres, but not on smaller properties?

- If you do decide to bury your loved one on private property, will you have her body embalmed first? If so, have you considered the effects of the embalming fluids leaking (eventually) into the surrounding soil?

- Thinking long-term, if you decide to bury a loved one on your private property, will the grave's presence make future sale of the property difficult?

Pricing

In truth, I am not sure whether charging for burial on private land is permissible, and, if it is, if it is permissible in all states and counties. Generally speaking, states have laws governing cemeteries. Hypothetically speaking, by charging you for a "plot", the land owner may be in danger of calling his/her land a de facto cemetery. If the land owner did not apply for and receive approval for the land to be used as a cemetery, then he/she may be breaking the law.

Depending upon your state, county and town, there may be fees associated with re-zoning land for cemetery use. At a minimum, you may have to pay a registrar's fee for the right to do so, or a recording fee so that the county keeps records of the plot. Contact your local registrar's office to ask about any fees and regulations.

In addition to local government fees, you may have to hire a funeral home to transport the body to the site (in those states that limit transportation of bodies to funeral directors and embalmers).

You may also have to hire someone to dig the grave. Fees for that work are completely at the discretion of the individual you hire.

If you choose to have a member of the clergy oversee a graveside service, you should note that while many churches do not have set funeral service fees, a modest contribution is usually expected and gratefully accepted. Just as a point of reference, I donated $250 to the church where we held Jahmila's funeral service (and another $80 to the Music Director). That service was held in the church and I would have offered more had the pastor had to travel.

Odds & Ends - As a final note, if you do decide to bury your loved one on private land, you should ensure that the final resting spot is at least 150 feet from any water supply (so there will be no leakage into the water supply system), at least 25 feet from any power line (to avoid power companies from digging up the site while working on the lines – and to avoid you accidentally hitting a line when digging the grave) and at least 25 feet from any neighboring property line (unless local laws say differently, of course).

BURIAL IN A MAUSOLEUM

As an alternative to an in-ground burial, you can consider burial in a mausoleum. Historically, mausoleums were large, above-ground, ornate buildings where the remains of royalty and the ultra-wealthy were "buried." Perhaps the most famous of all mausoleums is the Taj Mahal, built by Shah Jahan in India to hold the remains of his beloved third wife, Mumtaz Mahal, who died during the birth of their 14th child. Over the years, mausoleums have generally been built on a much smaller scale, though they often remain ornate.

Family mausoleums have been popular throughout history. Whether located on family property or within a cemetery, family mausoleums allow the remains of a number of family members to be housed together "for all eternity."

Many of today's cemeteries offer mausoleum burial. While these are not restricted to family members (though you can purchase any number of vaults side-by-side or on top of one another), mausoleums offer several benefits over in-ground burial.

Mausoleums save space. Instead of one casket being buried per plot below ground, any number of caskets can be housed one above the other in a mausoleum.

Each space, called a "crypt", holds one or two caskets and, taken as a whole, the rows and columns of crypts resemble a large chest of drawers. Most mausoleums are built six or seven crypts high with any number of crypts spread out along a row. Usually, a small plaque is placed on the front panel of each crypt, detailing whose body lies inside. A vase to hold a small spray of flowers may also be attached to the front panel.

Because there are no ground maintenance or monument fees involved when burying someone in a mausoleum, and because the footprint of a crypt is smaller than that of a grave, mausoleum burials tend to be the less expensive alternative.

Local weather and water tables can become a consideration when deciding between in-ground burial and internment within a mausoleum crypt. In some locations, such as in and around New Orleans and in the Florida Keys, where the water tables are high, in-ground burial is not an option. In those locations, burial in a mausoleum makes perfect sense.

There are different kinds of mausoleums to choose from. Single crypts are above-ground buildings designed for one entombment. Double crypts are available in three different arrangements:

- **Tandem crypts** accommodate two entombments, positioned lengthwise,

- **Companion crypts** accommodate two entombments, positioned side-by-side,

- **Westminster crypts** position one entombment above ground and the other below.

When deciding whether to bury your loved one in the ground or in a mausoleum, there is one factor you should take into consideration. That is that, as a body decomposes, it gives off gases. "Sealed" caskets, which have been marketed as being able to "preserve" a body, actually trap the gases, which can build up until the casket becomes highly pressurized. Unfortunately, sealed caskets have been known to explode in an event called "exploding casket syndrome."

Exterior heat can add to the gas build-up. When a casket is buried in the ground, it is generally maintained at a cooler temperature than one kept above ground. Mausoleums, especially those located in warm climates without air-conditioning, then, are sometimes blamed as contributing to the syndrome.

Research indicates that today's casket makers, aware of the syndrome, now include a protective valve when designing caskets that allows gases to escape, but that keeps the elements from entering the casket. Further, well-built mausoleums are built with ventilation systems that release gases before they can build to explosive levels.

That being said, I've read accounts of mausoleum personnel opening caskets after the encryption ceremony when all the mourners have gone home. Why would they do this? Because there is a risk that the casket gasket, or burp-valve as it has been called, may fail. An explosion would not only destroy your loved one's casket (as well as your loved one's body), but could destroy the mausoleum itself.

If you decide to encrypt your loved one in a mausoleum, be sure to ask about their casket policies prior to purchasing a crypt.

Pricing

As with all things funeral, pricing depends on the supplier but, generally speaking, encryption in a mausoleum is less expensive than ground burial in a cemetery. A general figure for a single crypt seems to be about $2,000, though you may find crypts for much less, as well as for much more. As with in-ground burial, pricing depends on location, with interior crypts costing more than outdoor ones.

The biggest savings when choosing a mausoleum crypt over in-ground burial actually come from the things you won't have to buy, including a grave liner or vault, a headstone, or a sealer casket. Maintenance fees are also less expensive as grass does not need to be mowed, fertilized or de-bugged, as it must be over a grave. Further, encryption fees tend to be less than the fees cemeteries charge for opening and closing a grave.

Like in-ground cemetery burial, pricing may vary day to day, with weekend and holiday encryption being more expensive than regular weekday encryption, and encryption later in the day costing more than morning services.

Odds & Ends – The word "mausoleum" comes from the tomb of Mausolus, the ruler of Caria in southwestern Asia Minor. The tomb is one of the Seven Wonders of the World and was built between about 353 and 351 BC by Mausolus' sister and widow, Artemisia. Roman author Pliny the Elder (AD 23–79), described the monument as being almost square, with a total periphery of 411 feet (125 m). It was bounded by 36 columns, and the top formed a 24-step pyramid surmounted by a four-horse marble chariot. For some 17 centuries, the tomb overlooked the city of Halicarnassus, even after the city fell into ruin. The tomb was eventually destroyed in a series of earthquakes that shook the region. What remains of it can be viewed in the Mausoleum Room at the British Museum.

MILITARY BURIAL BENEFITS

The United States Department of Veterans Affairs oversees military burial benefits. These benefits are available to eligible veterans of the armed services, to their spouses, and to their dependents. Burial benefits are offered both in national cemeteries and in private cemeteries, though the family's obligations (and expenses) differ.

Burial in a National Cemetery includes:

- A gravesite in any of the 131 National Cemeteries (with space available),

- Opening and closing of the grave,

- Perpetual care,

- A government headstone or marker,

- A burial flag,

- A Presidential Memorial Certificate.

You should note that, while the above are provided at no cost to the family, the veteran must be eligible (below), must be approved, and the burial must be scheduled by the Department of Veterans Affairs' Scheduling Office. Further, these benefits are available to those who opt for cremation as well as to those who choose full body burial.

Those eligible for burial in a National Cemetery include:

- Veterans and Members of the Armed Forces (Navy, Army, Air Force, Marine Corps & Coast Guard).

- Any member of the Armed Forces who dies while on active duty.

- Any veteran discharged for any reason other than dishonorable (note, though, that post-1980 eligibility conditions require that the person served for 24 continuous months or for the entire term that the person was called to be on active duty).

- Any U.S. citizen who, at a time of war in which the U.S. was engaged, served in the Armed Forces of any Government which was an ally of the U.S. and who, at the times of enlistment and death, was a U.S. citizen. Discharge from said Armed Forces had to have been through death or through honorary discharge in order to qualify for U.S. military burial benefits.

- Members of Reserve Components or members of the Reserve Officers Training Corps.

- Reservists and National Guard members who were eligible for retirement pay, or who would have been but for being under the age of 60.

- Members of reserve components, and members of the Army National Guard or the Air National Guard who die:

  ♦ While hospitalized or undergoing treatment for injury or disease contracted while attending an authorized training camp or cruise,

  ♦ While performing authorized travel to or from that camp or cruise,

  ♦ Or while hospitalized or undergoing treatment at the expense of the United States for injury or disease contracted or incurred under honorable conditions while engaged in said activity.

- Members of reserve components who died or were disabled during:

  - ♦ A period of active duty for training,

  - ♦ From a disease or injury incurred or aggravated in line of duty,

  - ♦ A period of inactive duty training, from an injury or certain cardiovascular disorders incurred or aggravated in line of duty.

- Commissioned Officers of the National Oceanic and Atmospheric Administration who served on full-time duty on or after July 29, 1945,

- Or, a Commissioned Officer who served before July 29, 1945; and,

  - ♦ Was assigned to an area of immediate military hazard as determined by the Secretary of Defense while in time of war, or in a Presidentially declared national emergency; or,

  - ♦ Served in the Philippine Islands on December 7, 1941, and continuously in such islands thereafter.

- Public Health Services Officers including:

  - ♦ Commissioned Officers of the Regular or Reserve Corps of the Public Health Service who served on full-time duty on or after July 29, 1945.

♦ Commissioned Officers of the Regular or Reserve Corps of the Public Health Service who performed full-time duty prior to July 29, 1945:

◊ In time of war;

◊ On detail for duty with the Army, Navy, Air Force, Marine Corps, or Coast Guard; or,

◊ While the Service was part of the military forces of the United States pursuant to Executive Order of the President

◊ Commissioned Officers serving on inactive duty training as defined in section 101(23), title 38, United States Code, whose death resulted from an injury acquired or aggravated in the line of duty.

• United States Merchant Mariners with oceangoing service during the period of armed conflict, December 7, 1941, to December 31, 1946.

• United States Merchant Mariners who served on block-ships in support of Operation Mulberry during World War II.

• Any Philippine Veteran who was a citizen of the United States or an alien lawfully admitted for permanent residence in the United States at the time of their death; and resided in the United States at the time of their death; and,

a. was a person who served before July 1, 1946, in the organized military forces of the Government of the Commonwealth of the Philippines, while such forces were in the service of the Armed Forces of the United States pursuant to the military order of the President dated July 26, 1941, including organized guerilla forces under commanders appointed, designated, or subsequently recognized by the Commander in Chief, Southwest Pacific Area, or other competent authority in the Army of the United States, and who died on or after November 1, 2000; or,

b. was a person who enlisted between October 6, 1945, and June 30, 1947, with the Armed Forces of the United States with the consent of the Philippine government, pursuant to section 14 of the Armed Forces Voluntary Recruitment Act of 1945, and who died on or after December 16, 2003.

- The spouse or surviving spouse of an eligible Veteran is eligible for interment in a national cemetery even if that Veteran is not buried or memorialized in a national cemetery.

- The spouse or surviving spouse of a member of the Armed Forces of the United States whose remains are unavailable for burial is also eligible for burial.

- The surviving spouse of an eligible Veteran who had a subsequent remarriage to a non-Veteran and whose death occurred on or after January 1, 2000, is eligible for burial in a national cemetery, based on his or her marriage to the eligible Veteran.

- The minor children of an eligible Veteran. For purpose of burial in a national cemetery, a minor child is a child who is unmarried and:

a. who is under 21 years of age; or,

    b. who is under 23 years of age and pursuing a full-time course of instruction at an approved educational institution.

- The unmarried adult child of an eligible Veteran. For purpose of burial in a national cemetery, an unmarried adult child is:

  ♦ Of any age but became permanently physically or mentally disabled and incapable of self-support before reaching 21 years of age, or before reaching 23 years of age if pursuing a full-time course of instruction at an approved educational institution. Proper supporting documentation must be provided.

- Biological or adoptive parents, who died after October 13, 2010, and whose biological or adoptive child was a service member:

  a. whose death occurred on or after October 7, 2001, and,

  b. whose death was the result of a hostile casualty or a training-related injury, and,

  c. who is interred in a national cemetery, in a gravesite with available space for subsequent interment, and,

  d. at the time of the parent's death, had no spouse, surviving spouse, or child who is buried, or who, upon death, may be eligible for burial in a national cemetery.

- Such other persons or classes of persons as designated by the Secretary of Veterans Affairs (38 U.S.C. § 2402(6)) or the Secretary of Defense (Public Law 95-202, § 401, and

38 CFR § 3.7(x)).

Please note that the foregoing list of eligible persons was taken from the United States Department of Veterans Affairs website. To review this site, or to search for updates, please follow the link in the Military Burial Benefits Resources section at the back of this book.

If you have chosen to have your loved one buried in a National Cemetery, you will find a helpful Burial in a National Cemetery Checklist at the back of this book.

Military burial benefits are available to eligible veterans outside of national cemeteries (in private cemeteries), though the benefits are fewer and they do not extend to family members.

Veteran burial benefits, at no cost to the family, in private cemeteries include:

- A government headstone or marker

- A burial flag

- A Presidential Memorial Certificate

If you opt for a private cemetery, you should be aware that some cemeteries have taken advantage of veterans and their families in the past by offering "free" burial for veterans, but demanding that a second gravesite (or other products and/or services) be purchased at the time arrangements for the veteran are made. Therefore, if you opt for a private cemetery burial, be sure to ask, up front, for a full, itemized and detailed quotation. Other questions you should ask include:

- If a second gravesite purchase is required, where will it be located? Will it be next to the veteran's gravesite or will it be located in another part of the cemetery?

- Is a burial vault or liner required? If so, what is the price of same? Further, is there a fee for placing the vault or liner?

- If you must pre-pay for a second site, or other product/ service, what type of account will your funds be held in? Are the funds reimbursable and, if so, under what conditions?

- Are you free to sell the second site or products/services?

- Will the cemetery allow the government-issued marker or headstone? If so, is there a fee for placing it?

- If the government marker is not allowed, what do they require? And, must you purchase it through them or are you free to purchase the marker elsewhere?

Remember that the Funeral Rule does not extend to cemeteries and, because they are unregulated, you have to take extra care when making arrangements with a private cemetery.

If your loved one was an eligible veteran, or otherwise eligible for military burial benefits, and you have decided to take advantage of this benefit, you can make arrangements through your chosen funeral home. They, in turn, will contact the proper government offices. If you opt to oversee your own funeral arrangements, contact the Department of Veterans Affairs directly and ask for help making these arrangements. For links to helpful resources, please refer to the Military Burial Benefits link at the back of this book.

Pricing

While the National Cemetery costs are covered by the government for eligible veterans and their eligible family members, all other costs are borne by the family. These include transportation costs, embalming and other preparations of the body fees, any charges related to services you may hold in your loved one's honor and, if you have chosen it, all costs related to cremation. Further, plot/mausoleum and all other cemetery costs charged by other-than-National-Cemeteries are the family's expense.

MILITARY FUNERAL HONORS

If your loved one was an eligible veteran of the armed services, you may request Military Funeral Honors. This will include an Honor Guard detail of not less than two members of the Armed Forces. At least one of the service members will be from the veteran's parent Service. The service will (at least) consist of the folding of the American flag and presentation to next of kin and the playing of Taps (by a live bugler if available, or a recording if not).

Those eligible for Military Funeral Honors are:

- Military members on active duty or in the Selected Reserve,

- Former military members who served on active duty and departed under conditions other than dishonorable,

- Former military members who completed at least one term of enlistment or period of initial obligated service in the Selected Reserve and who departed under conditions other than dishonorable,

- Former military members discharged from the Selected Reserve due to a disability incurred or aggravated in the line of duty.

The Department of Defense (DOD) is responsible for providing Military Funeral Honors for eligible veterans. If you have hired a funeral director, he/she will contact the DOD to make the request on your behalf. If you are not using a funeral director, contact the DOD yourself. The Department of Veterans Affairs National Cemetery Administration cemetery staff can help to make the arrangements if your loved one is to be buried in a Veterans cemetery (contact info can be found in the <u>Military Funeral Honors Resources</u> section of this book).

Pricing

There is no charge for Military Funeral Honors for eligible veterans. Please contact the DOD with as much advance notice as possible, however, to ensure proper coordination.

Burial at Sea – Direct Sea Burial

In times past, on long ocean crossings, death was common and burial at sea was the only option available. Generally, bodies were wrapped in canvas shrouds or, on ships with a carpenter and spare wood, placed in coffins, and were then lowered beneath the waves after a ceremony.

Today, not much has changed. Except that burial at sea is now more an option than a necessity. And, of course, there are laws that govern where sea burials can take place.

In deciding if burial at sea is the best way to care for your loved one's remains, you must first decide whether burial at sea without cremation, also called "direct sea burial", is your preference (or was your loved one's preference), or whether your loved one's body should first be cremated.

In this section, we'll look at non-Navy direct sea burial (without cremation). In future sections, you can find information about Navy sea burials and sea burials after cremation (found in the chapter titled "Cremation").

In the United States, burial at sea is governed, at a minimum, by the Environmental Protection Agency (EPA). Some states and/ or counties may have additional regulations that regulate beyond the rules set by the EPA, including obtaining a burial permit prior to sea burial, a transportation permit to carry the body to the point of embarkation, or, if you live in one of the seven states that mandate hiring a funeral director (CT, IL, IN, LA, MI, NE, NY), that you do so.

That being said, the following are the general rules for direct sea burial you will have to comply with.

Who can transport the remains?

The EPA has issued a general permit to "all persons" for transporting human remains for purposes of burial at sea, subject to a few conditions (below). This means that you can use your own boat, a friend's boat or charter a boat.

Location requirements:

While the EPA allows just about anyone to take human remains out to sea for burial, it is very clear about how far out to sea you must go before releasing the body. According the Code of Federal Regulations Section 229.1 (40CFR229), burial of non-cremated human remains shall take place:

    a. At least 3 nautical miles from land, and,

    b.   In water at least 600 feet deep.

Exceptions are made for the following locations, where water must be at least 1,800 feet deep:

    ♦ Off St. Augustine and Cape Canaveral, Florida,

    ♦ Off the Dry Tortugas, Florida,

Off the Mississippi River Delta, Louisiana, to Pensacola, Florida.

If you are considering burial off the coast of California, you need to take into account that there are ocean areas set aside by the state as conservancy waters. Burial is not permitted in those areas, according to Dennis Longaberger, a boat captain in Santa Barbara. There are, however, a few areas where full-body sea burial is permitted and there are companies that provide the service. Captain Dennis' company, Coastal Sunset Memorials, is one of them.

One of the provisions for full body sea burials is that "all necessary measures shall be taken to ensure that the remains sink to the bottom rapidly and permanently." To ensure that your loved one's body sinks rapidly and permanently, the following steps should be taken.

For Casketed Remains

- The body should be placed in a metal casket weighing at least four times the body's weight. For example, a 150-pound body would require a casket weighing at least 600 pounds to compensate for buoyancy,

- If not using a coffin that weighs at least four times the body's weight, then ballast at least equal to that amount should be placed inside the casket,

- A minimum of six 3-inch in diameter holes should be drilled in the top of the casket (the side with the holes will face up – if you drill in the bottom, for instance, the casket will flip when hitting the water). This is meant to ensure the "rapid and permanent" sinking of the casket to the sea floor,

- All plastic and fabric materials must be removed from the casket prior to burial at sea (note, this is an EPA requirement),

- The casket must be secured lengthwise and from side to side. Stainless steel chains are recommended for this. As a note, shipping straps are decidedly not recommended due to their rapid deterioration in water,

- To further aid rapid sinking, extra weight can be added to the inside of the casket (cannonballs, cement blocks, barbells, sandbags, etc. – make sure it is of an approved material; i.e., metal or cement). The weight should be added to the foot of the casket (my note) so that the casket submerges feet first.

For Uncasketed Remains

Instead of a casket, you may choose to shroud your loved one's body. Traditionally, sail cloth is used as the shrouding material, though you may choose another biodegradable fabric.

- Enclose the body in the shroud in such a way that ocean movement cannot free the body from it,

- Cut at least 3 slits in the material so that air can vent,

- Attach ballast to the lower (foot) end of the shroud. This can be metal bars or sand bags sewn into the lower section

- Alternately, you can purchase a specially made "sea shroud", which is a cross between a casket and a shroud. Pricing for this, however, begins at about $1,495.

Flowers and/or Wreathes:

The EPA allows you to toss flowers and/or wreaths at the site of disposition. However, these must consist of "materials that are readily decomposable in the marine environment."

Notify the EPA within 30 days:

The EPA requires that you report the burial at sea to their offices within 30 days and that the report is in writing (no phone calls). When informing the EPA of the burial at sea, you will need to include specific information about the body, the location where the body was laid to rest and about the vessel used.

For those who live near a state line, the EPA office you should contact is the one that oversees the port from which the boat transporting the remains embarks. For a list of regional offices, consult the Burial at Sea Resources section of this book.

In the back of this book, I have included a Burial at Sea Checklist of information that you should include when mailing or faxing your notice to your EPA regional contact.

When considering direct sea burial for a loved one, you should take into consideration any religious mandates that would prevent this sort of disposition. Some religions do not have any mandates against sea burials. Others see it as only a last resort when it is entirely impractical to safely transport a body back to land.

Should you decide upon a direct sea burial, you can choose to transport your loved one's body yourself (as long as you follow the EPA's regulations above), or you can hire a funeral service company that specializes in sea burials.

Some burial-at-sea companies allow families to accompany the body out to sea. Others do not. Those that do not may offer to video tape the disposition (for a fee).

Another consideration when making burial at sea arrangements is whether you want a "green" sea burial. While the EPA regulates sea burials to ensure that as little damage as possible is done to the marine environment, there are some companies that go the extra mile. New England Burials at Sea, for instance, does not accept embalmed or casketed bodies. Instead, they require that bodies are wrapped in a biodegradable canvas burial shroud, which the owner of the company, Captain Brad White, had created just for that purpose. White's company recommends 37.5 pound cannonballs be used as ballast, just as they were in earlier centuries in Navy burials.

> "'We're into clean waters and clean oceans,' (White) says. His system is designed to be as biodegradable as possible. Grommets in the shroud 'help the body sink because air comes out. And when a body decomposes, body gases come out. It also allows sea life to go in and do what sea life does. What's left after everything degrades are the cannonballs, and they make their own reef.'"

If you choose to hire a burial-at-sea company, there are questions you should ask up front. These include:

- Who owns the company?

- How long has it been in business?

- Is the company affiliated with any reputable funeral associations (CANA, for instance)?

- Is the company locally-licensed or registered with the correct government agencies for this work?

- Are sea burials the only business performed by the company (in other words, does it offer fishing charters, etc., when not in use for a funeral)?

- Does the company accept embalmed bodies?

- What boat will my loved one be taken out on?

- Who will captain the boat?

- Is the captain licensed by the US Coast Guard?

- Can family members/friends attend the at-sea service?

- Can our religious leader attend the burial and perform a service?

- If we do not have a religious leader, do you offer any sort of service (prayer, hymns, etc.)?

- Do you take photos or videos of the event?

- Can we hire you to bury our loved one without a family member/friend being present (unattended burial)?

- How will I know that my loved one was buried according to my requests?

- Will your company inform the EPA of the event, or do I need to?

- Can my funeral director make arrangements with the company to have my loved one's body delivered to you?

- What are the fees for your services (detailed and in writing)?

Pricing

Prices for sea burials vary considerably. They are contingent upon such choices as whether family and friends will accompany the body, whether scattering ashes at sea or burying a full, casketed body, distance travelled, whether other services are requested (music, flowers, food, etc.), and whether additional personnel are requested (clergy, bagpipers, etc.).

An important consideration for full body sea burials is port of embarkation. The continental shelf off much of the east coast, for instance, means that a boat will have to travel about 35 miles out to sea to reach the 600 foot minimum depth required by the EPA. The need to travel such a distance adds considerably to the length of the trip and to your costs.

Sea burial companies are privately owned and so prices are individually set. When considering a sea burial, be sure to contact several different companies to ask about pricing, services and availability. Keep in mind that you can use your own boat for a sea burial, as long as you abide by local and EPA regulations. Doing so is probably your least expensive option.

Unlike funeral homes and crematoria, there are not (as yet and that I know of) any business alliances, associations or societies that offer recommended business practices for sea burial companies.

Below are prices I've obtained from a number of different sea burial companies. They are offered for reference purposes only.

- Unattended Ash Scattering, $195 to $395

- Attended Ash Scattering starting at $450 to $895 for up to 6 attendees, and starting at $1,000 for up to 20 attendees

- Attended Full Body Burial starting at $4,500 to $9,750

- Unattended Pet Ash Scattering $95

Further to these "starting" prices, you should note that it is customary to tip boat charter personnel. 18-20% is not uncommon and, in some cases, is automatically added to your bill.

NAVY BURIAL AT SEA

The Navy offers a special service to veterans and their family members who want to be buried at sea. The committal ceremony is performed aboard a US Navy ship while it is deployed. For that reason, family members cannot attend the service but will, instead, be notified of the time and date of the ceremony, as well as the latitude and longitude where the committal took place.

The burial at sea program is available to:

- Active duty members of the armed services (Navy, Air Force, Army, Marine Corps and Coast Guard),

- Retirees and veterans who were honorably discharged,

- U.S. civilian marine personnel of the Military Sealift Command,

- Dependent family members of active duty personnel, retirees and veterans of the uniformed military services.

If your loved one qualifies for this service and you are the Person Authorized to Direct Disposition (PADD), you should print out and complete a "Burial at Sea Request Form" (available through the United States Navy Mortuary Affairs Burial at Sea program).

When completed, attach the following documents to the request and contact the United States Navy Mortuary Affairs office:

- A photocopy of the death certificate,

- The burial transit permit or the cremation certificate,

- A copy of the DD Form 214, discharge certificate, or retirement order.

Once your request has been accepted, the Burial at Sea package will be sent to the port of embarkation. You can elect either burial of cremated remains or burial of a casketed body. If casketed body, then only a metal casket is allowed and the port of embarkation must be either Norfolk or San Diego.

If making arrangements for a casketed body, you will have to hire a funeral home near the port of embarkation to receive the body. It is important to note, however, that you should not forward the body to the funeral home until the burial at sea has been approved, a Navy coordinator has assigned a ship for the task, and the date of embarkation is known. Calling the coordinator to discuss the details is highly recommended before beginning the process.

The Navy will not accept bodies or caskets for burial at sea that do not meet their requirements (listed below). Further, prior to accepting your loved one's casketed remains, the casket will be inspected to ensure that the following requirements have been met:

- The remains must be in a state of preservation to ensure no odorous emissions or decomposition for a period of at least 60 days,

- The remains must be in a metal casket and all seals normally designed to inhibit the penetration of external elements into the casket must be removed (this means that you should not purchase a sealer casket for this form of final disposition),

- Casketed remains must weigh at least 300 pounds. Sandbags may be used for additional weight and, when placed inside the foot-end of the casket, will ensure "feet first" sinking,

- The casket is banded with a minimum of six (6) nylon or

metal bands, at least ¾ of an inch wide. The bands are placed: two around the head panel, two around the foot panel, one lengthwise, over and under, head to foot, and one horizontally head to foot. NOTE: Ensure bands are placed under the casket handles to allow continued use of handles,

- A total of 20, two-inch holes must be drilled in the casket. The holes are spaced to ensure there are four holes in the head panel; four in the foot panel; eight holes in the bottom and two in each end.

A U.S. burial flag is required for all Navy burial at sea committal services, with the exception of family members who are not authorized a flag. The flag will be flown during the committal ceremony. You can send the flag along with the burial at sea package and, if you do, it will be returned to you at a later date. If you do not provide a flag, the ship's flag will be flown (and you will not receive it).

In addition to this information, the Navy makes this recommendation:

"It is recommended that funeral homes responsible for preparing intact remains contact (the) Navy Mortuary Affairs at the Military Medical Support Office in Great Lakes, Illinois to receive the preparation requirements."

There may be expenses that you will be expected to cover, so be sure to discuss this with the Navy coordinator and/or funeral home ahead of time so that you will not be surprised.

For ports of embarkation, links to necessary forms, and contact information, please refer to the <u>Naval Burial at Sea Resources</u> section at the back of this book.

NOTE: The US Coast Guard may also offer burial at sea of cremated remains for eligible veterans and their spouses. Due to lack of space on Coast Guard cutters and lack of refrigeration, the Coast Guard cannot handle full body remains.

GREEN/NATURAL BURIAL

"In Australia, as in Europe and North America, [after World War 1] reminders of death were put to one side and muted. Death began to move out of the centre of life and out of the family home into special, contained, places created by the churches, the funeral industry and the medical profession. The funeral industry reflected the domestic nature of earlier funerals in designating their premises as 'funeral homes' or 'funeral parlours'...Death became increasingly taboo."

-Griffin, Graeme and Des Tobin
"In the Midst of Life: the Australian Response to Death"

Whether you care about the environment, want to use your loved one's funeral as a way of honoring her life, want to lower your funeral expenses, or are looking for a simpler final disposition of your loved one's remains, a green burial may be for you.

The funny thing about green burials, sometimes called "natural burials", is that they epitomize the saying, "what's old is new again." In fact, until the late-1800's when embalming came into fashion, all funerals were green. A person died, the family cared for his body and, possibly, placed it in a simple coffin, and he was lowered into the ground. A grave marker may or may not have been erected.

The idea of a green funeral nowadays seems strange to many. After a century and a half of moving away from a green, or natural, burial, the idea of removing all the products and services we've built into the event seems somewhat sacrilegious. In fact, if you visit a funeral home in the United States today, chances are pretty good that you will see a "traditional funeral" listed. Ask, and you will find that it is now considered "traditional" to include embalming, an expensive, manufactured casket replete with metal adornments and interior cushions, photo and video productions, musical arrangements and any number of different services (viewing, funeral, graveside service or cremation service).

So, what exactly is a green funeral?

According to the Green Burial Council, an independent, non-profit organization that promotes environmentally-sustainable death-care and environmentally sound burial practices, green burial is:

"a way of caring for the dead with minimal environmental impact that furthers legitimate ecological aims such as the conservation of natural resources, reduction of carbon emissions, protection of worker health, and the restoration and/or preservation of habitat."[25]

A green burial impacts on the environment as little as possible, honoring the deceased by returning her to the earth in a restorative manner. Further, a green burial also respects the living and attempts to help them find meaning through participation.

Sounds good, but what does it mean? Perhaps the best way to explain a green burial is through comparison to a traditional burial. Below are two hypothetical, but illustrative, versions of the burial of "Jane", first in a traditional cemetery, then as she would have been buried in a conservation burial ground.

Jane's Traditional Burial

After Jane died, at 82, at home, her family calls a local funeral home. Though it is the middle of the night, the funeral director assures the family he will be there within the hour. True to his word, he knocks on the door an hour later. Because her death had been expected and arrangements made, the funeral director does not have to consult with the family at this time but, rather, simply has come to pick up and transport her body back to the funeral home to be embalmed in the morning.

The funeral director rolls his gurney into the house and he and his assistant lift Jane's body onto it. Out of respect for the family, they do not zip her into a body bag but, after placing an identification marker around her ankle, cover her in a white sheet, which they tuck under her to keep it in place. After strapping her body to the gurney, they slip it into the back of a van and drive away.

The next morning, the embalmer arrives to prepare Jane's body. He flips on the fluorescent light in the tiled room, rolls the gurney out of the walk-in refrigerator and, with the help of the funeral director, who was just walking by to get another cup of coffee, lifts Jane's body onto the preparation table.

The embalmer uncovers Jane and, because rigor mortis has set in, he opts to cut her nightgown from her body. He sprays her down with disinfectant, paying special attention to her eyes and mouth where decomposition could ruin her "memory picture."

Jane's mouth hangs open, but it is locked by rigor. He wets his gloved hands with water and adds liquid soap. Using this as a sort of massage cream, he works the lower jaw until he is able to break its rigor. He then moves on to her other joints, working each until she is no longer stiff.

Because the embalming fluid will freeze Jane into position, he now positions the body. Her straightens her legs and binds her ankles together with a length of tape. He uses a positioning bar to position her hands over her stomach, right over left. He places her head on a block and angles it 15 degrees to the right. She is small-breasted so he does not have to sew her breasts into place, but he opts to use a little tape to center them on her chest.

He reaches for his needle injector driver gun and, pulling back Jane's bottom lip, shoots a needle into her lower gum and then another just above her upper teeth. He does the same on the other side of her mouth.

Because she has her own teeth, he does not have to worry too much about sunken, hollowed out cheeks. He opts to stuff her mouth with cotton. This will both plug any purge that might seep up her esophagus, and add fullness to her cheeks.

Her eyelids are open. He wipes her eyeballs. They are dry but beginning to sink. He places a small dab of "stay cream" on each eyeball and presses an eye cap down onto it. The adhesive will keep the caps in place. He tugs a bit on her lower and upper lids. When her upper eyelid covers about two-thirds of her eye, the position most resembling slumber, he taps them down onto the eye caps whose angled barbs will keep the lids from opening. As an extra measure, he rims the lids with super glue.

Jane's face is covered in a fine layer of peach fuzz. He carefully shaves her so that the makeup he later applies to her does not clump. He squirts Nair to her nostrils, waits a few minutes, and wipes them clean. He trims her fingernails.

The embalmer cuts an incision in the side of her neck just above her right clavicle, locates her right common carotid artery, hooks it using an aneurism hook, and tugs it out. He carefully incises the artery, but does not cut all the way through it. He works a cannula-tipped tube into the opening and gently clamps it into place with a ligature. The tube is connected to the pump that will force embalming fluid through her vascular system. He finds her right internal jugular vein, the place where blood with drain from her body, and inserts and clamps a cannula in place.

When all is in place, he turns on the embalming machine. He has added pink dye to the arterial fluid, which he hopes will be enough to give Jane's pale, grey skin a rosier hue. Because of her age, he knows her capillary walls may be weak and he takes great care to monitor the pump's pressure.

When the last of her blood washes down the drain, the embalmer turns off the pump. He ties off the vein and artery, tucks them back inside her skin, sutures the incisions, and adds drying powder to the area to ensure there will be no leakage.

He reaches for the trocar, attaches it to the hydro-respirator, and turns on the aspirator. He pushes the pointed tip through her skin, just above her umbilicus. As the machine suctions, he moves it around to ensure maximum fluid removal. He uses the sharp metal tip of the trocar to puncture each organ, draining them of fluids and gas. He repositions the trocar and aspirates her lower organs, her bladder, large intestine and uterus. When he is done, he inserts the trocar into her nostril and pushes it into her cranial cavity. He aspirates that.

When aspiration is complete, the embalmer removes the trocar and attaches a bottle of cavity fluid to its end. Using the gravity method, he punctures and fills each organ, and the cavity itself, with the noxious fluid. When complete, he slips the trocar from her body and screws a plastic "trocar button" into the incision. He twists plastic A/V plugs into her anus and vagina.

The embalmer then checks the cotton in her mouth and finds it free of purge. He twists the wires that are threaded through the pins in her upper and lower jaws until he deems her mouth is just so, closed but not stern, and twists. He pushes cotton high up into her nostrils and into her ears, making sure no cotton is visible. He checks her positioning and notices that her fingertips are a bit shriveled. Using a hypodermic needle, he injects embalming fluid directly into each pad to plump it up. He curls her fingers around a roll of cotton so the position looks more "natural." Once she sets, he'll remove the cotton rolls.

He checks that her eyelids are properly closed and that her lips are curled into the barest hint of a smile. They are. He applies a bit of massage cream to her face and hands to prevent dehydration. He covers Jane with a sheet and leaves her for a few hours to allow the formaldehyde solution to fix her into position.

When he returns, the embalmer checks the cotton plugs in her nostrils and ears. They show no shadow of purge so he leaves them alone. He removes the tape from her breasts and ankles and then washes her body and hair. Her family has dropped off her funeral clothes, as well as a photo of her. He will use the photo as a guide when styling her hair.

Jane's body is now firmly locked into position. He uses scissors to slice the back of the dress her family has chosen for her and works the sleeves over her arms. He uses safety pins to pin the dress closed. Though her family won't see her feet, they have brought panty hose and shoes. He works the hose up her body. He has to slice the back of the shoes with a box cutter in order to work them over her feet.

The embalmer uses a light touch with the makeup. From the photo they have given him, he suspects the family would be surprised if her lips were too red or her lids too blue. The dye he used in the arterial fluid has lent a healthy flush to her skin but he adds a bit of rouge to her cheeks anyway. Not too much, though, because the soft pink light over her open casket will add even more color to her appearance. He styles her hair and then calls to the funeral director to bring her casket.

That afternoon, the family and a handful of friends gather for a viewing. They all agree that she looks great. Like she's sleeping. The embalmer has created a successful memory picture for the family to take comfort in over the days and years to come. The pillowed interior of her casket even looks comfortable. On the other hand, Jane's skin is hard and dry, and gives off a harsh, pungent odor.

The next day, the funeral director delivers Jane, in her casket, to the church where her funeral service is held. Afterwards, the casket is sealed, ensuring that no moisture seeps inside. A hearse delivers it to the municipal cemetery. There, the grave has already been opened. Earlier that morning, the grave digger used a back hoe to dig the trench. The machine is now out of view and the pile of dirt is covered with a rug of Astroturf.

Prayers are said over Jane's body and, with the use of a mechanical winch, her casket is lowered into the ground. Each family member tosses a handful of dirt onto her casket. Her daughter throws in a rose she took from one of the many funeral wreaths sent to the church. After the family leaves, the gravedigger will return with his backhoe to lower a reinforced concrete grave liner into the hole and to fill the rest with dirt. In a month, he will return again to install the granite grave marker.

Jane's body will take many years to decompose. The sealer casket keeps out the moisture and microbes that would normally help to break it down. Regardless, the casket is buried deep in the ground where there is no air. Aerobic decomposition would be difficult at that depth anyway. And, besides, the cemetery adds so many herbicides and fungicides to the grass to keep it bug-free, that the soil itself is all but dead. The embalming fluid killed off much of the bacteria that would work inside the casket. Regardless, enough survive. Over time, her remains will putrefy and, years later when her casket is moved, the grave digger will hear a swishing sound from inside. Decades after that, when her casket begins to break down, the lacquer that beautified it and the adhesives that held it together will mix with Jane's remains and form a bit of a toxic sludge.

In all, Jane's traditional burial, including embalming, transportation, cemetery plot, casket, flowers, grave marker, and opening and closing fees cost the family $12,360.

Jane's Green Burial

After Jane died, at 82, at home, her daughters gather to prepare her body for burial. It is early spring so they crack a window to allow the room to cool. They remove the soiled linens under her body and cover her bed with a plastic sheet. Using a sponge and a bowl of soapy water, they clean her body and wash her hair. One daughter moistens a cotton ball with Listerine and swabs out her mother's mouth. When Jane's body is dry, her other daughter works a disposable diaper up over her hips.

The girls rub a combination of massage oil and essential oil of Lavender into their mother's skin. They rub massage cream into her eyelids and shut her eyes.

Because her body is still pliable, Jane's daughters are able to dress her in her funeral clothes. When clothed, they roll her body to one side, put down fresh linens, and then roll her body to the other side to pull the sheet taut.

While the girls attend their mother, her sons drive to a local ice plant and purchase dry ice. When they return to the house, Jane's body is already dressed. They place blocks of ice under her torso and at her sides. They placed one on her stomach, several next to her legs and one under her neck. They cover the ice with a sheet so as not to burn her skin and to protect visitors, and then position her body on top of it.

Jane's children cover their mother's body, up to her chest, in her favorite quilt. This they will later use as a burial shroud for her. They cross her hands, right over left, on her stomach and tuck a rolled towel under her chin. They brush her hair and arrange it around her face.

One of her sons turns on a CD player and soft music fills the room. The other brings two chairs into her bedroom so visitors can sit with her if they wish. One of Jane's daughters lights fragrant candles while the other places framed photos of Jane and her family on the bedside table and dresser.

Later that day, friends and family begin to arrive. Some sit with Jane's body, caressing her exposed arms, while others simply pay their respects, perhaps saying a last goodbye or kissing her forehead. The family doctor comes by and fills out the death certificate. With that in hand, two of her children go to the Registrar's office and apply for transmit and burial permits. Neighbors bring food, and the family settles in for one last night with Jane's body.

The following morning, Jane's children wrap their mother's

body in her favorite quilt and place her in the simple pine box one of her sons had made the week before. The family places the casket in the back of a van borrowed from a neighbor and they drive to a conservation burial ground where they know their mother's body will never be disturbed.

Months before her death, Jane had visited the conservation burial ground where she'd walked through the wooded preserve and had chosen the place she wanted to be buried. The morning of her burial, three of her grandchildren go to the burial ground and, along with the founder of the preserve, dig her grave. They're careful to place the plants that had covered that ground aside so they can later replant them.

Family and friends gather in the chapel for a brief service. There, each of her children shares a special memory of their mother, prayers are said, and a hymn is sung. When they are ready, her grandchildren grasp the rope handles of her casket and carry their grandmother's body to its place of burial. Using long woven straps, they lower their grandmother's casket into its grave, and cover it with twelve inches of soil. They plant a tree over the grave and replant the plants that had been moved when digging the grave.

Over the coming years, the simple wooden casket will disintegrate, as will the quilt Jane was wrapped in. Her body, though, has already begun to break down into the organic matter that will nourish the tree and other plants above her. A few weeks after her death, one of her children will return to the spot to place an engraved native stone next to Jane's tree.

In all, Jane's green burial, including transportation, the simple casket, the marker inscription, opening and closing the grave, the tree the family planted, and the plot itself, costs the family about $3,000.

<u>Considerations for a Green Burial</u>

If you would like to plan a green burial for your loved one and you choose a green burial cemetery or preserve, you will have to comply with its rules which probably include some, if not all, of these best practices:

- A green burial should not use noxious, toxic or otherwise harmful chemicals. Formaldehyde embalming fluid, then, is not used, as it is harmful both to the environment, as well as to the people who work with it,

- A green burial should use a casket or shroud that is made of sustainable (meaning its use won't deplete a natural resource), nontoxic, biodegradable, natural material, such as a linen burial shroud or a woven casket,

- If a casket is desired, it should be made of plant-derived, recycled plant-derived, natural, animal, or unfired earthen materials,

- A casket should not be overly-embellished (as everything added to it is just one more thing that needs to biodegrade),

- Finishes and adhesives should not release toxic by-products,

- A casket or urn should not be made from plastics, acrylics, or similar synthetic polymeric materials,

- A green burial should not use a concrete casket liner, burial vault, lid or slab,

- Ideally, a green burial would not include a grave marker, unless it be a tree, bush or other plant indigenous to and reflective of the local environment.

The Green Burial Council certifies funeral products, services and burial grounds as to their "green-ness." This eco-rating system offers three ratings (four if you consider "not-green"), symbolized by one, two, or three leaves.

Take, for instance, burial sites. The Green Burial Council recognizes three levels of "green-ness." These are:

- **Hybrid Burial Grounds** (one leaf rating)

- **Natural Burial Grounds** (two leaf rating)

- **Conservation Burial Grounds** (three leaf rating)

A Hybrid Burial Ground is one that shares space with a traditional cemetery. It is often a section set aside by the cemetery from its "traditional" space. To be certified as a Hybrid Burial Ground by the GBC, the cemetery must provide options that include burial areas where:

- A concrete slab, vault, lid, liner or partition does not have to be used,

- Embalming is not required,

- An eco-friendly casket or shroud may be used.

A Natural Burial Ground is considerably "greener" than a Hybrid Burial Ground. For a burial ground to be certified as Natural by the GBC, it does not provide "options." Rather, the use of concrete slabs, vaults, lids, liners or partitions is prohibited, as is embalming with toxic chemicals. A burial container, if used, must be made of natural, plant-derived materials. In addition, a Natural Burial Ground:

- Must integrate practices and protocols in its business practice that promote energy conservation, waste management, and that ban toxic chemical use,

- Should "look" natural. That is, it integrates native plants and materials that fit naturally into the landscape. The landscape is not manicured but, rather, appears untouched, except by nature,

- Employs an Integrated Pest Management system so pesticides are not used (except when needed to eradicate invasive species).

To be recognized by the GBC as a Conservation Burial Ground, further steps must be taken. In addition to the above practices, a Conservation Burial Ground:

- Must be deeded in perpetuity as conservation land (so it can never be developed),

- Must be managed by an established conservation organization.

While the foregoing establishes the certification requirements set forth by the Green Burial Council, this in no way means that you must bury your loved one in GBC-certified land in order for his or her burial to be considered "green."

As long as you abide by the basic good practices set forth by the GBC (no toxic chemicals, all natural and biodegradable materials, a natural, un-manicured setting), you can give your loved one a green burial.

So, why hold a green burial?

Because what are now considered "traditional funerals" wreak havoc on the environment. According to statistics compiled by the Casket and Funeral Association of America, the Cremation Association of North America, Doric Inc., The Rainforest Action Network, and Mary Woodsen, Vice-President of the Pre-Posthumous Society, each year 22,500 cemeteries across the United States bury approximately:

- 30 million board feet (70,000 m³) of hardwoods, much of it tropical such as Mahogany (in caskets)

- 90,272 tons of steel (in caskets)

- 14,000 tons of steel (used in reinforced vaults)

- 2,700 tons of copper and bronze (in caskets)

- 1,636,000 tons of concrete (used in reinforced vaults)

- 827,060 US gallons (3,130 m³) of embalming fluid, which most commonly includes formaldehyde

According to Curiosity.com, from Discovery, this represents enough steel to build a new Golden Gate bridge each year and enough concrete to lay down a 535-mile highway. It is enough embalming fluid to fill one and a quarter Olympic-sized swimming pools.

As for cremation, long touted as being more environmentally "friendly" than traditional burial, it too negatively impacts the environment. Megan Love Huffman, from the University of Virginia, explains:

"In addition to harmless compounds such as water vapor ($H2O$), emissions include the greenhouse gas carbon dioxide ($CO2$); pollutants and carcinogens carbon monoxide (CO), nitrogen oxide ($NO2$), and sulfur oxide ($SO2$); volatile acids such as hydrogen chloride (HCl) and hydrogen fluoride (HF), both of which form during vaporization of plastics or insulation; and mercury (often from dental fillings). Organic compounds such as benzenes, furans and acetone are also emitted and react with HCl and HF under combustion conditions to form polychlorinated dibenzodioxins (PCDDs) and polychlorinated dibenzofurans (PCDFs), both of which are carcinogens. Hg, PCDDs, and PCDFs are of special concern because they are susceptible to bioaccu)mulation. A study by the Cremation Association of North America has found that filtering crematorium fumes has little effect on the toxins released."

On a more personal level, family members of those who have been laid to rest in a green burial often speak of the quiet simplicity and beauty of such an event. Their loved ones' bodies, they know, will eventually break down into their most basic molecules, carbon, nitrogen and calcium, and will re-enter the life cycle. There is comfort in that.

For areas that are high on population density and low on space, green burial may make sense. New York City, for instance, which is reaching crisis stage as it runs out of burial grounds, has seen graveyard plot prices explode. There, an above-ground mausoleum might sell for tens of thousands of dollars, while some cemeteries have resorted to multiple depth burials, to selling pathway space for burial, and to allowing families to have their loved ones dug up so they can re-sell the spot at a steep profit.

Of course, you might wonder why a green burial would save space, given that a grave is still needed. Actually, a lot less space is needed for a green burial as the body is placed in the ground without a large casket and larger concrete burial vault. Further, a body returned to the earth will decompose and re-enter the life cycle a lot more quickly than an embalmed body protected by a casket and concrete.

Price may be a factor for you when burying your loved one, and a green burial may make the most sense. A no-frills burial in a traditional cemetery will likely cost upwards of $7,000 while a green burial on private land can be as low as several hundred dollars, and up to a couple of thousand in a natural burial ground or conservation burial ground.

You can find links to Green Burial Resources at the back of this book, as well as a listing of Green Burial Cemeteries.

CASKET CHOICES

The casket is often the most expensive part of burial. Happily, The Funeral Rule gives consumers the right to choose. Before the rule was put in place, funeral homes could limit consumers to purchasing from only amongst the caskets they offered. As you can imagine, the caskets offered tended to be higher end models.

Today, consumers can shop for caskets from funeral homes, from casket stores, online, and even at big box stores such as Costco and Walmart.

A casket's price can be affected by the material it is made from and the hardware it sports. Embellishments, adornments and specialty designs can increase the price, as can interior padding, fabrics, and pillows.

Wood caskets range from pressboard (which, by the way, is not easily biodegradable) to tropical hardwoods. Pine is often used, and is often the least expensive of wood choices. Metal caskets are made from copper, bronze or stainless steel. Copper and bronze caskets are priced by weight, while steel is priced by gauge.

It is important to recognize that the casket you purchase in no way reflects your love for the person who died. Unfortunately, however, the two are often subtly connected in casket marketing material. The consumer can be made to feel that purchasing a low-end or mid-range model announces to the world that she is cheap or that she did not love the person who died. I'll give you an example.

Years ago, I knew a family in North Carolina. They were far from well-off and some weeks they found it difficult to even put food on the table. And then my friend's mother became ill and it became apparent she would soon die.

The lady in question was a lovely person who'd lived a long, good life and who'd enjoyed good health through most of it. She'd long had fondness for blue and prior to her death, she purchased a blue dress which, she informed everyone, she wanted to be buried in. But, that wasn't all. She insisted to her children that she had to be buried in a blue casket. She'd seen one once and it was her dream to ride out eternity in a baby blue box.

When she died, her children went to the local funeral home to look at caskets. The only baby blue one cost more than $5,000. Now, as I mentioned, there were weeks when they struggled to put food on the table. On the other hand, Mama really had wanted a blue casket. My friends began scrounging for money.

When asked, my friends admitted that they would be very embarrassed if they did not send Mama off in the blue casket she coveted. After all, Mama had mentioned her desire to just about everyone in town.

Now, these were not stupid people. They were (are) good, hard-working and honest. In this case, though, they'd allowed themselves to be guilt-ed into making a poor financial decision. They'd allowed guilt to make them feel as though the price of the casket reflected the amount of love they had for their mother.

I believe that people would have understood had they buried their mother in a well-made, but simple pine box. They did not think so. They borrowed the money and buried their Mama in blue. As the casket was lowered into the ground, everyone got a last glimpse of that glistening blue box. And then earth was thrown on top and it has never been seen again. Is Mama, wherever she is, thrilled that she got her wish? I don't know. What I do know is that it took a very long time for my friends to pay back all the people they'd borrowed from.

I recount this as a cautionary tale only. If you want to purchase a $20,000 casket for your loved one and that will bring you comfort in the years to come, then certainly do so. Don't, however, make that choice out of guilt or because you are afraid of what the neighbors will think.

In general, caskets can be divided into four types: Traditional, Non-Traditional, Green/Natural, and Homemade.

<u>Traditional Caskets</u>

Traditional caskets are generally made of wood or metal, though fiberglass is gaining in popularity. They are rectangular in design and may be square or round-cornered. The interior is most often lined with padded silk or satin. They usually have a two-part lid so that just the upper half can be opened for a viewing, as well as a tilted floor that raises the body for better viewing. Traditional caskets are equipped with a handrail or handles that pall-bearers can hold when lifting and carrying it. The casket may be embellished, or not. In short, when most people think of a casket, they are thinking of a traditional-style container.

According to the Casket and Funeral Supply Association of America, "personalization" is a growing trend. Batesville Casket Company, the largest casket maker in the U.S., offers "Commemorative Panels", which are embroidered "patches" applied to the interior lid of the casket that "highlight a loved one's interests." Choices include spiritual symbols, organizational emblems, favorite pastimes, or special relationships. The company also created a line of "LifeSymbols®", which are small "enhancement" statues that fit into special corner niches of the casket. Available themes include patriotism, gardening, sports, family relationships, and spirituality.

The company has also pioneered memento drawers and shelves so that you can send personal items and tributes with your loved one. The built-in MemorySafe® drawer is a place where you can tuck away private messages and small items. The MemoryShelf® feature is a small interior corner shelf where you can display small mementoes during viewing and visitation.

As part of my training as a hospice volunteer, I visited a local funeral home to learn about their side of the business. There, I learned that Red Sox coffins and urns are big sellers (I live in New England). Apparently, the various sports clubs license their logos to casket makers, much as movie companies license their characters to McDonald's and Burger King. NASCAR was represented, as well, with a black-and-white Finish Line flag airbrushed on the inside of the lid. Waterloo Casket Company even offers RealTree™ AP camouflage caskets for hunters.

Personalized caskets are not limited to sports fans. There are caskets that feature paintings of favorite rock bands. Some feature lovely "heavenly" themes with harp-playing cherubs. One even played Pachelbel's Canon when a button was pushed. I don't know what happens when the batteries run out.

So-called "sealer" caskets are also trending higher in the industry. Those caskets come lined with a rubber gasket meant to keep moisture and contaminants from seeping into the casket once it has been buried.

You should understand that "sealer" caskets offer huge profits to casket retailers. The gasket, which is similar to those used to seal refrigerator doors, wholesale for about $8.00, according to the Funeral Consumers Alliance, a non-profit consumer advocacy group. They add about $800.00 to the retail price of a casket, however. As you can imagine, casket retailers really push sealer caskets to grieving families with claims that they will "protect" their loved one from the elements.

If you plan to encrypt your loved one in a mausoleum and would like to purchase a sealer casket, you should first contact the mausoleum offices. Sealer caskets are not allowed in some mausoleums because of the slim chance that pent up gases inside the casket will cause it to explode.

A variation on the traditional casket is one used in a conservative Jewish funeral. Those caskets must be fully made of wood and metal is not allowed, even for nails, screws or other fasteners. The reason for this is that a wood casket does not interfere with the natural process of returning to the earth. Further, a conservative Jewish casket must be simple and free of ostentation. When arranging a conservative Jewish funeral, it is best to consult a conservative Rabbi as casket choice is but one small part of the ritual.

Non-traditional Caskets

Non-traditional caskets are available in a seemingly endless variety of shapes and styles. Some are designed by artists, others by quirky casket makers, and others still are designed to reflect the tastes of the recently deceased.

Some people have strange requests for their final resting home. With enough money and the right craftsman, you can bury your loved one in a guitar-shaped (and painted) box, in a hot dog shaped coffin, in a corkscrew-shaped casket, in one shaped like a shoe, or a Coke bottle, or even in a piano (yes, a real one). Truly, the shape is limited only by your imagination, your wallet, and the ability of a craftsman to turn your vision into reality.

Another option in non-traditional caskets is to hire an artist to custom paint a casket for you. You can request a reproduction (of Monet's water lilies, for instance) or request a one-of-a-kind. Some families choose to purchase simple, undecorated and unvarnished pine boxes and then, with a bit of paint and imagination, they decorate it themselves, leaving messages of love and drawings.

While you can easily look up traditional casket sellers online, finding some of the more interesting non-traditional craftsmen might be a bit more difficult. For that reason, I have included the contact information for a number of <u>Non-Traditional Burial Container Suppliers</u> section at the back of this book.

Green/Natural Caskets

Whether you like the simplicity of a green burial, or you are worried about the effect of burying so many bodies in elaborate, non-biodegradable caskets (not to mention the concrete vaults and casket liners) on the environment, you may want to consider a green, or "natural", casket for your loved one.

Green caskets are made from earth-friendly, bio-degradable, toxic-free, renewable resources that allow a body to return to the earth with minimum impact on the surrounding soil, water table, or air. They are often made of pine or other renewable woods, and usually do not employ metal nails or hinges (wooden dowels are used instead). Natural material, such as hemp rope, is used for the handles.

Not all natural caskets are in the form of wooden boxes. Some are body-shaped baskets woven out of renewable reeds and fibers, while others are made from unglazed clay and even from paper mâché.

Besides the environmental benefits of choosing a green casket, many families find that they are often much less expensive than those purchased from funeral homes or casket retailers. Some natural options are available for less than $500 for a casket and less than $100 for a biodegradable urn.

A burial shroud may also be an option for you. Made from biodegradable fabrics, often linen or cotton, burial shrouds can be the most earth-friendly burial container for your loved one's body as they do not place a barrier between the body and the surrounding soil. This, of course, allows your loved one's body to more quickly return to the life cycle.

For green/natural casket and urn resources, refer to the <u>Green Burial Resources</u> section of this book.

Homemade Caskets

Some families choose to make their own caskets. Doing so can actually be quite therapeutic, as the process becomes a sort of meditation on the life of the person just lost and the decisions (design, materials, etc.) are made to reflect the unique personality of that person.

Homemade casket (as well as urn and shroud) designs vary greatly and are often dependent upon those building or creating them. While you can find plans online (search for "casket plans"), there is nothing that says that you cannot get creative and design your own.

If you do decide to design your own, there are a number of things you should take into consideration, including:

- Place of burial: if you are burying your loved one in a cemetery, there may be specific prohibitions you should be aware of. If, on the other hand, you are burying your loved one in a green cemetery, your material choices may be limited.

- Size and weight of your loved one: make sure you make the casket big enough inside to hold your loved one's body. Likewise, test the casket's holding capacity by filling it with an equal weight of bricks or some other material before placing your loved one's body inside and lifting.

- Decoration: if you will be decorating your loved one's

casket, make sure you make choices appropriate to the burial grounds (non-toxic paint, for instance, may be OK for green cemeteries).

Pricing

The casket is usually considered the single most expensive funeral item. It is also considered one of the most expensive purchases a person will make in their lifetime. While the Funeral Rule gives consumers choices, it does not take away from the fact that caskets are often marked up as much as 300% to 800%.

According to AARP, an 18-gauge steel casket, which is a common choice in metal caskets, costs around $2,300. Some caskets, however, can cost upwards of $12,000. A mahogany Masterpiece casket by Batesville, for instance, retails in the range of $17,890. The Promethean, a copper casket with 14k gold hardware retails for $21,980.

Casket pricing depends on many different factors including:

- Composition,

- Hardware,

- Size (over-sized caskets cost more, while infant or child-size caskets are generally less expensive),

- Whether the casket is "traditional" or custom-made,

- Whether it is easily biodegradable or made to withstand the elements,

- Interior amenities, such as pillows, padding, shelves, drawers, icons, etc.,

- Whether it is seal-able or not,

- Whether you purchase from a funeral home, online, or from a wholesale big box store such as Costco or Walmart.

Two types of caskets that are generally inexpensive are cremation containers and cloth-covered caskets. Cremation containers carry the body into the cremation retort and are burned with the body. While intended for cremation, they are often used in green burials because their cardboard construction easily biodegrades. Cloth-covered caskets are made from corrugated fiberboard, pressed wood or softwoods, which are then covered with cloth and have finished interiors.

Of solid wood caskets, those made of poplar, willow or pine are less expensive than those made of cherry, black walnut or mahogany. Simple pine caskets can be had for as little as $375.00, though you can make your own for less than $100.00 in supplies. Alternately, you can purchase casket plans online for as little as $30.00 and casket kits can be found for as little as $150.00.

Odds & Ends – The size of the average American adult is growing. To keep abreast of this growing trend, the major casket companies have begun to introduce larger caskets. The Batesville Casket Company released its Dimensions® line in 2004 with 53 oversized models. Goliath Casket, meanwhile, offers the largest of the large with some models running more than 8 feet in length and stretching as far as 52 inches in width. A standard casket, in comparison is about 6.5 feet long and 28 inches wide.

Odds & Ends – The terms "casket" and "coffin" are not interchangeable (though many people do use one when they mean the other). Coffins are shaped along the lines of a human form, with the widest part at the shoulders and the ends tapering towards the head and feet. A casket, on the other hand, is shaped like a rectangle.

Odds & Ends – Shawn M. Smith, Funeral Director of Connecticut Funeral Home, who I interviewed for this book, cautioned that families who want to hold in-home wakes or other services should be sure to choose the casket wisely. Today's caskets are often larger than customary door widths. Better to make sure the casket can fit through doors than to realize it can't at an inopportune time.

Odds & Ends – Batesville Casket Company, founded in 1906 and traded on the NYSE, sells approximately 45% of the caskets in the

United States (about 800,000 per year). The company's most recent quarter revenues were reported at $212 Million, with a net income of some $20 Million.

CREMATION

Cremation does not have the long, rich history that burial does, nor has it been practiced as extensively around the world. That is not to say that it has not been practiced in the past – in fact, cremated human remains have been found dating as far back as 20,000 years ago. It is simply that burial has been the preferred method of caring for bodies across the majority of cultures and religions, with a few notable exceptions, including Hinduism.

In modern times, cremation has been gaining in popularity and it is estimated that, as the population grows and land becomes more precious, cremation will become the preferred means of caring for the dead.

Cremation is the process through which a body is exposed to extreme heat – usually between 1600 and 2000 degrees Fahrenheit – for two hours or more in order to reduce it to bone. While cremated remains are often referred to as "ashes", they are really bone and tooth fragments.

After the cremated remains, or "cremains", cool sufficiently, they are inspected visually and/or passed through a strong magnet in order to remove non-consumed items such as bridgework, artificial joints, and metal parts of clothing. The cremated remains are usually mechanically crushed post-cremation in order to reduce them to tiny, sand-like particles.

There are many reasons to consider cremation for your loved one. One of the best reasons, of course, is that she indicated that was her desire. Another is to minimize the impact on the environment. It is a simple fact that burials require a great deal more space than do cremated remains. Add to the size of a casket the concrete grave liner or vault which is often required by cemeteries, and multiply that by millions, and there is just not enough ground space to bury the world's growing population.

Unfortunately, the choice between cremation and burial cannot be minimized to a simple issue of space. There are pros and cons of each to consider, including the effect that each has on the environment, as well as the costs involved.

Those pro-cremation point out that a disintegrating casket (which often contains formaldehyde resin) and body, especially if it was embalmed, can poison the surrounding soil and, in some places, those toxins can enter the water table. Metal caskets and concrete vault liners will slow, but not permanently halt, that process.

You should know, however, that cremation is not totally "clean" and it does, indeed, have a negative impact on the environment.

Heating a cremation chamber up to about 1800 degrees Fahrenheit and maintaining that temperature over several hours requires a great deal of energy. Some environmental analysts have calculated that this process sends approximately 573 pounds of carbon into the atmosphere, hardly an insubstantial amount, especially when multiplied over the number of cremations performed annually.

Mercury is another issue to consider when deciding whether to have your loved one cremated. Mercury, which was used in old-style dental fillings (amalgams), is released during cremation and the harmful vapors can find their way into the atmosphere. An article in the Minnesota Star Tribune pointed out that:

> "Dental amalgam fillings (sometimes called silver fillings) contain mercury. As solids in the mouth, they are considered inert and not a hazard, but when exposed to high temperatures, the mercury vaporizes and becomes airborne, contributing to mercury pollution in the state and beyond.

> "While there isn't a large amount of mercury in any one body, the state estimates that, all together, cremation emits about 80 pounds of mercury a year in Minnesota," said Ned Brooks of the Minnesota Pollution Control Agency. The aging baby boomer population tends to have lots of these fillings and as more people choose cremation, pollution isn't

expected to drop.

"Just a little mercury released into the air can cause problems. Mercury makes its way through the food chain through fish and then into the people and wildlife that eat the fish. Mercury builds up in the human body, where it can harm the brain and nervous system."

Unlike at least eight European countries, including Germany and Sweden, the United States does not currently regulate mercury emissions from crematoria, though in 2010 Congressman Dennis J. Kucinich, as Chairman of the Domestic Policy Subcommittee, asked the EPA to become involved. As he pointed out, in 2005 more than 6,600 pounds of mercury was released into the atmosphere as a direct result of cremation. Nationally, over 30% of Americans are cremated, a figure expected to rise to 43% by 2025, which will further stress the environment if controls are not set and enforced. In its reply to the Congressman, the EPA indicated that the agency does not feel that regulation falls under the umbrella of the Clean Air Act.

A further impact of cremation on the environment is that the combustion of embalming chemicals can add to air pollution and, of course, burning, in and of itself, releases a myriad of gases into the air. Other unhealthy substances released during the process include including dioxin, hydrochloric acid, sulfur dioxide, and climate-changing carbon dioxide.

Professor Roger Short, of the University of Melbourne (Australia) reports that cremation can create up to 350 pounds of greenhouse gases, including the remains of the cremation container.

This does not mean you should avoid cremation. Rather, you should weigh the pros and cons of any type of final disposition.

Cost can be a determining factor when choosing between burial and cremation. Burial requires a casket, which can be extremely expensive. In the United States, most states only require that a body is placed in a combustible container prior to cremation. That container can be as simple as a cardboard box (some other countries require, at the minimum, a wooden box).

Added to the cost of a casket is the price of a burial plot, a grave liner or vault, a marker and, in many cemeteries, perpetual care fees. Cremation, on the other hand, is a one-time fee and the remains are generally returned to the family in a simple, plastic-lined cardboard box.

While minimizing the effect on the environment and cost differences are two important factors in choosing between burial and cremation, there are a number of other considerations involved. These include:

- **Your loved one's religion**. Some religions expressly forbid cremation. Orthodox Judaism and Islam are two examples. Other religions frown on the practice. Roman Catholicism, for instance, has only recently eased its restrictions against cremation. If you are unsure how your loved one's religion views cremation, it is important that you find out prior to making your decision.

- **Location can be a consideration**. In the past, when people spent their entire lives living in one geographical area, burial was an obvious choice as family members could visit and tend their ancestors' graves. Today, that is not always practical. If you, or another family member or friend, feel strongly about keeping your loved one's remains close to you, cremation may be your better choice.

- **Cultural views can play a part in your decision**. Some countries, with limited land resources, promote cremation as the method of choice. Cremation, then, has become a cultural preference.

- **Size/Weight**. Your loved one's size must be taken into consideration before making cremation arrangements as not all crematoria can handle bodies over 300 pounds. One consideration, of course, is that the body must be able to fit into the retort with at least one inch of space on the sides and top. More importantly, however, is the fact that human fat has an excessively high combustion rate. It has a BTU nearly 17 times that of normal tissue. This means that the remains put off enough heat themselves to sustain the process without the burners being necessary at all times. If not carefully monitored, the heat could damage the retort.

Pricing

Pricing will vary from company to company and the type and number of services you choose will impact your bottom line. Direct cremation, when a body is taken from place of death directly to the crematorium without embalming or services, is the most cost-effective choice. Families on budgets often choose this option and hold a memorial service at a later time.

If you are a member of (or can join) a cremation society, you may find more inexpensive services than those charged to the general public. Cremation societies are groups that arrange special pricing for their members.

Matthews International's Cremation Division (a crematory supply company) reports that basic cremation services average around $425.00. The National Cremation Research Council (an independent research organization dedicated to conducting, compiling and analyzing consumer trends towards cremation), however, reports the following from their January 2011 survey of more than 80 cremation societies:

- The average cost of direct cremation is $1,110.95

- The median (middle) price is $1,079.50

- The mode (most repeated) price is, $1,295.00

The Neptune Society, which bills itself as "the largest provider of affordable cremation services in the nation" charges $1,499 for direct cremation (with charges escalating as different services are chosen).

The Cremation Association of North America, with more than 1,500 members worldwide, reports that the average cost of cremation is about $1,600., with prices ranging from less than $1,000 to over $5,000.

Note: If you are planning the cremation of a young child or infant, you should know that you may not receive cremated remains back from the crematorium. This is because the bones of very young children have not hardened enough and may be wholly burned in the process.

Odds & Ends – According to the Cremation Association of North America, the three primary reasons people choose cremation over burial are:

- To save money (30%)

- Because it is simpler, less emotional and more convenient (14%)

- To save land (13%)

Odds & Ends – Prior to cremation, any pacemaker, implant or radiation producing device may have to be removed from the body because these can damage the crematorium.

Odds & Ends – Depending upon your state, a casket may or may not be required for cremation. Indiana, for instance, does not require a casket, but does require a "sturdy, leak-proof container." Some states only require a "container" which may be cardboard, wood, or other material.

Odds & Ends – You can purchase an urn to hold the ashes of two individuals. If considering doing so, be sure to take into account the size/weight of both and purchase an urn that will hold the combined remains.

THE ASHES: WHAT TO DO WITH THEM

If you have chosen cremation for your loved one, at some point his cremated remains will be returned to you. This usually happens within days or, possibly, a few weeks. Regardless, at some point, you will receive them and you will have to decide what to do with them.

Unless you've purchased an urn and delivered it to the crematorium for inurnment, the remains will be returned in a temporary container. This is often a heavy-duty cardboard box with an interior plastic bag. If your plans are to simply bury the remains, you really don't need to do anything, though you may elect to remove the plastic bag if you are concerned about its environmental impact.

Scatter the Ashes in a Special Place

Many families choose to scatter the ashes, either in a garden, at sea, or in a place that held special meaning for their loved one, say at a park, or along a hiking trail.

Families of sports fans often scatter their loved one's ashes on home-team turf. Until several years ago, for instance, the Boston Red Sox permitted the scattering of ashes on the field at Fenway Park. Sometimes they even arranged a short ceremony to be held on the field when the team was not playing. That has changed, however. Due to an increasing number of requests, the practice is no longer allowed. At least, not officially.

"'We had to implement a change in that policy,' said vice president of media relations John Blake. 'We were concerned that we were getting too many requests.'"

That does not mean it doesn't happen. Park security is aware that fervent fans continue the practice, if on the sly.

Besides sports stadiums, amusement parks are often the site of illegal scatterings. Dubbed "wildcat scatterings" because of the covert tactics employed by scatterers, the practice of spreading cremated remains on private property without permission is illegal in some states. Regardless of the law, it happens. And often.

Not surprisingly, many people choose to scatter their loved ones' ashes at Disney theme parks. I was first alerted to this phenomenon by my husband who informed me that the "It's a Small World After All" ride is known to be the final resting ground for many (but, that song!). According to recent articles in the Wall Street Journal and Obit-Mag, the Haunted Mansion and Pirates of the Caribbean ride also receive their (un)fair share (so much so that Disney has standardized cleanup procedures that include special HEPA-filtered vacuum cleaners for cleaning Aunt Mary off the mannequins).

With cremation rates on the rise (about 39% of Americans choose cremation today, according to the Cremation Society of America, a rate that is expected to rise to 60% in the coming years), urn burial prices high (though still much lower than full-body burial fees), and more and more people bucking tradition, it's no wonder that cremated remains are showing up in strange places.

Some people are surprised by the amount of remains returned to them and opt for multiple scattering sites. An average adult body will result in about five pounds of cremated remains, similar in volume to a five pound bag of flour. One woman mentioned in the WSJ article decided to scatter her husband's remains "in beautiful places he would have liked to have seen." To that end, she's sent a bit of him along for the ride with eleven of her friends. So far, he's been to Rome, Namibia, Hemingway's home in Cuba, Rockefeller Center, and Disney, among other locations. She has plans to scatter the rest of him in Paris on what would have been his 50th birthday. The long process "has prolonged my goodbye," she stated.

Scatter the Ashes at Sea

Some families want to scatter their loved one's ashes at sea. Scattering ashes at sea can be as simple as holding a seaside ceremony and dispersing the ashes into a seaward-blowing wind. If you choose to do this, you really should check into local laws. Many places do not allow the scattering of ashes so close to shore. California, for instance, mandates that ashes cannot be scattered at sea closer than 500 yards from shore. That state also requires that you advise the county registrar of the scattering.

An alternative to a beachside service is to take a boat out to sea to scatter the ashes farther from land. The fact that you may not own a boat or know anyone who owns a boat should not deter you if that is what you want to do. You can hire a boat to take you and your family out for a couple of hours, or you can hire a service that scatters the ashes at sea on your behalf (you can find contact information in the Burial at Sea Resources section of this book). Again, though, inquire about local registration. Companies that advertise and charge for ash scattering in California must hold a Cremated Remains Disposer license.

Scatter the Ashes from an Airplane

If your loved one was a pilot or simply loved to fly, releasing his ashes from an airplane might be a fitting tribute. There are a number of companies that provide this service, either with family members on board, or not, and scatterings can be done over land or sea. There are, however, a couple of caveats that you should take into consideration. The first is that it is important to inform the crematorium of your decision. Large bone fragments or metal can damage the airplane and so it is a good idea to make sure the cremated remains are processed through a cremulator to ensure the pieces are small and ash-like. Passing them under a magnet is another good idea so that any metal pieces are removed.

You should be aware that while scattering over a national park is generally permitted, each park superintendent can set limitations as to location and whether a permit is needed. Scattering at sea, on the other hand, is permitted, as long as the airplane is out at least three nautical miles from the coast. As far as scattering over inland waters, a permit is definitely needed as inland waters are governed by the Clean Water Act.

Ash scattering from an airplane can be difficult with blowback common. There are measures a pilot can take that will ensure that the remains fully scatter outside of the plane rather than blowing back inside. Be sure to discuss this with any pilot you've considered hiring.

Pricing varies from pilot to pilot and company to company. Accompanied flights may cost more than unaccompanied and distance to location will factor into the pricing as well. I have seen prices range from about $250 and up. When discussing pricing, be sure to ask if the company/pilot offers discounts for military veterans, as some do. One company, Final Flight, even performs the service for free if the decedent was a Metal of Honor recipient.

Send the Ashes into Space

Land and sea scatterings are not your only alternatives. If your loved one was a space aficionado, sending his ashes into orbit may be a more meaningful way for you to memorialize him. Celestis, for instance, is a company that can arrange for a "Memorial Spaceflight." Starting at $995 (at the time of this writing), Celestis can send a lipstick-sized portion of your loved one's ashes into space to be returned to you post-flight, into orbit, onto the moon's surface, or into deep space. To learn more about space options, please visit the Spaceflight Resources section of this book.

Send the Ashes up in A Helium Balloon

When I initially heard about this option, I thought, "no, no, no." First of all, I worried that a meaningful balloon ride for one would eventually become someone else's roadside trash. Worse, that the balloon would fall into the ocean only to be eaten by a sea turtle (it happens, and a lot more frequently than you would imagine.) Then, I worried that the balloon wouldn't break but would, instead, float back to the ground where some unsuspecting child would gleefully catch it and tote grandpa home.

Suffice to say that my imagination worked overtime for no good reason.

The company that invented (and patented) a way to send cremated remains up in a balloon is called Eternal Ascent. The owners, Clyde and Joanie West, who own a gift balloon shop, came up with the idea when Clyde told his brother, "I don't care what you do with me - just have me cremated and send me up in a balloon."

Upon release, the balloons rise to a height of 30,000 – 40,000 feet where the temperatures are about 40 degrees below 0. At that temperature, the balloon crystalizes and fractures, sending the ashes scattering.

The balloons used by Eternal Ascent are five feet in diameter (when inflated) and are made of latex, a natural derivative of rubber trees. According to the company website,

> "Scientific research, most notably by D.K. Burchette in, 'A Study of the Effect of Balloon Releases on the Environment,' demonstrates that latex balloons decompose at a rate equal to - or faster than - an oak leaf under similar conditions."

Pricing varies greatly for this memorial option, with rates ranging between $995 and $2,500. The company explains that this variation is the result of individual prices set by company franchisees. To find out more, please refer to the <u>Helium Balloon Scattering Resources</u> section of this book.

Cremation Fireworks

A number of companies will pack your loved one's ashes into fireworks. Options include inland fireworks displays, beachfront displays and marine displays (off a yacht). Some companies will arrange for the fireworks permits, while others require you to obtain them (so make sure you ask). You must also make sure that ash scatterings are allowed by local law. While some states allow scatterings over public land, this varies considerably.

The author of *Fear and Loathing in Las Vegas*, Hunter S. Thompson, chose cremation fireworks as his exit from this world. The display, hosted by his friend Johnny Depp, was probably the most famous cremation fireworks display on record (to date). "I just want to send my pal out the way he wants to go out," Depp told a reporter at the time. The service was attended by a number of luminaries including Senator John Kerry, Charlie Rose, and actors Jack Nicholson, Bill Murray, Benicio del Toro and Sean Penn.

Prices vary according to the provider. Some prices I've found place inland fireworks displays at about $4,000 and marine display packages beginning at $5,500. For a partial listing of providers, please see the Cremation Fireworks Resources section.

Include the Ashes in an Artificial Reef

For those who love the ocean, a fitting memorial might be to have a loved one's ashes turned into an artificial reef. Generally-speaking, the cremated remains are mixed in with concrete and formed into a structure that will withstand underwater forces. Currently, there are a number of artificial reef companies that offer this service. One such company is Georgia-based Eternal Reef, which creates "reef balls", formations that mimic natural reef structures.

Another company, Florida-based Great Burial Reef, creates "Living Urns" and "Classic Reef" formations that encourage marine life to grow around them. Yet another memorial reef company, the Neptune Society, is turning 16 barren acres off the Florida Keys into an artistic, underwater garden. Cremated remains are included in molds of seashells, leaping dolphins, lions, chariots, benches and columns.

> "'I was trying to achieve some sort of sunken city, but not Atlantis,' (Key Largo artist Kim) Brandell says, calling his architectural style futuristic rather than classical."

Regardless of the artificial reef company you choose, there are benefits to this type of final disposition. These include:

- Oftentimes, this type of final disposition is less expensive than a traditional, cemetery burial,

- Your loved one's ashes help the oceans by forming the basis of a new, living reef,

- Most companies include a plaque with your loved one's name and provide you with GPS coordinates in the event you wish to visit the site, or scuba dive down to it,

- Once your loved one is cremated, you can hold onto the ashes for as long as you want or need to and can take time to consider your memorial options,

- Many of the companies are recognized by The Green Burial Council as providing an environmentally-friendly "green" service.

Pricing varies from company to company, but I've included some of the more popular items below. Please note that, in most cases, you will be responsible for your own transportation to and from the place of embarkation, as well as for any other personal charges (hotel, etc.).

- Eternal Reef's "Reef Balls" vary in size. The Mariner is 4' high by 6' wide and weighs between 3,800 and 4,000 pounds. It can hold the remains of up to four people. $6,995.

- The Nautilus is 3' x 4' and weighs between 1,200 – 1,500 pounds. It can accommodate the remains of two people. $4,995.

- The Aquarius is 2' x 3' and weighs 350 to 400 pounds. $3,995.

- The Sea Oats Community Reef accommodates a number of people's remains – you should note that this is a "community" reef where the remains of various people will be mixed together. $2,995.

- The Neptune Memorial Reef is a man-made reef off Key Biscayne, Florida being designed by the Neptune Society, a company that offers cremation services. The reef features statues, columns, lions, benches, archways, etc. and is billed as, "a classical re-creation of the Lost City, 40 feet under the sea." Cremated remains are mixed in with the various statues and forms. You will have to contact the company for pricing as it varies according to the mold (seashell, column, etc.) you would like for your loved one's remains.

- Reef Maker, a company out of Alabama, offers to create a memorial reef using your loved one's cremated remains (mixed with concrete) for about $1,595.

- Great Burial Reef, a Florida company, creates "ocean cremation urns" which look a little like a multi-headed mushroom or a cement version of a Dr. Seuss tree (one look at a photo and you will know what I mean). They offer cement-based urns into which you can blend your loved one's ashes in two sizes – a 600- pound urn for $3,999 and a 60-pound urn for $999. For an additional $169 per person (with a minimum of six people), you and your family can accompany the urn on its voyage to its final placement.

- Poseidon's Garden, a Florida company, creates large blocks reminiscent of oversize Legos out of cement and your loved one's remains. Pricing is about $1,800.

You can find links to a number of the memorial reef companies in the Memorial Reef Resources section at the back of this book.

Turn the Ashes into Memorial Jewelry

One way to memorialize a loved one is by incorporating some of his cremated remains in a piece of memorial jewelry. Ashes can be incorporated into glass, metal, man-made crystals, synthetic stones, and even into "created diamonds."

Created diamonds are man-made diamonds which are said to be structurally identical to diamonds found in nature. Pricing ranges from about $2,690 for a .10 to .19 carat stone up to more than $20,000 for a 1.0 carat stone.

If you do decide to have jewelry made from your loved one's remains, you should do your homework. Just a little bit of research uncovers hundreds of companies that offer memorial jewelry options.

Some of the options are quite expensive and I highly recommend price comparison.

You will find <u>Memorial Jewelry Resources</u> at the back of this book.

Other ways to Incorporate Ashes

While those listed above seem to be the more "common" ways to memorialize a loved one by using his ashes, there have been (and, I'm sure, will continue to be) unique, even bizarre, methods using cremated remains. These include:

- Adding the ashes to ink or paint to create a one-of-a-kind "masterpiece",

- Adding the ashes to tattoo ink,

- Adding them to plastic to make "memorial Frisbees",

- Adding them to ammunition to honor a hunter.

Keep the Ashes in an Urn

One of the most common methods of handling ashes, of course, is to place them in an urn and keep them at home, or place them in a columbarium.

As cremation rates steadily increase, the urn industry grows accordingly. Nowadays, you can find urns made from many different types of material including pottery, wood, metal and plastic. A simple urn can retail for as little as $19.95. More elaborate ones, or those made by an artisan rather than mass produced, will cost much more.

Urns can be decorative, or can reflect your loved one's personality. Sports urns, for instance, are big sellers. For around $799, you can place your loved one's ashes in an urn decorated with his favorite ball team's logo.

Like caskets, you do not need to rely on your local funeral home's choice of urns. You can purchase them from a retail store, ask an artist-friend to create one for you, or buy one online. When purchasing an urn, there are several things to consider. These include:

- Body size at time of death, and the sex of the decedent. Larger bodies will create more remains and will thus require a larger urn to hold them. Because soft tissues such as fat and muscle are fully burned, body weight at time of death is not a great indicator of the weight and volume of the cremated remains. Height and sex are better indicators with the cremated remains of an average sized adult female weighing in at about four pounds and those of an average sized adult male weighing in at about 6 – 8 pounds. Make sure you order an urn that will hold the correct amount of remains,

- You can purchase an urn that will hold two sets of remains. If, for instance, your spouse died first and you know that you will want your own remains mixed in with his, purchase an urn that will hold both of your remains,

- Neck opening may be a factor to consider. If, for instance, you want to add a religious token to the remains, or a wedding ring (you won't want to send either through the cremation process as they will melt or burn), make sure you choose an urn with a wide neck,

- If you plan to bury the urn and you are concerned about the environment, make sure to choose an urn that is biodegradable.

It is in the crematorium's interest to sell you an urn, though you should not feel pressured to purchase one from their stock as there are many online retailers that might offer something more in line with your loved one's personality. Alternately, you can make your own or purchase a container that was not necessarily meant to be used as an urn but which is more to your liking. If, for instance, you will be keeping your loved one's cremation remains at home, you might want to choose a lidded vase from Pier One or another home products store of your choice.

Place the Ashes in a Columbarium

If you do not want to keep your loved one's ashes at home or to bury them, you might consider placing them in a columbarium. Similar to a mausoleum that holds any number of caskets, a columbarium contains niches for any number of urns. You can find columbaria at cemeteries and religious houses. The cremated remains of my father and grandparents, for instance, are in a columbarium in Florida. My mother purchased four niches there (hers will be added one day) in a sort of "family plot."

When considering a columbarium, you need to take into account the dimensions of the niche. If you have already placed your loved one's ashes in an urn, it may not fit into the small vault. If that is the case, you can find out if there are interior liners you can move his remains to, or what other options the facility offers.

Odds & Ends – So-called cremation "ashes" are not ashes in the usual sense. Instead, they are dry bone and tooth fragments. These are pulverized into an ash-like powder either by a mechanical device called a "cremulator", or by hand.

ALKALINE HYDROLYSIS

As the world's population swells, our carbon footprint grows, the costs of traditional funerals skyrocket, and land becomes increasingly precious, the funeral industry is looking at new ways to care for the dead. Cremation, which is gaining in popularity in the United States, both for its lower costs and its smaller carbon footprint (than traditional burial with embalming), has its own drawbacks.

Cremation requires a great deal of energy, which it gets from fossil fuels. Because laws limit the number of bodies that can be cremated at a time (to one), the system is highly inefficient (though compassionate for that very same reason). Some estimates indicate that a mid-size car could drive coast to coast and halfway back again on the amount of fuel needed in just one cremation cycle. Further, cremation releases a number of toxic gases into the atmosphere. Scrubbers, which could be installed in crematories to cleanse the emissions, are extremely expensive and some of the older crematories cannot be retrofitted to accommodate them.

In response to the negative aspects of cremation, Resomation LTD, a company in Scotland, has created a new technique for reducing bodies to "bone ash" just as cremation does. The process goes by a number of names. In Europe, it is referred to as "Resomation" after the company that created it. In the States, it is called "Bio-Cremation" by the Mathews Corporation, the US distributors of the technique. "Alkaline hydrolysis" is the scientific name for the process that it employs, though "water reduction" and "aquamation" are used as well.

The term "alkaline hydrolysis" refers to the use of an alkali, lye, known also by its chemical name, potassium hydroxide, and water (hydro). To understand how lye works, you must first remember your high school chemistry class when pH was explained.

pH refers to the parts-hydrogen in a compound. The pH scale runs between 1 and 14, with something having a pH of 7 considered neutral. Everything with a pH of 1-6 is called an acid, while everything with a pH of 8 – 14 considered a "base." Lye is a base, with a pH of about 14. As such, it is extremely caustic.

You have probably heard of lye before. It is one of the main ingredients in soap. To make soap, lye is combined with a fatty substance (often animal fat or, more recently, vegetable oils, such as coconut oil). The resulting product is a salt, which we call soap.

Lye reacts well with water. As you know, humans are made up of about 65% water. When we die, the bindings that hold all our disparate molecules together eventually break apart. Over time, we are returned to our elemental state. Lye accelerates this natural process as it is able to break the molecular bonds quickly. Or, as Sandy Sullivan, the Managing Director of the Scottish company, Resomation, that pioneered the process for final disposition of human remains, explains it:

> "Scientifically, the process involved is called alkaline hydrolysis. When human tissues are built, elements get bound together by the removal of water molecules. Hydrolysis puts the water back in – and unzips the tissue molecules."

In alkaline hydrolysis, a body is put into a metal tube-shaped container. Water and lye are added and the liquid is heated to about 350 degrees Fahrenheit, far below the 1,100 – 1,800 F degrees needed during cremation. The unit is placed under high pressure, which speeds up the process, and the body is reduced to bone. The bone is then pulverized, just as in cremation, and the resulting "ashes" are returned to the family.

Because alkaline hydrolysis and cremation offer the same outputs–reduction to bone matter–it is often referred to as "bio-cremation." For alkaline hydrolysis proponents, this is an important inclusion.

In some states, statutes limit the disposition of human remains to either burial or cremation. Rather than go about the difficult process of opening allowable forms of disposition up to other practices, alkaline hydrolysis advocates have found it easier to have this process recognized as a form of cremation.

Alkaline hydrolysis does offer a number of benefits over heated cremation and traditional burial. These include:

- No emissions are released, including mercury emissions (teeth with amalgams can be separated out from the bone material afterwards),

- Retains 20 – 30% more bone fragments than flame cremation (to be returned to the family, if requested),

- No cremation container emissions (from a burning cremation container),

- Lower operating costs,

- Smaller carbon footprint (reduces carbon emissions of flame cremation by 90%),

- Minimum energy requirements (about 20% of the energy required by heated cremation),[40]

- No need to remove medical implants prior to the process (such as pacemakers),

- Does not require land, as a traditional cemetery does,

- Completely destroys pathogens, including prions,

- Mimics much of the natural decomposition processes of a natural, green burial when alkali in the soil and water in soil help to break down a body,

- Is relatively quick, requiring only 2 – 3 hours.

Alkaline hydrolysis is not entirely new to the United States. In fact, it has been in use by The University of Florida, Gainesville and The Mayo Clinic in Minnesota since the mid-1990s and 2006 respectively. Those institutes have been using the process to dispose of cadavers donated to science. According to Brad Crain, President of BioSafe Engineering, a company that makes alkaline hydrolysis cylinders for alkaline hydrolysis machines not used by the funeral industry, there are between 20 and 40 other facilities in the United States that use the process for human medical waste, to dispose of animal carcasses, or both. Those facilities include veterinary schools, mortuaries, health care facilities, agricultural facilities, pharmaceutical companies, universities, and the U.S. Government.

Resomation, the Scottish company that first began advocating for the process to be used by the funeral industry, has its roots in the veterinary waste industry. When cows in Britain were infected by Mad Cow Disease and a great number had to be disposed of in a relatively short amount of time, alkaline hydrolysis was used. The process effectively destroyed the prions that caused the outbreak and halted the spread of the disease. That is because the alkali concentrations and the temperature conditions used in the process destroy the protein coats of viruses and the peptide bonds of prions.

What this means, is that the process sterilizes the leftover bone matter, as well as the liquid matter it creates.

As much as alkaline hydrolysis solves many of the problems created by traditional burials and cremation, the process does have its detractors. The loudest voices against its use seem to be most bothered by the idea that the liquid created by the process is washed down the drain.

This, it seems, is more of an *eww*-factor reaction than one of scientific concern. When handled correctly (correct mix of water to alkali, correct temperature, correct pressure, correct time), the resulting liquid is sterile, and so there is no risk of it causing contagion (remember, also, that embalming releases the blood displaced by arterial fluid, as well as some embalming fluid, directly into the sewage system).

If there is any concern, it may be that the pH level of the effluent does not meet local sewage district codes. This can be resolved by bubbling carbon dioxide through the liquid prior to dispensing it to lower the pH into an acceptable range.

David Humphries, a former funeral director and now Chief Executive of Aquamation Industries, an alkaline hydrolysis company in Australia, recommends adding vinegar or citric acid to the liquid.

"By that time," he says, "it's safe enough to pour on the rose bushes." And, some advocate that you do just that. In fact, the liquid collected in veterinary aquamation is used as fertilizer.

It should be noted, that in Australia, "resomation" is considered a bit different than "aquamation." There, resomation refers to the process that heats the bath to about 350 degrees Fahrenheit, while in aquamation, the water is heated to just about 200 degrees. The outcome is the same, but the added temperature speeds up the process.

From the family members' points of view, alkaline hydrolysis should be no different than cremation. They would spend time with their loved one's body during a viewing or visitation, the body could be present during religious services, and they would be offered the chance for a final goodbye.

The process has only recently been introduced in the United States as a choice for final disposition of loved ones. Currently, it is not accepted in all states, though it is under consideration by quite a few.

Some states, such as Colorado, simply had to re-word the state's definition of cremation. In Colorado, the term "direct exposure to intense heat" was removed from the code as a description of cremation. Other states have followed suit, borrowing language proposed by the Cremation Association of North America (CANA) to include alkaline hydrolysis as a form of cremation.

States that have changed laws, or that are in the process of changing their laws to include alkaline hydrolysis as an acceptable form of final disposition include Colorado, California, Florida, Kansas, Maine, Minnesota, Oregon and Washington. The process is under consideration in Arizona, Illinois, Massachusetts, Michigan, Nebraska, New Jersey, New York, North Carolina, Oklahoma, Pennsylvania, Tennessee, Texas, Virginia, Washington, and Wisconsin.

In February of 2011, Ohio's Board of Embalmers and Funeral Directors issued a written statement that determined that alkaline hydrolysis is not an authorized form of disposition.

Because the United States is just now entering into the world of alkaline hydrolysis, pricing for the service is still not known. Technically, it should be cheaper even than flame cremation as it uses fewer resources and requires less maintenance (a crematorium must be re-bricked after so many hours).

Unfortunately, the equipment is expensive, requiring an initial investment by a funeral home in the range of $200,000 to $400,000, which is about 3 – 5 times that of a crematory retort, or crematorium. This, of course, could come down as production increases. In the meantime, however, funeral homes will be looking for a return on their investment.

Curt Rostad, Executive Director of the Indiana Funeral Directors Association, understands that because this is a new service, those who are the first to offer it will be setting the pricing. For now, he "sees little choice for funeral homes that invest in the technology other than to base initial pricing on costs. 'Right now, the major cost is in equipment,' he said. 'I understand [the number] of man hours required [for the process] is similar and the cost of gas vs. chemicals is within a few dollars of each other. If public acceptance of the process grows and the units become more mass produced, we can expect the cost to eventually come down so maybe the costs will be comparable.'"

So, what is the future of bio-crenation? In the September 2010 issue of "American Funeral Director" magazine John Ross, who is the executive director of the Cremation Association of North America, predicted that, "within 10 years, alkaline hydrolysis could be a significant portion of overall disposition - perhaps in the 5 to 10 percent range. In 25 years, it will probably be an even larger percent – it could be as much as half in some point of time, but it really depends on the market."

To learn more about bio-cremation, please see the links to Alkaline Hydrolysis Resources at the back of this book.

Odds & Ends – Lye, the alkali used in alkaline hydrolysis, is extremely caustic and can cause chemical burns on contact. Strangely, however, it is used in a number of household items, most notably in certain soap products and hair relaxers, as well as in some foods. Yes, foods. Lye is used to cure olives (black olives result from soaking green olives in a lye and water bath) and to give pretzels their crusty texture.

PROMESSION

Promession is a new method of final disposition that, at the time of this writing, is not yet available in the United States (but soon should be) and that is only just becoming available in other countries including the UK, South Africa and South Korea. It is a mechanized process that uses a "promator" to break a body down into its essential organic matter, without polluting the air (as crematoria do), the earth (as traditional funerals do), or the water table (as both cremation and traditional burial can).

To fully understand and appreciate the simple elegance of promession, it is important, first, to understand a bit about its inventor, Swedish biologist and avid gardener, Susanne Wiigh-*Mäsak*, as well as to understand basic biology.

From a very early age, Wiigh-*Mäsak* has had two passions – gardening and science. Of particular interest to her is the art and science of composting, and how, when done right, composting breaks organic material (once living) down to a nutrient level that can be used to nourish and replenish the earth.

When correctly employed, composting requires moisture, oxygen and temperature (heat). These three, working together and when applied to organic material, break the material into smaller and smaller units. When any one of these is absent, say when organic material is dumped in a heap and is not turned over, a process which aerates it, the material will break down, but the result will be a smelly, rotten mess rather than soluble organic matter.

Further to the fundamentals of composting, Wiigh-*Mäsak*

understood that all organic material is made of basic building blocks, or elements, including oxygen, carbon, hydrogen, nitrogen, calcium, and phosphorus. In the normal course of things, when something dies, it decomposes from organic material into organic matter, the state at which no further decomposition occurs. At that point, the elements can be released into the soil to be absorbed by plants, and so become again a part of the life cycle.

At some time over the twenty-odd years that Wiigh-*Mäsak* thought about composting and about biology, she began to wonder if composting methods could be utilized by the funeral industry to rapidly turn bodies into organic matter rather than incinerating them or sealing them in coffins, neither of which returns "earth to earth."

The idea, of course, was simple, yet brilliant. Neither cremation nor traditional burial returns bodies to the earth and, because they do not, these methods somehow rob the earth of necessary elements. Cremation incinerates just about all the elements except calcium, while traditional burial seals the body off from nature.

Of course, there are some fundamental problems with composting human remains. Who, after all, wants to stick their loved one's body in a pile of kitchen refuse and to turn it every few days in order to aerate it? Surely no one.

The other problem with composting human remains is that, while the bodies they are generally large, they have a relatively small surface area. Because moisture, oxygen and temperature work on the surface area, the larger it is, the slower the process. Wiigh-*Mäsak*'s challenge, then, was to come up with a way to break organic material down into organic matter in an intellectually and emotionally acceptable process, without causing pollution of any kind.

Eventually, Wiigh-*Mäsak* developed a method that would meet these goals. The process, which she named "Promession" (after the word "promise"), breaks the body down into organic matter without taking anything from it other than water and metals, and without polluting the earth, air or water. What is returned to family members is a fine dust-like substance that can be buried directly in the earth, or that can be placed in a biodegradable container prior to burial. Unlike the "ashes" of cremation, the powder from promession is rich organic matter.

According to Promessa Organic AB of Sweden, the company

that offers the promession method of final disposition, the promession process is carried out in a number of automated steps:

- After a viewing or final goodbye, your loved one's body is frozen to minus 18 degrees Celsius, which is about 0 degrees Fahrenheit,

- Once frozen, it is exposed to liquid nitrogen, which crystalizes it,

- The table the body is lying upon is gently vibrated, causing the crystals to break down into an organic powder,

- The powder is place in a vacuum chamber that removes all moisture from it (freeze drying),

- The dry powder is passed through a metal separator that removes any metals from it, including mercury,

- The powder is then placed in a biodegradable container made from corn starch,

- The container is buried in living topsoil (where there is oxygen, unlike traditional burial where the casket is buried so deep there is no oxygen to encourage decomposition),

- Over the next 6 – 12 months, the container and its contests are broken down into their basic elements, which replenish and renew the surrounding soil.

Because one of the fundamental ideas of Promession is that death is a part of the life cycle, the company recommends planting a memorial tree over the burial site which will then be fed by the composted organic matter.

Promession is being touted as the most "green of green" forms of final disposition. "The non-polluting green burial method of Promession allows the body to be fully restored to the earth as naturally as possible," Promessa's UK partner's website explains.

At the time of this writing, Promessa is not yet available to the public. The first "Promatorium" is, however, due to open in Sweden, with sites approved in both the UK and in South Korea.

If you are interested in promession for your loved one, please contact the company through the links in the <u>Promession Resources</u> section of this book.

<u>Questions You May Have About Promession</u>

Why is the body broken down into powder? Can't it simply be freeze dried?

Yes, it can, but the powder will have a greater surface area than the body did. Oxygen, moisture and temperature work on the surface area to decompose (compost) the organic material. By breaking the body down, the entire process is greatly accelerated and your loved one's remains can re-enter the life cycle that much more quickly.

Is Promession equal to or better than green burial?

"Equal to" and "better" are subjective words. While one person might find it "better" to bury an in-tact body in a conservation burial ground, another might prefer the idea that their loved one's remains will more quickly re-enter the life cycle through promession.

On the other hand, from a purely "green" point of view, promession may often be "better." That is because organic material and organic matter need to be buried in living soil where oxygen is present. Oftentimes, bodies are buried too deeply, where there is no oxygen available to help break it down. While there are microbes that can survive in an anaerobic environment and these will eventually break down the body, the process takes a very long time.

Promated remains, because they are dust-like, can be buried in living soil (about the top 6 inches) without fear that they will be dug up or disturbed. This allows oxygen, moisture and heat to work to quickly reduce them to their elements so that they can re-enter the life cycle.

When will Promession be available in the United States?

In July, 2011, I heard from Peter *Mäsak*, Susanne Wiigh-*Mäsak*'s husband. He gave me this update:

"We did already start the commercialization process by signing license agreements with territories as South Korea, UK, South Africa, and we are negotiating with parties in different states in the US, Germany, Norway... We have seen an interest from several states in the US, i.e. Texas and Oregon, but in California the interest seems to be 'something beyond the ordinary' - still we do not have any licensee in the US, but we will certainly have (one) very soon."

It is likely that the European Union will turn to Promession in a big way soon as they have banned mercury emissions and because there is a large (and loud) green funeral movement afoot. Land-challenged countries such as Japan will likely begin implementing the method soon as well as.

The United States, with its disparate funeral laws, may lag behind these other countries simply because each state will have to adopt changes to its individual list of acceptable methods of final disposition in order to make the process legal. That means that fifty separate state agencies will have to first learn about and then vote to approve Promession.

Odds & Ends – According HowStuffWorks.com, a casketed human body can take 40 to 50 years to fully decompose to bone. Of course, a number of factors will affect this process, including whether the casket is buried too deeply in the ground (most bacteria need oxygen) and the ambient moisture content. An un-casketed, unburied body exposed to the elements will decompose and return to the life cycle much more quickly, though bone fragments may remain for hundreds of years. Promession fully returns a human body to the life cycle within 6 – 12 months.

CRYONICS

Cryonics, or cryo-preservation, is the method of preserving bodies indefinitely in a frozen state. Proponents of cryonics, who call it a "life extension" method, argue that at some time in the future, technology will find a way to "unfreeze" the bodies, to cure whatever caused the person to die (or, if the person died of "old age," to have discovered ways to live longer), and to give those frozen a second chance at life.

The cryonics movement started in the early 1960's with the private release of Michigan College physics professor, Robert Ettinger's, book, *The Prospect of Immortality*. In it, he argued that while freezing a body is fatal, what is considered fatal today may not be so in the future. Central to the premise of cryonics is the idea that personality, identity, and memories are held, and can be frozen within, the physical, durable, cell-structures of the brain.

Science seems to support this premise, to an extent.

> "We know that secondary memory does not depend on continued activity of the nervous system, because the brain can be totally inactivated by cooling, by general anesthesia, by hypoxia, by ischemia, or by any method, and yet secondary memories that have been previously stored are still retained when the brain becomes active once again. Therefore, secondary memory must result from some actual alterations of the synapses, either physical or chemical."

You have, no doubt, heard the news stories of people who have survived profound hypothermia, such as children who have fallen through ice and been rescued and revived up to a couple of hours later. While those stories are extremely rare, they do happen.

The term "cryonics" comes from the Greek word, kryos, which means "icy cold." When a person is cryogenically frozen, his body temperature is lowered to about 77.15 Kelvin, the boiling point of liquid nitrogen, or -320.8 degrees Fahrenheit/-196 degrees Celsius. It is at that temperature that the opportunity for physical decay ceases.

A person can elect to have his full body frozen, or just his head. Freezing a head is, of course, less expensive due to the smaller storage space and equipment required. Proponents argue that as long as the memory, personality and identity remain intact within the brain, at some point in the future the technology will exist to transfer those to a new body, or that it will be medically possible to attach a head to a new body.

The biggest challenge to the successful freezing of a body is in doing so in such a way that moisture in the cells does not turn into ice, which can damage and destroy cell structures. To circumvent the formation of ice crystals, cryoprotectants are pumped into the body. These, acting as a sort of antifreeze, prevent the formation of ice as the body's temperature is progressively lowered.

If you want your loved one's remains to be cryonically frozen, hopefully you have made the arrangements prior to death. The reason for this is that tissue preservation is best when the body is prepared immediately after brain death has occurred. If that is not possible, you may request that your loved one's body be placed on machines to maintain oxygen and blood flow so that his tissues will remain viable until his body can be taken to a cryonics facility.

Of course, death does not always occur in hospitals or other facilities where a heart/lung machine is available. According to The Cryonics Society, if your loved one has elected for cryonics (or if you have elected for the method on his behalf), it is important that you take all measures to keep his body cooled until "suspension service" members can be contacted.

To cool your loved one's body, submerge him in a cold bath. If possible, pack his body (beneath, at the sides, and on top) with ice, paying particular attention to keeping his head cold. If you know CPR, perform it until the suspension services arrive to take over. This will ensure that oxygen and blood keep flowing throughout your loved one's body.

Questions You May Have about Cryonics

How popular is cryonics?

While Mike Meyers as Austin Powers made cryonics famous, its popularity in the real world is really infinitesimal. 2010 estimates note that just about 200 people (and pets) have been frozen. There are, however, some notables amongst them, including baseball great, Ted Williams (whose head was frozen). Robert Ettinger, the founder of the method, and both his wives are also frozen.

Alcor, one of the leaders in cryonics, states that as of June 2011, it has 948 "members" (those who have made plans and paid for the service) and 106 "patients" (those who have already been frozen).

Are there any estimates as to when technology will be available to "un-freeze" the dead?

To date, no. While there have been huge advances in other cryo-industries, we are not yet medically able to reanimate the dead, and there are no realistic estimates (that I can find) that indicate when this may be possible.

Is this method used in other ways?

Yes, absolutely. For decades, similar methods have been used to freeze human eggs and sperm for later donation and implantation. Because the method is relatively new (just decades old), we do not yet know how long the cells will remain viable, though some suggest that "indefinitely" is a good estimate.

How much does this cost?

As you can guess, it is expensive. Alcor, which is one of the leading cryonic suppliers in the United States, states that life insurance is the best way to pay for cryo-preservation. It recommends at minimum a policy of at least $200,000 for full body freezing and $80,000 for "neuropreservation" (just the head or brain itself).

The American Cryonics Society offers two "plans" – the "Standard Plan" and the "California Plan." Their fees range from $33,000 to $155,000.

For more information on cryonics, please refer to the <u>Cryonics Resources</u> section of this book.

Odds & Ends – Cryonics is not the same as "cryogenics", though the two are often confused. Cryogenics is the branch of physics that studies extremely low temperatures and its effects. Cryonics, on the other hand, depends on the belief that a body can be frozen and later returned to life, a belief that many in the cryogenics field find untenable.

PLASTINATION

Plastination is a preservation method developed in 1977 by German anatomist, Gunther von Hagens. Originally intended as a way to preserve biological specimens (such as hearts and lungs) for educational study, the process is now used to preserve whole bodies.

Plastination infuses bodies with polymers (silicone, epoxy or polyester-copolymer) in a four-step process that begins with formaldehyde embalming. Depending upon the polymer used, the resulting "specimen" will be either soft and flexible or hard, and either opaque or clear.

While plasticized anatomical specimens have greatly improved education, the plastination of whole human bodies has drawn controversy. In 1995, Von Hagens put his first plastinized human bodies on display in Japan. Since then, more than 32 million visitors have seen his exhibits. The show, called *Body Worlds*, travels throughout the world and is displayed at both art and science museums.

Body Worlds does not simply display human corpses. Rather, the bodies are frozen in any number of dynamic poses. There is a display of three bodies playing cards at a table, one player leaning forward, cards in hand, another nonchalantly leaning back in his chair, the third watching the other two, his face clearly displaying anticipation. Another exhibit shows a rider on the back of a plasticized galloping horse. Until recently the most controversial exhibit was of a reclining 8-months pregnant woman, her fetus curled in her belly.

After a body is embalmed, it is placed in an acetone bath, which dissolves water and soluble fats. Next, a vacuum process forces the exchange of acetone with the selected polymer. Von Hagens' teams then position the body using wires, clamps and foam blocks. Once perfectly positioned, the body goes through a hardening process that cures, or "freezes", it in the desired dynamic position. Most are plasticized with appropriate expressions on their faces. A tennis player, for instance, stretching for a ball, looks as if he is grimacing.

There have been many complaints about the displaying of corpses, but, apparently, it is quite legal, especially as the show is advertised as "educational" and all of the people displayed donated their bodies for just that procedure.

Plastination of whole bodies requires hundreds of hours of work. One display, of a giraffe, required more than 4,000 hours.

More than forty medical and veterinary schools use the method to create educational specimens. While von Hagens was the first to use the method for show purposes, he was not the last. A number of companies now "plastinate" whole human corpses for body exhibitions.

If plastination appeals to you as a form of final disposition of your loved one (or for yourself, for that matter), you will need to decide if this full-body donation is meant for educational purposes, or for display purposes. Some universities, including Michigan University's Division of Anatomical Sciences, accept bodies specifically for plastination purposes. If your preference is, instead, for the body to be used as part of an anatomical exhibition, like *Body Worlds*, then you would contact one of the companies that prepares bodies for exhibit.

Odds & Ends - *Body Worlds* features plastinated animals as well as humans. The displays include an elephant, giraffe and horse, among others. Currently, the most controversial of *Body Worlds* poses is that of a copulating couple. The couple, who did not know one another in life, is frozen mid-copulation. According to the company, two-thirds of the men and one-third of the women who have donated their bodies to *Body Worlds* agreed (while they were still living and able to do so) to have their bodies placed in a sexual position.

MUMMIFICATION

As strange as it may seem, mummification is alive and well in Salt Lake City, Utah, where the company, Summum, will mummify your loved one's body for a mere $67,000 (starting price).

Mummification is an ancient practice of preservation. The Ancient Egyptians believed that the body was the home of the soul, or spirit, and that if the body were destroyed, the spirit might be lost. To preserve the spirit, then, they devised ways of preserving the body.

The first mummifications were probably accidental as bodies, buried in shallow, sandy graves, naturally dried out in the desert Egyptian environment. Later, Egyptian priests began to devise ways to intentionally dry and mummify a body. The best practice was very involved and required months to accomplish.

The first step of mummification was to remove all moisture from the body. Because internal organs contain much moisture and also account for much of the initial decomposition, the ancient Egyptians removed them to be dried separately from the body itself. The priest embalmers then coated the body, inside and out, as well as the separated organs with natron, a type of salt that has great drying properties.

When the body was desiccated, it was washed and the organs were replaced inside of it (though sometimes, they were left in ceremonial jars, called canopic jars, to be kept with the body). The body was then wrapped in hundreds of yards of linen. Every so many windings, the linen-coated body was coated with resin, and then wrapped some more. Finally, the "mummy" was placed in its sarcophagus, a stone coffin often elaborately inscribed and decorated.

Today's mummification is probably similar to that used by the ancient Egyptians. Though Summum will not disclose its exact methods and is quite cagey about its practice, calling the mummification process "Transference" and describing the desiccation procedure as "immersion in a baptismal font" with "a special preservation solution made up of certain fluids, some of which are chemicals used in genetic engineering", the company does describe the winding of linens and application of resins.

Once a body is mummified, or "Transferred", it is placed in a bronze or stainless steel "Mummiform", the company's specially designed sarcophagus. "Amber" resin is then poured around the mummy and the Mummiform is welded shut.

If you would prefer a standard casket to a Mummiform, you may choose one. In any case, the Mummiform or casket will need to be sealed within a burial container. Summun recommends the Wilber Bronze, a burial vault that retails for about $9,850. This, then, can be enshrined in the cemetery or mausoleum of your choice, as long as the surrounding temperature does not fall below freezing or rise above 72 degrees Fahrenheit.

In a CBS look at new funeral practices, titled "Not Your Parents' Funeral", Corky Ra, of Summum (as well as its first mummy), called its Mummification of Transference Service the "Rolls Royce of the funeral industry." Currently, the company earns its living from pet mummifications, which cost from $4,000 for a pet up to 15 pounds (and another $2,000 to $14,000 for the Mummiform) to $28,000 for a pet weighing up to 100 pounds (with another $50,000 to $100,000 for the Mummiform). According to Ra, however, the company has 1,400 humans signed and paid up for the process.

If you choose mummification for your loved one, there are a number of considerations to undertake, including:

- **Spiritual Will**. The company requires that your loved have a Spiritual Will detailing "things you want read to you during the Transference." According to Summum, "everyone has an essence that will begin a journey upon the death of the body. The start of this journey signals the beginning of a transition to a new destination.... it is important and necessary that you compile and put into written form things that will be read to you while Summum conducts your Mummification and Transference... <u>Your essence will be fully aware of things going on</u> (note, Summum's link, not mine), and your Spiritual Will will play an indispensable role during your Transference."

- **Last Will & Testament** - As legal protection for the company, your loved one will be required to include mummification instructions in his/her Last Will & Testament.

- **Power of Attorney** - Again, as legal protection for the company, it requires that your loved one signs/has signed a Power of Attorney allowing the company to make decisions on his/her behalf.

- **Body Release Documents** - These documents are meant to prevent any member of your loved one's family from countermanding the mummification request.

- **No Embalming Allowed** - The company requires that a body be neither embalmed nor autopsied prior to mummification. Note, some states will not allow an unembalmed body to be transported across state lines or via common carrier.

- **Donation** - Probably because "mummification" is not an acceptable form of final disposition in any state, those who want to be mummified, or to have their loved ones mummified, will have to "donate" their bodies to Summum, much as those who choose plastination must donate their bodies to a medical school that offers the process or to *Body Worlds* (or another plastinized body exhibition company).

- **Proof** - Please note that I have absolutely no way of knowing if Summum's process works. Besides the company's secrecy, the bodies are placed inside a casket or "Mummiform", which in turn is welded inside a metal casket vault. I have included this choice for final disposition simply because it is available to you.

Caution

Please conduct your own research if this option appeals to you. I have not been able to find much information regarding it and the company is currently not taking questions from or giving interviews to the media. I have decided to include information about it, nonetheless, simply because it seems to be a legitimate non-profit and a number of large media companies (ABC, CBS, etc.), as well as a number of books and magazines, have discussed it. Again, please do your own due diligence.

Obviously, if your loved one did not make arrangements for mummification prior to death, you will not be able to provide the necessary forms. If, however, you are the person who is legally qualified to make final disposition arrangements on your loved one's behalf, you should be able to do so. If you have any doubts or questions, you should consult an attorney.

For more on mummification, please see the Mummification Resources section.

Pricing

Mummification is not cheap. The most basic human mummification service begins at $67,000 within the United States. To that you will have to add the costs of hiring a local funeral home to prepare the body for transport, transportation fees to Utah, transportation fees from Utah back to place of burial, burial plot or mausoleum fees, a burial vault (the $9,850 Wilbert Bronze is recommended), as well as any services you will want held in your loved one's honor.

PART II:
Preparing the Services

STEPS FOR ARRANGING A HOME FUNERAL

If you have made the decision to keep your loved one's body at home for a wake, vigil, home funeral or other service, there are steps you can take to ensure all goes smoothly.

First, of course, you will have to determine if a home funeral is allowed in your state (at the time of this writing, Connecticut, Delaware, Indiana, Nebraska and New York do not allow it). In a previous chapter, I pointed out the states that require that you hire a funeral director regardless of your preferences. If you are still unsure, you can contact your state's supervising authority (contact information is in the Funeral Law State-by-State resource section of this book), or contact one of the Home Funeral resources also listed at the back of this book.

Now, let's first understand that there is no strict definition of "home funeral." It can be as simple as holding a memorial service in your home, or as complete as preparing your loved one's body at home with the help of other family members and friends, holding a funeral service in your back yard, and, possibly, if you have enough land, burying your loved one on your property.

You may decide to work with a funeral director to handle some of the arrangements (in some states, you will HAVE to hire a funeral director), such as body preparation or cremation. If so, make sure that the agreement you reach reflects the amount of work you will do yourself. For instance, if you will be placing notices in your local newspapers, make sure the cost to do so is taken off your bill.

You may choose to contact a "death midwife." These are people who specialize in helping loved ones prepare home funerals and who have access to many of the local resources that will make this move more smoothly for you. If you do not know a death midwife, you may be able to find one through the Resources section.

If you do decide to hold a home funeral and caring for your loved one's body is part of your decision, the following should help.

The items you may need:

- A table or bed to lay the body out on

- A casket if you will lay the body out in one

- Sheet(s) to lay the body on, roll the body and/or to cover dry ice packs

- Blanket(s)

- A small pillow to place behind her head

- Q-tips to swab mouth

- Cotton for packing orifices

- Disposable gloves for placing of cotton

- Soft cloths or sponges for cleansing the body

- Vinegar

- Mouthwash

- Body Soap

- Shampoo if washing her hair

- Water in a basin

- Towels

- Scarf for tying her mouth closed

- Hand towel to roll under her chin

- Oil to rub on eyelids

- Moisturizing lotion to keep skin from drying out

- Lavender Essential Oil

- Nail clippers

- Cedar wood chips (like those found in a pet store), sawdust or cat litter

- Dry Ice (about 30 pounds per day for an average adult-sized body) - if possible, have them cut into 1-inch thick blocks, or,

- Gel ice packs, or,

- Zip-lock bags of ice - fill zip lock bags with water and freeze them in flat blocks

- Leather gloves and apron to protect you when handling dry ice

- An ice pick and/or hammer for breaking up ice

- Pillow cases or towels to wrap dry ice in

- A non-plastic container for storing extra dry ice (do not keep it in your freezer)

- Scissors if it becomes necessary to cut off clothing

- Plastic-lined diapers and/or mat for placing under the body, or,

- Sanitary pads

- Makeup if you wish to touch up your loved one's face a bit

- Scented candles or essential oil dispensers

- Flowers

- Framed photos

- Music

- An air conditioner to keep the room cool

- Chairs for visitors to sit in

- A casket, burial shroud or other appropriate container

- Transportation for the body – truck, van, SUV, station wagon, etc.

Steps in Preparing the Body and Services:

Take your time. There is much to do, but do give yourself time to sit with your loved one's body and to reflect. Nothing needs to be done for an hour or so, so take the time to grieve in privacy, if that makes sense to you.

Call your local authorities. If death was expected or your loved one was under medical care, call the doctor or nurse practitioner. Or call your local coroner. For the death certificate to be prepared, the death will need to be "pronounced" by an appropriate medical representative or authority.

Swab out her mouth. Moisten a cotton ball or soft cloth with mouthwash or vinegar. Use this to gently swab out her mouth. If she wore dentures in life, clean these and then put these in her mouth for a more natural look.

Close her mouth. Because the muscles are no longer working to keep the mouth closed, it may hang open. Loop a soft scarf under her chin and tie it over her head until rigor sets. Alternately, roll a hand towel up and tuck it under her chin to keep her mouth closed.

Close her eyes. You may have to repeat this step a number of times as the lids may pull back, especially as they dry out. To avoid this, try dabbing a small amount of oil on the lids to soften them enough so that they stay closed. Understand that you may not be able to fully close the eyes.

Empty her bladder. There may be urine in her bladder and/or urethra. Place an absorbent towel under her body and gently press down on the bladder area so that the fluid releases.

Wash her body. If you have access to Lavender Essential Oil, you can add some to a bowl of clean water and use it to rinse off your loved one's body. The essential oil has mild antiseptic qualities and should also help to mask any odors. If not, choose a mild cleanser and gently wipe your loved one's body down.

Expect fluids to leak from the body. You should understand that fluids will leak from your loved one's body. For that reason, you should don disposable latex gloves and pack absorbent cotton into her rectum and vagina. Until burial, keep an absorbent towel or blanket under her body. You may choose to dress your loved one in diapers until burial. If you are planning a fully "green" burial, any plastic lining will have to be removed prior to placing her in the ground. As an alternative to "diapers", you can use sanitary pads.

Trim any facial hair and clip finger and toe nails. Contrary to old wives' tales, nails do not continue to grow after death. The body, however, begins to dehydrate, which makes nails look longer.

Dress her. Dress her in clothing she would have worn in life – not funeral black. Let her clothing be yet another reminder of the person she was. To cover any bruising or scars, drape a scarf around her neck. If she lost her hair due to illness, wrap a scarf around her head (if that is what she did in life) or cover her head with a wig (again, if that was her preference in life).

Groom her. Brush her hair in a style she wore in life. If it makes you feel better, apply a bit of makeup to her face.

Prepare the Casket. If you are going to place your loved one's body in a casket for the Viewing or Home Funeral, you may want to first line the bottom of the casket with cedar wood chips, saw dust or cat litter. These will help to absorb any fluids and to mask any odors.

Place her body on a sheet. The sheet will be used to lift and move her body. Generally, four people will each take a corner and lift together. The sheet will also drape the dry ice (if used).

Position her hands. If you so wish, and before rigor mortis sets in, place a precious item in her hands, be it a religious book, a bouquet of flowers, a stuffed animal, or a rosary.

Expect rigor mortis to set in. Rigor mortis will set in within a few hours so dress your loved one and lay her body out beforehand. You might place a small pillow behind her neck and cross her arms over her stomach. Note: rigor will pass within 36 hours, after which her body will loosen. At that point, you may need to prop her body up.

Keep the body cool. As soon as possible after the death, you will want to make every attempt to keep your loved one's body cool. You can do this by turning on an air conditioner to its lowest setting or using dry ice to keep the body cool (note, be very careful when handling dry ice as it can burn you. Wear protective gloves, preferably durable leather, and a heavy-duty apron). If using dry ice, you will need about 30 pounds for an average-sized adult. You will want to place the dry ice both under and alongside your loved one's body, particularly under the torso.

One of the benefits of dry ice is that it evaporates rather than melts so you do not have to worry about dripping water. However, breathing the released carbon dioxide can make you feel light-headed and ill. It is always a good idea to crack open a window in the room where you will be laying out the body. If you do not have access to dry ice, freeze plastic water bottles or fill Ziplock bags and freeze them, and pack these around her body. Unlike dry ice, these will "sweat" and you will have to dry up any puddles.

Remove signs of illness. Before visitors arrive, remove any signs of illness from bedside tables. These may include medicines, IV lines, oxygen tanks or even hospital beds or wheelchairs.

Personalize the space. Use candles, arrange framed photos of your loved one on nearby tables, arrange flowers in vases, or cover her with a favorite blanket. You may choose to play soft music in the background, or to play videos of your loved on a TV. An aromatherapy diffuser or scented candles may be helpful.

Decide upon the service(s) you want to conduct. Set a date and time and begin calling those who you would like to attend.

Coordinate the service(s). Decide how long the service(s) will be (an hour is a common length for a funeral service, while visitation is usually several hours long), decide who will speak, and what they will say (for instance, will they say a prayer? Give a eulogy? Read from scripture?), and in which order.

Place a notice in your local newspaper. Additionally, if appropriate, post notices on social sites, such as Facebook or MySpace. As strange as this may sound, some people are more likely to find out about the death and any scheduled services through social media rather than through a local newspaper.

Decide upon food and beverages. If you will be providing nourishment for those who attend, make the arrangements to do so.

Contact your local Registrar's office. Ask about obtaining a transportation permit (if you will be transporting the body to the place of burial).

Arrange transportation. If a certain type of transport vehicle is needed (for instance, some states require a closed vehicle), arrange to rent or borrow one.

Burial container. Decide upon a casket, urn, or burial shroud. If this is to be a green burial, you may make your own casket or urn, purchase one online made of reeds or other easily biodegradable material, or settle on a simple, natural-fiber burial shroud.

Choose a burial location. If on private land, you may have to contact local authorities about having a designated area zoned as a burial ground or family cemetery.

Order flowers.

Prepare the service(s). Who will speak? Will a poem and/or verses be read? Will someone sing? Or will music be provided by another means? What (if any) prayers would you like spoken?

Order, or make, a marker. If you are burying your loved one in a cemetery, there may be restrictions as to the size and type of marker allowed. You will have to contact the cemetery to inquire. If you are burying your loved one in a green cemetery, markers may not be allowed, but planting a tree or other plant may be. Again, simply inquire. You should know that you do not have to do this immediately. Grave markers are often installed months after a burial.

Death Midwives, Burial Societies

A number of religions have incorporated burial societies into their community outreach programs. The Jewish faith has for centuries relied on the Chevra kadisha (Khevra kadishah), a society that ensures that the bodies of those of the faith are tended according to Jewish law. The Muslim and Mormon religions have their own burial societies.

Tending to the dead is considered an honorable, laudable and selfless act as the dead can never return the favor. Caring for the dead usually includes a purification ritual (cleansing), dressing, and preparing the body for a funeral service.

Death midwives are a small, but growing, group who help families to care for their own dead. They help with everything from preparation of any necessary paperwork, to cleansing and grooming the body, to locating appropriate burial products (for instance, green caskets for green funerals, etc.).

If you would like to hold a home funeral, but do not know where to start, you should consider reaching out to a local death midwife. While there are not yet so many in the United States that you will always find one available, you should certainly try. At the very least, one midwife can put you in contact with another, or point you in the direction of resources that can help.

Two organizations are at the forefront of death midwifery in the United States. They are Final Passages, an organization begun by Jerrigrace Lyons, and Crossings, an organization begun by Beth Knox.

You can find links to both Final Passages and Crossings in the Resources section of this book.

THE VIEWING

Sometimes called "visitation," the viewing is an arranged time when visitors can go to the funeral home (or wherever the body is being kept) in order to pay final respects to the family of the deceased, and to say a last goodbye to the deceased him/herself. In the United States, it is common that the body, having been "restored" (made up, hair washed and arranged, dressed, etc.), looks as life-like as possible and is on display in an open casket.

While there are no state or federal laws that require embalming, many funeral homes do require the procedure if a body is to be displayed to the public. If you are using a funeral home, then, but do not want your loved one's body embalmed, inquire as to your options. The funeral home may allow for dry ice preservation (though this is not likely), or, at the least, may offer the use of non-formaldehyde embalming fluids, such as the essential-oil-based Enigma line.

Many funeral homes have rooms where a variety of services can be held. These are generally set up with a place at the front of the room where the casketed body can be placed. Most will have pews or rows of seats where visitors can sit in silence, meditation or prayer. Some may even have a dais or podium from which a service can be held or words spoken.

Most funeral homes will also have on hand small tables and easels to hold wreaths and flower arrangements. It is not uncommon for families to arrange photos of the deceased on the tables as well, or to position a large, framed headshot of the deceased on an easel next to the casket.

If you are planning to hold a viewing in your home, or in a private venue, you might want to borrow or rent folding chairs that can be set up to give visitors a place to sit. Likewise, you may want to have small tables on hand to display flowers sent to the family.

If the decedent was religious or if you expect the guests to be religious, you may want to arrange for a kneeler to be placed in front of the casket where visitors can kneel and say a prayer.

I have been to a number of viewings and have noticed that a family member of the deceased often takes up a position next to the casket where he/she can accept the condolences of those who decide to approach the deceased.

When preparing for a viewing, you should expect that some, at least, will not want to approach your loved one's body. They may show up in order to offer their condolences to the family, but might prefer to take a seat at the back of the room, or not to enter the room where the body is on display at all. For that reason, it is recommended that you have a greeter or greeters at the door who can represent the family and who can accept condolences on the family's behalf without forcing visitors to enter the viewing chamber in order to do so.

It has become more and more common for photo montages of the deceased's life to be shown during viewing time. Many funeral homes offer screens or televisions on which these can be played and they can be set to loop upon themselves over and over until turned off.

Photo montages are fairly easy to set up, whether in PowerPoint or similar program. If you are not familiar with doing so and do not know anyone who can, ask the funeral director for help. Oftentimes this will be a service offered by the funeral home – for a fee, of course.

In addition to video, you may want to set up an audio track. This can be a collection of songs your loved one particularly liked, or songs you have chosen to reflect your own feelings for the decedent. Many funeral homes have the equipment to play the audio, but you should inquire as to the format they accept, be it straight from an iPod or other MP3 player, or from a CD.

You may want to have a guest book at the viewing (as well as at any other service). If you are planning to write thank you cards to those who have attended, a guest book helps greatly in remembering who came. While some people might jot down a small remembrance or comment in a guest book, a better idea would be to also have a memory book that can be passed around, along with a pen. Reading other people's memories and comments about your loved one can be extremely comforting later on.

It is a good idea to offer a funeral or burial notice to guests at a viewing. Simply print up a small note with all the pertinent details and set these alongside the guest book. If it is possible that not all your guests will know how to get to the place of the funeral or burial, you might even include a map, or directions, on the back of the notice.

Generally speaking, food and drinks are not served at a viewing (as opposed to a wake). That is not to say that you can't, especially if the viewing is being held in your home. If it is being held in a funeral home, however, be sure to inquire ahead of time if this is allowed before planning to offer food and drinks.

If you are holding a viewing at a funeral, home, be sure you are given the total pricing up front. Many funeral homes charge by the hour for room usage. Others charge by a block of time (say, a four-hour period). Be sure you know what the charge will be if the viewing should go over that time limit.

You also need to be aware of the cost for funeral home personnel who remain available during the viewing. They may be needed to escort guests to the viewing chamber, to get more chairs or easels, or to help in any other way that may come up. While their job is to be of service to you and to your family, you want to make sure the number of attendants fits the event. You don't, for instance, want to pay for five attendants to be on call when one or two would suffice.

Also be sure to ask about rental fees. Does the funeral home provide an unlimited number of easels for your use, or do they charge a rental fee per easel? Likewise, how do they charge for display tables? For that matter, what type of table do they provide? Do they require table skirts or cloths and, if so, what are the rental charges for same?

Some people choose to have a viewing even if the body will be cremated. It makes no sense, then, to purchase an expensive casket for the viewing when it will no longer be needed. For this reason, many funeral homes offer rental caskets for the viewing. If your loved one is to be cremated, be sure to ask about the possibility of renting a casket for the viewing.

You should know that when renting a casket for viewing purposes, most funeral homes require that you purchase the inner padding and pillows. While you should not expect to get these back, you should ask about the fees involved as these will add to your bottom line.

THE FUNERAL SERVICE

The funeral service you design for your loved one will depend upon a number of factors including your loved one's faith, your faith, your loved one's community standing, your personality, your loved one's personality, yours and your loved one's customs, and budget.

Your Loved One's Faith - Religion, or faith, is a defining factor in many people's lives, and may have been in your loved one's life. A similarity among most religions is that they promote some idea about what happens to the soul upon death. Some believe that the soul goes to "heaven", while others believe it is reincarnated in another body. Regardless, most religions promote the idea of preparing the body in a certain way so as to help the soul on its final journey. The funeral, then, for many, is the final ceremony that releases the soul to the hereafter.

If your loved one held a certain religious belief, you should familiarize yourself with the customs of his religion. If he was Catholic, for instance, a funeral Mass "should" be held, with his whole body present (not cremated, at that point, if cremation is the eventual plan).

Oftentimes, planning a funeral is easier if your loved one held to a religious belief. That is because the funeral has already become ritualized and you are simply expected to adhere to the tenets of the ritual. Further, because it is a ritual, there are often religious leaders to help you through the process.

Your faith - You probably won't hear this often, but your faith, as the one arranging the funeral, may also come into play. If, for example, your loved one had no religious beliefs with rituals you can fall back on, but you do, you may find it helpful to reach out to your own religious leaders for guidance and help. That is, of course, unless your loved one expressly desired otherwise.

Funerals are as much for the living as for the dead. They force the living to accept that, yes, this really is happening, and offer an opportunity for a final goodbye. As such, they can as much be a celebration of your loved one's life, as of your love for him.

Community – You may feel that your loved one's death hit you the hardest, and it may have. Don't forget, however, that he had a life within a community as well. He may have been a civic leader, or an employer. He may have been an employee or a good neighbor. Regardless of who he was and what he did, there are other people who will want to say their goodbyes at a funeral service.

This does not mean that you arrange a funeral for the community. By this I mean that you should not design an ostentatious funeral because of his standing within the community when a simple service would better celebrate the person he was. Rather, it means that there are factors to take into consideration.

The venue, for instance, is important. If your loved one was a community leader, you can expect that there will be a great number of attendees. That means that you will have to make arrangements for the service in a place that can accommodate them. On the other hand, if your loved one was an environmentalist and you are planning a green burial on conservation land with the service held graveside, you will have to consider transportation to the site, not only of the body, but of the attendees (four wheel drive vehicles may be necessary, for instance).

Further, communities have customs. An example would be if your loved one was a member of the Knights of Columbus. They hold a ceremony for their members. Whether this is held separately from the funeral or incorporated into it is a choice you will have to make, but it is something you will have to consider, nonetheless.

Your Personality - I am going to confess something to you here. My husband and I have not agreed upon funeral arrangements. We actually have not spoken much about it. He is Catholic and, while I was baptized in the Catholic Church, I was not raised Catholic. In fact, I was not raised to "be" any religion whatsoever.

When my husband dies, and if he dies before me, I am assuming he will want a Catholic funeral service, complete with a funeral Mass. While I fully respect and would adhere to his wishes, I think I would have to "tweak" the funeral just a bit.

The Catholic Funeral Mass is a ritualized service that is more about the religion than it is about the person. A ritualized service that does not speak to the wonderful, unique individual who is my husband would not sit well with me. I am not sure how I would tweak the service, but I would find a way to do so because, to my mind, a funeral is as much about the living who loved the dead, as it is about the dead themselves.

Your Loved One's Personality - Much of a funeral is about honoring the dead and celebrating the newly departed's life. It is important, then, that the service reflects your loved one's personality. For you, as much as for him. Why? Because a generic service will not reflect your loved one's life and, as such, will not give you the opportunity to do something special for him.

I will give you an example. When my niece, Jahmila, was killed, she was just eighteen. She was so full of life and joy that I can hardly remember ever seeing her without a huge grin on her face. She was also one of four sisters and, to this day, I cannot reconcile myself to the idea that there are now just three. She was a daughter of a single mother, a mother who lives for her children. She was also a much loved granddaughter, niece and cousin. She was an employee of a local grocery store, and a college student. She was a friend to many.

A generic funeral service that did not honor all who she was and that did not include all who knew and loved her, or that did not reflect her individual personality, would not have done her justice and would have left the rest of us even emptier.

The funeral we planned included an hour of contemplation before the actual service, for anyone who wanted to attend. During that hour, a slideshow of photos of her life played on a large screen at the front of the church. There were photos of her with her sisters, with her mother and father, with her grandparents, with her aunts and uncle, her many cousins, her many friends and co-workers. Everyone who saw those photos was reminded of their own special moments with Jahmila.

We also played music. Not staid "church" music, because that would not have reflected her. We played Dave Matthew's, a family favorite, and other songs she cherished. We did play some hymns, such as "Swing Low Sweet Chariot", but we chose an upbeat version we were sure she would have loved. Likewise, we chose the Bolivian flute version of "El Condor Pasa" to honor her Bolivian roots.

Her three sisters and her cousin, Dean, who was like a brother to her, were all speakers, as was her mother, her uncle (my brother) and I. Her mother spoke of her life. I read a poem that expressed the loss we all felt and the belief that she is, somehow, with us still. Her uncle, my brother Sergio, told a story, a very poignant and funny story, of an event the two shared.

Solemnity would not have suited Jahmila in life, and it would not have honored her in death. By designing a service that celebrated her, we all felt closer to her than we would have had the service been generic. I like to believe that she would have approved.

Customs – Like religion, or faith, many people have customs that may be important to consider when planning your loved one's funeral. In New Orleans, for instance, it is customary to have a funeral procession, complete with a Jazz band, accompany the body to the graveyard.

Your loved one may have customs important to him that you can incorporate into his funeral service as a way of honoring him. Customs do not have to be communal or religion-based, though they certainly can be. At a Jewish funeral, for instance, it is customary for all men to cover their heads, even men not of the Jewish faith. For that reason, guest yarmulkes are offered to the men who do not have their own.

You might have customs that you and your loved one practiced together that may be meaningful to incorporate in the service. If you are burying a child, for instance, to whom you read a certain story at bedtime, you might choose a passage from that to read during the service.

However they develop, whether they are community driven, religion-based, or family-created, customs help to define each of us as individuals and they can be extremely comforting when saying goodbye.

Budget – This is a touchy subject because too often we are made to feel as if the amount we spend on our loved ones is a reflection of our feelings for them. In life, this is often manifested by parents who buy lavish gifts for their children or spouses, when something simpler and more personal might have meant more. In death, we often feel, or are made to feel, that a top-of-the line, designer casket lets the world know we really, really, really loved the one recently deceased. Likewise, we feel (or are made to feel) that we have to hire a choir, when recorded music or an organist will do.

Please understand that, while you want the funeral service to be special, over-spending will not help your loved one and, ultimately, it will hurt you, something your loved one most likely would not have wanted.

Something else that you should keep in mind is that simplicity can be more dignified than ostentation. The "fluff" can actually take the focus away from the memory of your loved one. Attendees, instead of focusing of the wonderful life now ended, would instead focus on the price, the decorations, the show.

The saddest part about designing an over-the-top funeral, of course, is that your loved one will still be gone.

THE GRAVESIDE SERVICE

Some people opt to forego a church, temple or mosque (or other religious venue) service altogether and, instead, prefer a graveside service. Others choose both.

If you have held a funeral service already, but have invited attendees to accompany your loved one's body to a cemetery or other resting place, you might choose to have a prayer said graveside, or to have one or two people speak a few words. Generally, however, the bulk of the service will be over and anything said or done graveside will be secondary, and shorter.

There are those, on the other hand, who opt to forego a traditional funeral service and instead hold a graveside service. When my grandfather died, for instance, we held a viewing in a local funeral home. Music was played (bagpipes), prayers were said, and many of us shared stories and memories. He was not a particularly religious person, however, and he did not attend a church where he died (in Missouri). We did not even know what we wanted at that time and the only thing we could all agree upon was that he wanted to be cremated and to have his ashes buried on family property in North Carolina. So, we agreed to meet some months later in North Carolina.

My grandparents had five children and numerous grandchildren and great-grandchildren. My parents owned about fourteen of the most beautiful acres imaginable on top of a mountain in North Carolina. When it came time to bury my grandfather's ashes, it was there that we met on a sun-splashed summer weekend.

We chose a spot under a sprawling oak tree and dug a small grave. Everyone who wanted to dug a shovelful. One of my aunts chose to scatter some of his ashes in the rose bushes and then, with the urn re-sealed, we laid his ashes to rest. We then planted an evergreen next to the site. We are an informal family and this was an informal gathering. Whoever wanted to share a memory did so. Whoever wanted to help bury the urn did so. At the conclusion, standing in a circle, holding hands, we said a prayer.

You may choose a more formal graveside gathering for your loved one. If you are burying him in a traditional cemetery, there may be rules that you have to adhere to, or at the least, hours that you have to abide by. If you are going to ask for a religious leader to be present (or, for military honors to be given), you will have to coordinate those services as well.

Most cemeteries have opening and closing fees. This means that cemetery personnel will dig the grave and cover it back up. You may, of course, toss in a handful of soil or a flower or two on the casket once it has been placed in the grave, but after all the attendees have left, cemetery personnel will do the big job of installing a grave liner, and refilling the grave, often with the use of heavy equipment.

It is becoming more and more popular today to hold a green burial, oftentimes in a conservation burial ground. These are not always easy to get to on foot, and you may have to make arrangements for four wheel drive vehicles to get you and the funeral party to the burial site. Or, you may have to carry the body in. If that is the case, using a light (but sturdy) casket is something you should consider, or even a burial shroud.

If you are going to bury your loved one in a green burial ground, be sure you ask who will dig the grave. This may be something that you will be expected to do (and so you should be prepared with shovels), or might be a service provided by the management for a fee.

One thing you definitely need to take into consideration, especially in the north, is weather. Some cemeteries have "holding areas" where casketed bodies are temporarily stored until spring thaws the ground. If that is the case, you might hold the funeral service a few days after your loved one died, and hold a graveside service in the spring or summer.

THE MEMORIAL SERVICE

Memorial services are often held sometime after a person has died, even months or years later. The reasons for this are many. Some cultures, in fact, hold memorial services rather than funeral services. Others choose to hold memorial services for purely practical reasons including that more family and friends can gather during a certain time of year, or as a yearly tribute to the one now deceased.

Without the pressure to bury a body, or to adhere to a religious time table, such as the mandate that those of the Jewish faith be buried as soon after death as practical, preferably within 24 hours of death, more thought and preparation can go into a memorial service than can into a funeral service.

The first step in preparing a memorial service is to decide upon a date, time and venue. The date will likely be dependent on convenience to you and your family or possibly timed to coincide with a special anniversary. The time may depend upon availability of a venue (for instance if being held in a church, you will have to arrange the service around the church's availability). The venue, of course, is a highly personal choice. Venue ideas include:

- A Church, Temple, Mosque or other place of worship,

- Your home or the home of the deceased,

- A meeting place, such as a club house, social venue or even a hotel ballroom,

- Someone's back yard,

- A ferry or rented boat (if your loved one loved the ocean or lake),

- A restaurant that your loved one enjoyed

- A golf clubhouse if your loved one was a golfer,

- A concert if he loved a particular band (with the memorial part taking place while tailgating, perhaps),

- A campsite or fishing hole your loved one often visited

- A beach,

- A park.

Memorial services do not have to be ceremonial, or even formal. They can be a special weekend that all those who loved him are invited to participate in. You may choose to go on a cruise, to rent vacation homes, to go on a special outing. Over the course of that day, or weekend, many instances to share your cherished memories will come up.

If you prefer a more organized memorial service, you might consider preparing a video presentation of your loved one's life, whether in "movie" format or as a slideshow. Or, you can pass around photo albums and play background music that is meaningful. At some point, you can have pre-chosen speakers stand up to talk about their most precious memories, to read a poem, or to say a prayer.

You might consider preparing a keepsake for all the guests to take home with them. My extended family (aunts, uncles, cousins, etc.), for instance, meets twice yearly for family reunions. At the first reunion after my niece's death, my sister passed out lime green (Jahmila's favorite color) rubber bracelets with her name and a personal message on them (similar to the yellow Livestrong bracelets). In fact, even as I write this, my green bracelet is on my right arm.

Once you have the memorial service planned out, you may want to have a "program" printed up. This simply informs the attendees of what is going to happen next. A program can be just as helpful during a church service where it tells attendees which hymn to sing next, as on a family cruise which tells attendees which dining room to meet in.

The most important thing about planning a memorial service is to remember that it is a way to celebrate your loved one's life. Therefore, it should be a reflection of who he or she was as an individual.

PERSONALIZING THE SERVICES

Funerals and other services are not just about doing something with the earthly remains. If they were, we'd have services in place that would pick up bodies and dispose of them while the rest of us would carry on with our lives.

Funerals, memorial services, viewings and all the other possible services really have two fundamental reasons for being: 1) they allow the living to come to terms with their loss and, 2) they celebrate the life of the recently dead and remind the world of how important she was. What happens to the body, then, is somewhat incidental.

When someone dies, it is very important for the living to remember and to reminisce. Yes, our memories will further remind us how much worse off we are, but they will also underscore how much better our lives are for having known and loved the one who has just died. Fourteen years later, I have not reconciled myself to my father's death. By that I mean that I don't think it was OK, and I probably never will. But, I do know how very lucky I was to have gotten him for a father. If given the choice ahead of time, I would have gratefully accepted the 33 years I had him in my life over having any other father for 100 years. The same with Jahmila.

Looking back, I would have made very different decisions for my father's funeral service. It was a bit staid and, while it was a decent service, it did not do my father justice. On the other hand, his burial six months later (we had to wait for the ground to thaw at our vacation home in North Carolina) was pure Peter (my father's name). And twice a year when all my cousins get together, "Uncle Peter" is often the topic of conversation. Why? Because he was hilarious and outgoing and joyful. Everyone who knew him felt better off for having spent time with him. Even some of the younger kids in my family who never had the chance to meet him tell stories about him as if they'd grown up at his side. That is an amazing memorial.

When planning the various services surrounding your loved one's death, it is important that you find ways to personalize them, to remind the world of the unique individual who was. In other words, don't settle for the generic.

Some religions have ritualized all the various services that they deem important when a person dies. That is to say that if arranging your loved one's service(s) according to a religion's tenets, you may not have much room for personalization. That being said, you can often find moments or activities when personalization is appropriate and possible.

When personalizing the services, you should try to come up with traits that made your loved one special and unique. This can be by listing his interests and hobbies, his beliefs, his personality traits, what was important to him, and even sayings and comments that he was known to repeat.

Your loved one might have been a ham radio operator, for instance, who loved fly fishing. He could have been a practical joker. Maybe he was fastidious, or was a great cook. He may have been a family man whose highlight of his day was coming home to his spouse and kids.

Oftentimes, you will get your best ideas for personalizing a service by speaking with his friends and family. Each person he interacted with in life will have a slightly different take on who he was. Ask others to share their ideas and, in the end, you might find the perfect ways to personalize the services so that they best reflect your loved one as he was in life. To help you get started, ask yourself (and others) these questions:

- What were his hobbies?

- What was his profession?

- Did he hold any position within the community?

- Was he religious?

- What were his family ties?

- Where was he born?

- Where did he choose to live as an adult?

- What was his personality?

- Did he own pets?

- What were his favorite possessions?

- What was his favorite color? Food? Song? Book? Movie?

- How did he like to spend his free time?

- Who were his best friends?

- Had he won any awards?

- What sports did he play?

- Which languages did he speak?

- What were his political views?

- What was he most proud of?

While it may seem ridiculous to you to go through this exercise because you feel that you know what would have been important to him, it is nevertheless a worthy technique for developing a "theme" for the memorial service and for coming up with ideas to best memorialize your loved one as the unique individual he was.

When you have your ideas together, ask yourself who would best be able to convey a sense of the person he was to an audience? Would his best friend? A cousin, perhaps? If he was in the military, perhaps his commanding officer? Whoever can best remind the attendees of what a unique, wonderful, full person your loved one was, consider inviting those people to speak at the service. Or, if it is more important that the audience hear from those closest to him in life, ask his spouse, his children, his parents and/or his siblings.

Remember to focus on how much better life was when your loved one was here, rather than how empty life is now that he is gone. This is a celebratory service, not one meant to leave the attendees feeling lost and depressed.

When you have the date, time, venue, theme and speakers arranged, begin to plan the event itself. What will come first? What will follow? Will you open with a prayer? A poem? A song? A video? Will there be food and drink and, if so, what will it be and how and when will it be served? How will the service wrap up? Will the attendees leave with keepsakes?

Maybe instead of leaving with a keepsake, you've asked all the attendees to bring something – a written memory. If so, you can gather all of these into a book, or make copies of all the memories for the attendees to take away with them.

Some people like to incorporate symbolism in funeral/memorial services. For instance, could you release doves (or butterflies or balloons) to symbolize the release of your loved one's soul? Would the lighting of candles symbolize unity and community?

When thinking about personalizing the services, I recommend that you think about the five senses. These, of course, are Sight, Sound, Touch, Taste and Smell.

For many years I worked as a spa director and it was there that I learned the importance of enlivening all five of the physical senses in order to transport our guests. To that end, I designed the spas with pleasing colors and textures, soothing sounds, the softest of linens. We used different essential oils to either enliven or to relax and added cucumbers or lemons to our water to ease and refresh our guests.

You can use these same techniques to make your loved one's services more memorable or poignant. For instance, by including a photo montage or picture board, you have included visual memories. Music that was important to your loved one or is a tribute to her enlivens auditory memory. Serving a special dish or drink during a wake brings in the sense of taste. For example, if your loved one had a special recipe for which she was known, you might consider including that – and then sending the attendees home with a copy of the recipe. Spritzing the funeral program with her favorite perfume will enrich the experience for the attendees and will awaken scent-based memories. If your loved one was a hobbyist, say a woodworker or needle-pointer, displaying a small selection of her work can allow the attendees to pick them up, to handle them, and to reminisce.

Use the senses as a way of personalizing the services you will hold for your loved one. These will trigger memories and discussions about him or her. What better way to celebrate a life than to have the living keep his or her memory alive?

READINGS

During the various services that surround the death of a loved one, there often comes a time for the reading of special words. This can be during the funeral service itself, when prayers are often read, during the memorial service when someone elects to read an essay they have written, or at a graveside service.

The time surrounding a death is often so emotional for the living that they do not have the wherewithal to come up with words of their own that they feel adequately expresses their love and loss. Some may even feel that they do not have the talent to equal some of the beautiful words already written by others.

If the services you are arranging are of a religious nature, finding appropriate readings should not be too difficult as you can always turn to scripture. If you are having difficulty locating the perfect piece, ask a member of the clergy to guide you. They are familiar with scripture and should be able to point out one or two passages that beautifully reflect your feelings.

For those who want to find something not particularly religious in nature, the internet is a wonderful source. You can simply search for "poems for death of a grandmother" or something similar and you will find many to choose from. Or, you can choose, instead, to read a poem or prayer that was particularly important to your loved one. It need not have anything to do with loss or saying goodbye. The simple fact that your loved one loved it is reason enough to share it at her funeral.

Music is another source you can turn to. After all, many songs are really poems put to music. Or, you can quote a song that was particularly important to your loved one and that you feel reflects her spirit and outlook on life.

If you are so inclined, you can write your own essay or poem for the occasion. Or, you can read something your loved one wrote. At my niece's funeral, one of her sisters read a poem that Jahmila had written and that we found among her things after her death. Hearing her very words spoken was akin to receiving an important message straight from her.

One thing I would caution against is to allow yourself to sink into melancholy, or to become maudlin. Yes, you are sad. Yes, you are depressed. That is very understandable. Remember, though, that your focus (for now) should be on celebrating your loved one's life rather than demanding that the world focus on you. While you will have plenty of time to share your grief, at this moment, at least, it's really not about you.

THE EULOGY

The eulogy is an important part of many funerals. While different speakers may reflect on their loved one, might share a memory or read a poem, the person giving the eulogy is tasked with a very specific job – to remind the attendees of who that person was in life and to celebrate that life.

If you have been tasked with writing a eulogy, congratulations! I know that sounds strange, but really, it is a great honor to be chosen to do so because you have now been trusted with celebrating your loved one's life in words. On the other hand, you have been given a great burden, not a bad burden, but a large and important one. You have been trusted with celebrating your loved one's life in words.

While each eulogy will be different, there are a number of styles that you can choose from to help you get started.

Life History - Life history is often the easiest eulogy to write. After all, you begin at the beginning and work your way through the end, highlighting the important parts in between. If you are not careful, however, a life history can come off as a dull, bulleted list that misses the essential life force you are trying to celebrate. If you have chosen to write in the Life History style, use the bullet points in your early drafts, but expand upon them in your later ones. Here is an example:

- Born June 16, 1928, the youngest of 10 kids in Tennessee

- Parents (list names) and siblings (list names)

- Early years (family's place in society, how they spent their time, important events)

- Teenage years (important events)

- Education (where, when and what degrees, if any)

- Twenties (important relationship, i.e. spouse, children, etc.)

- Career (jobs, promotions, etc.)

- Community (clubs, politics, place in society, etc.)

- And so on…

If this were your bullet list, you wouldn't want to read it as such, "John was born on June, 16, 1928 in Tennessee. He had nine older brothers and sisters. His parents were Tom and Viola Henderson. His siblings were…"

Instead, try to bring your essay to life: "The Big Flood of 1928 carried away half of Elmsboro, Tennessee. Its muddy waters washed in and through John and Viola Henderson's modest wood home and would have washed them away, along with their nine kids, if they hadn't been tied to the rafters in the attic. Of course, logic should have dictated that the family get out just as soon as the warning was given that the river had overflowed its banks. Only, logic wasn't an option. By the time the warning came, Viola was in hard labor. Quick thinking Tom tied the older kids to the rafters and then carried his wife to the small widow's walk on the roof of the house. It was there, around sunset, that John Edmund Henderson came into this wide, wet world. It's no wonder that, seventeen years later, he took to the sea."

Shared Memories and Recollections - Some speakers use memories of times shared to remind the audience of who their loved one was in life. This type of eulogy is both easy and difficult to write. Easy because you were there and you can re-tell the event(s). Difficult because it is not always easy to capture in words the important aspects of an event.

My brother chose to write this kind of eulogy for our niece's funeral. He related the story of an interchange between him and Jahmila that had the audience laughing through its tears. The story captured her perfectly - her wit and timing, her ability to trump her uncle, her charm and intelligence. It was one of the saddest essays I have ever heard because it brought home how much we had lost. It was one of the most wonderful essays I had ever heard because, for those moments, Jahmila was back with us (I have included a copy of Sergio's eulogy for Jahmila in the <u>Samples section</u> of this book).

Writing a shared memory eulogy about a loved one may seem an insurmountable task. It isn't. The key is to show, not tell. To those of you who are writers, you will know what I mean (that is the number one rule of writing). To others, I mean simply this: do not tell the audience that your loved one was "funny", instead choose a memory of a time when she said or did something surprising and hilarious. Picture it in your mind's eye. Replay it over and over until you understand why that moment was particularly humorous. And then, write it down.

You will have to edit several times. Each time, take out the unessential. Remove everything that does not move the essay forward, that is a side-story to the event you are recreating. Look at the verbs you have chosen. Choose expressive verbs over mundane ones. For instance, if she "laughed loudly", write instead that she "howled with laughter." If, during the event the two of you were walking down the street and she was known for walking fast, don't write, "she walked quickly." Instead, choose something like, "she galloped."

The point is to bring your loved one to life, to reveal to your audience the events that unfolded that day so that they, too, can feel as if they were there. Of course, don't choose words that would not have fit your loved one's personality, either. Simply choose the words that best reveal your loved one as she was in life. A thesaurus can be a big help.

A Tribute – Tributes are often somewhat formal eulogies. Rather than sharing a memory or taking the audience through the person's life, a tribute focuses on her achievements. While her struggles might be alluded to, they are included only to make a point of how and why her achievements were so noteworthy.

Legacy – Rather than focusing on the achievements of a person's life (though those can certainly be mentioned), a legacy eulogy focuses on the differences a person made in life and how those differences will affect the world going forward. Eunice Kennedy Shriver, for instance, started the Special Olympics in 1968. While that great woman accomplished a lot in her lifetime, the Special Olympics will impact millions going forward. The Special Olympics, then, are her legacy and focusing on them and how they will affect others is a celebration of her, their founder.

When writing a eulogy, keep the following in mind:

- This is a celebration of your loved one's life. Therefore, leave out the negative. If the person overcame great barriers, don't focus on the barrier, focus instead on her triumph.

- A eulogy is meant to be uplifting and inspirational. Focus on the special qualities of your loved one - and remember, "special" doesn't have to be earth-shattering. Being a faithful, loving partner is special. Being a truthful, loyal friend is special. Being a caring, uplifting parent is special.

- Keep the eulogy to 3 – 10 minutes. This means that you will have to practice it out loud. When doing so, try to pause at different points to find the ones that are most effective. Choose the pace of your speech and enunciate each word.

- Choose a style. If you are going to write a warm and loving eulogy, one spattered with humor, don't sink into melancholy.

- Build to a climax. No, this is not a novel, but sound storytelling can add impact and dimension. Set the stage in the first paragraph and then work up to the punch line, or climax, or point.

- When you have polished your essay, ask others to read it and to help you through a final edit. Then, practice it out loud. It will sound very different than it does in your head.

It is an honor to be asked to speak at a funeral and you should treat that honor with deep respect. For that reason, take your time in choosing the right words, in putting them in the best order, in revealing your loved one as you had known her.

MUSIC

Music often accompanies the various elements of a funeral. Hymns are sung in religious services, bagpipes are often played when the person was of Scottish descent, as is "Taps" in a military funeral, a soloist is sometimes asked to sing. Music touches a place deep inside of us and can add beauty and meaning to any memorial.

When choosing music, there are several things to take into consideration. These include:

- Music your loved one loved

- Music that is spiritual in nature

- Music that transports

- Music that reminds you of your loved one

- Whether it will be live or recorded

- Whether it is appropriate to the event

- How it fits in with the other elements of the service

- Who will choose and prepare it

- Your budget

Music Your Loved One Loved - Each of us goes through life collecting songs and music. We perk up when we hear "our song" on the radio, play it incessantly ourselves, sing or whistle along with it. There are some songs that come and go and those that stay with us throughout. My niece, Jahmila, loved the Disney song, "Hakuna Matata." Not only did it bring a smile to her lips every time it played, but she took its meaning to heart.

The song is derived from a Swahili phrase that, taken literally, means "there are no worries." And, while she was alive, there weren't. When we planned the music for Jahmila's funeral, then, it was only natural that we chose this as one of the songs to play, not only during the video montage of her life, but also as the concluding, exit song of her funeral service.

Some may think that a happy, upbeat song is inappropriate to a funeral. I beg to differ. A head-banging song about devastation and destruction I would call inappropriate at an event that celebrates a life. One about living worry free and keeping a positive attitude is fully appropriate and was a perfect reflection of the life we were honoring.

Did your loved one have a favorite song, or songs? Is there a moment when it would be appropriate and uplifting to play it?

Music That is Spiritual in Nature – There are countless hymns that celebrate religious beliefs and attitudes. If your loved one was spiritual or religious, including one or two hymns or other spiritual music would be very appropriate as a way of celebrating that aspect of her.

My father was not particularly religious. He was, however, Catholic and, while he did not actively practice his religion, it was a part of who he was. Moreover, his mother (also Catholic) attended his funeral. For her, who had lost her child, including aspects of Catholicism in his funeral service was important. We chose "Ave Maria," a hauntingly beautiful prayer set to music that soothed my grandmother and that honored my father.

Music that transports – For the non-religious who attended my father's funeral, the choice of "Ave Maria" may have seemed wholly moving. It is, after all, both magical and haunting. You do not have to look to religious themes, however, to find music that transports the listener. "Taps", a haunting tune of loss that is played at military funerals, does this as do many songs played on bagpipes. "The Wind Beneath My Wings" by Bette Midler is often played at funerals because it is both meaningful and moving.

Music that reminds you of your loved one – You might know a song that, whenever you hear it, reminds you of your loved one. Even though that may not have been a particular favorite of hers, you can certainly include it in honor of her. As I mentioned before, we chose "El Condor Pasa", the original Bolivian flute version that Simon and Garfunkel later recreated as "If I Could", to honor the Bolivian in both my father and Jahmila.

Whether it will be live or recorded – My brother's mother-in-law plays the harp. I have always thought that it would make a wonderful addition to any funeral service (as it did at my brother and sister-in-law's wedding). If you know someone who is musically talented, you may ask him or her to play a live version of a meaningful song at your loved one's funeral. If you are arranging a service within a place of worship, you can inquire about hiring the organist, choir, soloist or music director. Or, you can look into the possibility of hiring a local band to play live music.

When live music is not a possibility, you can always resort to recorded music. Understand that there are often many different versions of the same song to choose from and search for the one that is most meaningful and inspirational.

Whether it is appropriate to the event – Even though I have recounted that my family is fairly easy-going and anything but uptight, I am sure there are some songs that we could have chosen that would have been inappropriate at our various funeral services. The Eminem and Rihanna song, "Love the Way You Lie", for instance, is a great-to-sing-along-with song. Its lyrics, though, that glorify domestic violence, would have been inappropriate at a funeral, regardless of the fact that my niece liked it.

When choosing music for the various services, then, make sure you take the time to read through the lyrics of the songs you choose to include. Remember, this is a celebration of your loved one's life and depressing, downbeat lyrics, even set to an upbeat tune, should probably be avoided.

How it fits in with the other elements of the service
– Think of the service you are preparing as a whole. While you are not planning a wedding or a birthday party with a theme in mind, you should consider the overall tone of the event. Will it be solemn? Joyful? Uplifting or melancholy? Whatever you plan it to be, ask yourself if your music choices enhance that tone or grate against it.

Who will choose and prepare it? – Think about important
life events. Births, birthdays, anniversaries, weddings, funerals. What makes funerals different? Your immediate answer might be "the mood" but, while true, that is not the answer I am seeking. The answer (in this case) is, "the time to prepare for it."

Think about it. You have nine months to prepare for the birth of a child, to buy all that you need to buy, to inform all who need to be notified. You have at least a full year to plan for a birthday or anniversary celebration, multi-years (in some cases) to plan for a wedding. For funerals, though, you often have only days. And, believe me, there are at least as many details that go into planning a funeral as go into the most extravagant of weddings.

When planning a funeral, it is extremely important that you delegate. As a control-freak myself, I know how difficult this can be. Especially when your heart is so deeply involved. Regardless, you have to let go of some of the preparations and, unless it is something you are the best at, you might consider letting go of the music. Not necessarily the choice of music, but the preparation of it.

For Jahmila's services, we had two lists of music. One included some forty songs to be played during the viewing the day before her funeral service, as well as during the video homage to her life played the hour before her funeral service began. Our second list consisted of three songs chosen to be played at different times during the funeral service itself.

My sister Liz, Jahmila's three sisters and I spent many hours putting together the first list of songs. Over the next couple of days, other family members and friends added to it. My cousin Theresa, Liz and I listened to countless versions of the three songs chosen for the funeral service on a long drive we took out to the crash site where Jahmila died. When we had our two lists, we turned them over to Jahmila's soon-to-be brother-in-law, Reggie. It was his job, then, to find the songs, to copy them to a file, to purchase them if necessary, and to arrange them and burn them to CDs. It was a time-consuming and thankless job for which I am extremely thankful.

What I am saying by this example is that coming up with the song-list itself is easy, though it may take you several hours. Actually locating the recordings (and choosing between versions), arranging them and burning them to CDs is a headache waiting to happen. When preparing your loved one's funeral, do not become bogged down in all the preparation. Delegate the time-consuming jobs and move on to the next detail on your list.

Budget – As with all aspects of funeral preparation, your budget should be taken into consideration when deciding upon the music. Hiring a band is more expensive, generally, than hiring a soloist. Playing recorded music is often more inexpensive than hiring an organist (unless the organist offers her services for free). Just about every choice you make during the preparations will have an associated price tag. Make sure you keep on top of the little things, like music, as well as the big things, because these can add up.

VIDEO MEMORIALS

It probably seems obvious to the YouTube generation, but for some of us, incorporating video into funeral services might be one of those, "Now why didn't I think of that?" moments.

Video is a wonderful way to celebrate a loved one's life. After all, it gives those who loved him the opportunity to see him again, to hear his voice, to share a bit of his life with him.

Happily for us, Jahmila was in a lot of videos. She and her sisters were made to be in front of cameras and they haven't lost an opportunity to preserve their memories on film (or, to digitize them). We have videos of her goofing off, at family celebrations, as part of a larger group, and of her alone. But, we did not incorporate any of the videos into her services.

Why? Because there were so many hours of video to go through, and then they would have needed to be edited, and, really, there was just not enough time to do so.

We did, however, create a photo montage of her life, which we made into a video. We showed it during her viewing and, again, right before her funeral service. We also had it playing, over and over again, at my brother's house in the days that led up to her funeral. Every time I saw it, I fixed on a different photo or series of photos, and was returned to a specific place and time.

Watching other people watch the video was a healing experience. Because I had moved out of state a few years before her death, I was not familiar with some of her many friends. I watched them watch the video of her life, however, and was sadly pleased every time someone would say, "Oh, I remember that. Do you remember when we…?"

If you are planning services for your loved one, you might want to consider incorporating video. While time consuming, the process of turning printed photos into a video montage is fairly easy and straightforward (and you can always delegate it to someone). If you happen to have videos of events your loved one took part in, even better. Again, if you can delegate the editing, adding music (if appropriate), etc., to someone else, go ahead and do so.

If you like the idea of incorporating video, but do not know how to do so yourself, or do not know of anyone you can delegate this task to, speak with your funeral director. They often offer this service for a fee. Otherwise, call your local photo shops and ask if they know a person who can quickly scan and digitize your photos for you.

As a final note – you can opt to set the photo montage to music, or play music separately.

PHOTOGRAPHS

Photographs are a wonderful way to remind the attendees of your loved one, of her/his life and experiences. There are many ways to incorporate photographs and I've included some of those ideas here.

I do recommend that you ask others to give you copies of photos that they may have. You will be surprised how many people have photographs of your loved one on their cell phones or who may have copies on their social networking pages. While you may not use them all during the services, they will be a comfort to you in the days to come.

As a final note, make sure you check your loved one's cell phone as well. My niece had more than 200 photos on her cell phone. Because we did not have her phone's password to access the file, we took it to Verizon. After my sister explained why we wanted access, a salesman at Verizon very graciously unlocked her phone for us. Some of the most endearing photographs I have of Jahmila came from her phone.

Framed on Easels - If you have ever been to a funeral (visitation, memorial, etc.) service, you have probably seen a large (8 x 10 or 11 x 14) framed and matted photo of the deceased placed on an easel near the casket. Generally, a head shot is chosen, though there are no rules. Further, don't limit yourself to just one photo if you want to display more. You can have a photo enlarged for very little at most big name pharmacies (CVS, Walgreens, etc.) or even at an office supply store such as Office Depot or Office Max. My cousin Tisa and I found a Staples next to a Michael's art supply store in Wellington, Florida. That made it very easy to take the photos next door for framing.

Photo Boards – You can purchase display boards at most office/school supply stores. Because they have three sides, you can open up the "wings" and stand them on a table (or easel). Use this to display a number of photos from your loved one's life.

Photo Album – Have a photo album of your loved one's life available at any visitation/viewing or memorial service. The attendees will enjoy browsing through it and it will remind them of some of the wonderful times they spent with your loved one.

CD Photo Display – You can scan any number of photos of your loved one to a CD. Set to music, this can be played on a projection screen or monitor during any of the services. If you do not know how to scan to CD, simply take your photos to a chain pharmacy that has a photo department and ask that it be done for you. If appropriate and within your budget, you can order copies of the CD to give to family members and friends, or even to attendees.

Funeral Program Cover - If you choose to create a funeral program, choose a wonderful photo of your loved one and place it on the cover of the program.

Keepsakes – If you have a photo of your loved one that you particularly love, have it copied on card stock with your loved one's name written underneath. Have these available for attendees to take home with them.

Thank You Cards – More than likely, you will have people to thank. Those who brought food, who sent flowers, who helped you with the myriad tasks. Take a photo of your loved one to an office supply store, such as Staples or Office Depot, and ask if they can create a bi-fold card with your loved one's photo on the front.

Inside, arrange to have a thank you message printed.

Social Media – If you are going to use social media to memorialize your loved one, you can post the photos to the web. We set up a memorial site for my niece on Facebook, for instance (more about that in "Social Media"). There, her friends and family can post photographs and leave messages. This has been a wonderful way for those who love her to see photos of her life that we ourselves did not take and to read about experiences we were not party to.

THE FUNERAL (OR MEMORIAL) PROGRAM

The funeral program is a simple brochure that informs service attendees about what to expect and alerts them to hymns they can participate in. At its most simple, it is an 11.5 x 8 page folded in half to form a four-page 5.75 x 8 booklet.

You can design and print the funeral program yourself if you have a computer and basic software such as Microsoft Publisher. Or, you can take your ideas to a local office supply store and ask for help. We designed Jahmila's program ourselves and then took it to Staples in Wellington, Florida on a memory stick. There, we met a wonderful woman, Karen Hausman, who helped us to format and print our design in full color.

If design is not your forte, you can purchase programs online. While this seems like a great idea, there are a couple of disadvantages you should be aware of:

- **Price** – even if the price is cheaper per unit than at your local office supply store, you have to factor in shipping and handling, which can be relatively hefty,

- **Delivery** – Unless you are ordering the programs for a memorial service, there just may not be enough time between your order and the funeral service to ensure you receive the programs on time,

- **Changes** – If you change your mind about the music, speakers or any other element of the service, you will not have time to make the changes to the program.

There are a number of companies that sell brochure templates. Priced at about $30 each, you can download the template to your computer and insert the information about the service you are preparing. Templates generally have space for a photo on the front and often include a background design. The templates are available for use on either a Mac or PC, and can be printed at home. You will find a few online template suppliers listed in the <u>Resources section</u> of this book.

CLERGY AND CELEBRANTS

Please note that I am using the term "clergy" to refer to the spiritual leaders of any religion.

Your loved one may or may not have been religious. If she was, and was a member of a congregation, contacting her place of worship seems the likely place to find a member of the clergy who can lead the service(s). If she was not religious, you have the option of holding a non-denominational service, or contacting a member of the clergy if you would like to arrange a religious service regardless.

Even if your loved one was a faithful member of a place of worship, you might find that your funeral plans conflict with the clergy's schedules. Such was the case when we tried to arrange the funeral service for my niece. All the clergy at her house of worship were booked throughout the weekend after her death. We were offered a time/location mid-week the week following her death. My sister did not want to hold her daughter's funeral mid-week as she knew that would create a conflict for those who wished to attend but who could not get off work. And so, we began to look for a new venue.

My mother used to live in Wellington, Florida, where she was a member of the Episcopal Church. We contacted the priest there and asked about availability. Unfortunately, or so we thought at the time, there were scheduling conflicts there as well. We then stopped by a church my sister had attended once or twice before, but to which she had not been in several years.

The pastor, Ranier Richter, immediately invited us into his office. He listened to our needs and desires. He cleared his schedule. He called his Musical Director, Joseph Farrar, and explained what we wanted. After hours of people telling us "No", Pastor Richter said, "Yes."

Depending upon your loved one's religion, you may have to stick to a time-table for burial. Those of the Jewish faith, for instance, are supposed to be buried as soon as possible after death, even on the same day the death occurred, but not, with few exceptions, more than two days after death. That time constraint limits funeral planning. Of course, if such is the case (or similar) for your loved one, his/her religion more than likely takes into account the need for flexibility and his/her place of worship will most likely help to make sure all is arranged in a timely manner.

It sometimes happens that the deceased was not a religious person. If she left instructions for her funeral, your job is easier. If not, however, you will have to decide whether to arrange a non-denominational or non-sectarian service, or whether to go ahead with a religious service regardless.

For instance, your loved one may not have been religious or spiritual in any sense, but you and other family members are. It may, then, make sense for you to arrange a service that is in alignment with your own beliefs. You should be sure, however, that doing so will not offend mourners who have reason to believe that your loved one would have been against a religious service being held in his/her name.

The term "celebrant" is often used in a religious context, as the person who officiates at a religious ceremony. It can also be used, however, to refer to the person who leads a non-religious ceremony, and even to someone who simply participates in a ceremony. For the sake of this chapter, let's agree that it refers to someone who leads a non-religious ceremony.

If your loved one was not a religious person and you have reason to believe that he would not have wanted his life celebrated in a religious manner, you can always arrange for a non-religious funeral/memorial. In such a case, the decedent's life, his achievements and connections to the world and to those who loved him, are celebrated more than any spiritual beliefs he may have (or not) held.

When choosing a non-religious ceremony, it is often easiest to ask someone to act as Celebrant. That person will likely open the ceremony and will step up between speakers to introduce the next one. He/She may also be the person who offers the eulogy. While informal services are very appropriate to some funerals, having a recognized Celebrant can add order to those who find comfort in it.

MEMENTOES & KEEPSAKES

It is not uncommon to offer attendees a small memento or keepsake. This can be something as simple as a photo of your loved one to a more elaborate memory book. It can be a piece of jewelry or a simple bow pinned to a shirt.

In an earlier chapter, I mentioned that Jahmila's favorite color was lime green. At her funeral service, we handed out lime-green ribbons we'd spent the night before gluing to safety pins. Each attendee pinned a ribbon to his/her shirt and, months later, some of her closest friends still wear the ribbons in her memory. About a month after her death, we ordered lime-green bracelets with Jahmila's name stamped on them. They glow in the dark and, in the middle of the night, make me smile.

Jahmila's best friend, Mazelle, died in the same accident as my niece. Shortly before her death, she had a butterfly tattooed on her shoulder. Her mother Sue wanted those who attended her memorial service to leave with a keepsake of her beautiful daughter. As guests filed by photo boards depicting scenes from Mazelle's too-short life, they could choose a colorful clip-on butterfly from baskets Sue had placed around the room. As you can see, each memento was chosen to reflect the likes and personality of a particular loved one.

If you are interested in handing out mementoes to attendees, you may want to consider one (or more) of the following:

- Ribbons (styled after the breast-cancer pink ribbon)

- Photo card (printed on card stock, with your loved one's

name underneath)

- Prayer card (with a prayer on one side and your loved one's photo on the other),

- Bracelet (similar to the yellow Livestrong bracelet)

- A t-shirt with your loved one's photo on the front,

- A sapling (to be planted in your loved one's name),

- A stone (engraved with your loved one's name),

- A candle with your loved one's name printed on a ribbon or wrap,

- A memory card with your loved one's favorite poem or saying printed on the front,

- If your loved one was artistic, a copy of a painting or drawing she created.

THE OBITUARY

Unlike funeral notices, which simply state that so-an-so died and his services will be held at a certain place and time (and which are usually offered as a free service), an obituary is a short article that celebrates someone's life. True, it usually discusses funeral arrangements, but it also offers highlights of the person's life and discusses how he/she impacted those around him/her.

Newspapers often write the obituary of a person they consider significant and run it as a public service not dissimilar to a news story. While your local newspaper may not choose to write an obituary as a complementary (free) service to the community, there is nothing that stops you from doing so. You can, however, expect to pay for it.

You may write the obituary in any style you deem appropriate. You should be aware, however, that there is a somewhat standard format to obituaries. This format provides all the relevant details (date and location of birth, date and location of death, highlights of the person's life, next of kin, and place and time of funeral arrangements). The highlights, or achievements, you write about can be from his personal, professional, social, or community life. Or, all of the above.

If you have ever seen the obituary section of a newspaper, you have probably noticed that there are, in general, two types – one that is short and concise and may or may not include a small photo of the deceased, and one that is longer and reads like an article.

- The short and concise obituary usually includes:

- Full Name

- Age

- Place of residence

- Birth date

- Death date

- A very brief bio (1 – 2 sentences)

- Possibly spouse's name

- Information for funeral service(s)

The longer version may include the following:

- Full Name

- Age

- Place of residence

- Birth date and location

- Death date and location

- Spouse's name

- Circumstances of death

- Educational information (degrees earned, school names, honors received, etc.)

- Military service information and any honors earned

- Career information, as well as highlights of same (awards, years of service, etc.)

- Religious affiliation

- Community affiliations

- Information for funeral service(s)

I've included an obituary template in the <u>Samples section</u> at the back of this book to help you get started.

Note of caution: Some specialists who work to combat identity theft caution families not to divulge too much information in an obituary. Unfortunately, there are those who troll obituaries in order to steal the identities of those who have recently died. Including information such as the decedent's mother's maiden name, which banks and other institutions often use as a secondary form of ID, can help identity thieves steal your loved one's ID.

NOURISHMENT

Even when someone dies, the living need to eat. Over the centuries, a custom of dropping food off at the home of the bereaved family has become ingrained in many communities. This allows friends and community members to feel somewhat helpful and removes just one more chore that the family would otherwise have to accomplish.

I personally do not believe that bereaved families need to feel an obligation to feed visitors. Believe me when I tell you that this goes against everything I feel at any other point in time. I simply feel that the burden of grief erases the need to be an attentive hostess.

If a member of your family has died and a friend or neighbor offers to help, please do yourself the favor of asking that he or she be in charge of food and drink. If that person could simply make sure some sodas and fruit juices are available for those who come by to help in other ways and, possibly, a platter of sandwiches is available, that would be great.

As for food for your own family, yes, you will need to eat, too. Even if you think you will never be able to take another bite in your life, you should force yourself to do so. You are in for a rough week and should eat when you can. If you have kids to feed and your cupboards are bare, please ask someone to run to the grocery store for you. Believe me when I say that people want to help you. Let them.

Nourishment becomes a bit more complicated when you hold a wake or service at your house. Or if you invite attendees back to your home after the funeral or memorial service. In those cases, food for visitors is often expected.

Again, do not undertake this chore yourself. Asking a friend or family member to be in charge is not a burden. In a strange way, it reinforces how important that person is to you. Simply let that person know the number of visitors you expect and ask him or her to take care of it. He or she will figure it out.

TRANSPORTATION & ACCOMMODATIONS

If you expect people to travel in from out of town for the funeral, you may consider appointing someone to be in charge of transportation and accommodations. Like nourishment, I don't expect the immediate family to oversee these arrangements, but you can certainly hand this task off.

If you have been tasked with transportation and accommodation arrangements, below you will find some helpful tips to make your job easier:

- Contact local friends and family members and ask if anyone can spare a bed. Begin a list of who can offer accommodations and how many people they can put up. If they have a preference for no children or a gender preference, write that down. Make sure you note their contact information.

- Call local hotels and motels. Explain the situation and ask if they offer special bereavement pricing. If so, ask for a special code that attendees can use when making their reservations or ask whom attendees should contact. It is always a good idea to get information from a variety of hotels that offer rooms at different price points.

- Ask local friends and family members if anyone will be

available to provide transportation. If so, ask for details such as the type of transportation available, the days and hours available, the number of people that can be accommodated and whether they happen to have access to a car seat in case anyone is travelling in with a small child.

- Once you have the details, post a message on any social media sites that are being used for the funeral and include your contact information. Likewise, send out an email with your contact information.

- If you are coordinating any of the transportation arrangements for visitors, make sure you have their travel information, that you have informed them where they will be picked up and by whom, and that you have their contact information in case anything changes.

To make your job easier, use the Transportation & Accommodations Checklist at the back of this book to keep on top of everything.

UTILIZING SOCIAL MEDIA

As I am sure you are by now aware, social media is an extremely powerful tool. It is not only helpful for keeping connected with friends and family, but it can save you a great deal of time and energy when a loved one dies. Further, it can also bring you some level of comfort.

One of the big tasks when someone dies is to alert the world. This used to be accomplished by placing a death notice or obituary in the local newspaper. Nowadays, when more people go online for their news, newspaper notices no longer suffice.

If the task of informing family and friends of a death falls to you, use social media to get the news out faster and to spread it farther. Just as a note, though, it is probably best to call the friends and family members who were closest to your loved one. Opening up their Facebook pages to read about a death would be a bit too shocking for most.

- Compose a short message and email it to friends and family members. Something along the lines of, "It is with great sadness that I have to inform you that _____ died last night. This initial email is just to let you know of his/her death and tell you that I will send you more information and funeral details as I know them." In the email, ask recipients to pass the email along. This will save you having to track down email addresses you might not have access to.

- If your loved one used Facebook, MySpace, LinkedIn or any other social media venue, place a notice on your own page. Chances are that your page is linked to your loved ones and the news will spread.

- If you are familiar with YouTube and have a channel, consider placing a short video there.

As funeral and other services are planned, you can update these messages with the details. For instance, put the time, date and place of the upcoming funeral on Facebook. Again, the news will spread quickly.

Once the funeral is over, you might consider creating a memorial page on Facebook (or other site) or possibly a channel on YouTube dedicated to your loved one. After Jahmila died, for instance, we created a memorial page on Facebook. Entrance is by invitation only, something I highly recommend. Hardly a day goes by without someone posting a new message and/or photo. This has given those who love her access to areas and events in her life that we may not have known about otherwise. While that can never disperse the sadness, it often gives us cause to smile.

IN YOUR LOVED ONE'S NAME

In lieu of flowers..." You've probably heard that before. It is a notice that some families attached to funeral notices requesting that rather than sending flowers, attendees do something else in memory or honor of the recently deceased. This could be donating to a charity or medical research fund, contributing to a scholarship fund, purchasing books for a library, or sending food to a food bank.

In-lieu-of requests are generally set up to reflect some aspect of the decedent's life. If, for instance, he had a rare disease in life, setting up a fund to help research cures for the disease would be a fine memorial. On the other hand, if your loved one died young, setting up a scholarship in her name to help other young people afford college would be a lovely tribute.

There are any number of different charities you can request that donations be made to. Alternately, you can set up a fund or charity and name it after your loved one. Below are some of the different types of funds you might consider. I highly recommend that you consult an accountant if you do plan to set one up as different fund types may have different tax benefits and obligations.

Charitable Contributions (to an established cause)
– this is when you ask people to donate to an already-existing cause or charity. Some charities will allow you to set up a fund-within-a-fund to keep track of donations made in your loved one's name. Others don't track individual accounts. The "Susan G. Komen for the Cure",

for instance, offers the general public the opportunity to contribute to breast cancer research for a cure, but also partners with a number of organizations and individuals that have their own specific funds set up that channel donations to the larger foundation.

Scholarship Fund – this is when you set up a fund to help others afford school or some sort of scholastic, athletic or community activity. The family of Kimberly Cates, a New Hampshire woman who was murdered during a home invasion, has set up a scholarship in her name, the "Kimberly L. Cates Memorial Scholarship Fund", to help local kids interested in pursuing a career in medicine afford college. Similarly, my sister set up a scholarship in my niece's name, the "Jahmila Kyla Bertie-Mariaca Scholarship Fund", to help chronically ill kids attend summer camp.

The Kimberly L. Cates Memorial Scholarship Fund was set up under and is administered by a non-profit organization. In addition to ad hoc contributions to the scholarship, the administrators hold local events to raise money for the fund. In its first year of activity, the fund was able to help nine high school seniors pay for college.

The Jahmila Kyla Bertie-Mariaca Scholarship Fund is a scholarship offered through the larger organization, Brainy Camps Association, a non-profit organization that provides residential summer camps, family retreats, leadership training and transitional youth programs for children with severe chronic health conditions. In its first year of activity, the fund sent seven children to summer camp.

I have included links to each of these scholarships in the Resources section of this book. Visiting those sites may give you ideas for setting up your own scholarship or charitable program.

Private Foundation – according to The Foundation Center, private foundations "maintain or aid charitable, educational, religious, or other activities serving the public good, primarily through the making of grants to other nonprofit organizations. Every U.S. and foreign charity that qualifies under Section 501(c)(3) of the Internal Revenue Service Code as tax-exempt is a 'private foundation' unless it demonstrates to the IRS that it falls into another category." Private Foundations receive the bulk of their funding from a single family or corporation, and usually do not solicit public funds.

Public Charity – public charities "generally derive their funding or support primarily from the general public, receiving grants from individuals, government, and private foundations. Although some public charities engage in grant-making activities, most conduct direct service or other tax-exempt activities." The missions of these charities range from helping the poor to advancing science and education.

SAVING MONEY
WHEN A LOVED ONE DIES

According the National Funeral Directors Association, the average cost of a "regular adult funeral" in 2009 was $6,560. It must be noted, however that this average DID NOT include a vault or liner. With a vault, the price rose to an average of $7,755. And, it did not include any fees charged by a house of worship, musical directors, etc. Further, that "average" did not include cemetery costs (plot, opening and closing fees, grave marker, obituary notices, flowers, site preparation, etc.). With those additional items added, the cost of an "average adult funeral" exceeded $10,000.

In 2009, according to the US Census Bureau, the median household income was $49,777. That meant that a family faced with the death of a loved one in the United States that chose a traditional funeral (with in-ground cemetery burial) was faced with an often un-planned expense that represented at least 20% of their entire income for the year.

The death of a loved one can bankrupt families. Especially in today's terrible economic times. That is enough reason to find ways to save money when a loved one dies.

In the months I have been researching and writing this book, I have often been asked one of two questions:

1. Which is the "greenest" form of final disposition? and,

2. What is the least expensive way to lay the dead to rest?

Here are my answers:

- Promession with the remains buried on private land or on conservancy land, and,

- Whole body donation

My husband, who is an attorney, has challenged me on my first answer. He wants me to take into account the carbon footprint of running the Promession equipment, as well as the expenses required to produce the liquid nitrogen used in the freeze-drying process. While I have to concur that there is a minor use of electricity, I believe that the rapid reintegration of organic matter into the lifecycle (6 – 12 months as opposed to up to decades for a full adult body buried in aerobic soil to fully decompose) is of greater benefit to the ecosystem as a whole. As for why I think Promession is "greener" than alkaline hydrolysis or bio-cremation, that is because in bio-cremation the remains are washed into the sewage system, along with lye, a caustic chemical. Anyway, that's my opinion.

There can't be an argument about the least expensive form of final disposition. When whole body donation is chosen, the body is picked up by the procurement agency and taken away. The research facility that uses the body assumes all costs from that point forward, including (when requested) cremation and the return of cremains to the family. Of course, you might want to buy an urn.

Short of full body donation, there are many ways that you can control the costs associated with the final disposition of your loved one's remains. In most cases, this means that you will have to take on some of the tasks yourself.

Below, I've listed some ways to keep your expenses under control.

Direct Cremation – this is when your loved one's body is cremated without any services being performed, or any "preparations" made to the body (embalming, grooming, etc.). You can often find a crematorium that will perform this service for as little as $300. To keep the costs really low, offer to deliver the body to the crematorium yourself and, if a cremation container is required, opt for a simple cardboard box.

Direct Burial – like direct cremation, this option precludes any services being offered prior to the burial event (you can always opt for a memorial service later) or preparations made to the body. If you opt for direct burial, shop around for a cemetery that offers inexpensive plots, that does not require a burial liner or vault, and that does not require expensive markers. You must also inquire about opening and closing fees (digging the grave and filling it in again).

Green Burial – burial in a green cemetery or on conservancy land is often much less expensive than in a traditional cemetery. Bodies are not embalmed prior to green burials, which saves at least $650 (on average, according to the National Funeral Directors Association). Green burial grounds do not require burial vaults or liners (which can cost well over $1,000), nor are they routinely manicured, meaning "perpetual maintenance fees" are less, or at least minimal.

Home Burial – home burial on private land is probably the least expensive burial option, as the land is often "free" (you own it or a friend allowed you to bury your loved one on his/her property). If you live in a state where only funeral directors or embalmers are permitted to transport a body, you may have to hire one. Likewise, if you live in a state where a funeral director is needed to oversee burial, you may have to hire one, though you can often find one who works with families who want to take care of their own arrangements and who may be willing to sign off on your plans.

Choose a Shroud Instead of a Casket – burial shrouds can be as simple as a hand-sewn case tied with ribbon. Not only will the shroud decompose more easily than a standard casket (choose a natural fiber for the "greenest" effect), but it can cost less than $20 for material and supplies.

DIY Burial Containers – if you prefer to lay your loved one to rest in a casket rather than in a shroud, consider making the casket yourself. If you are good with tools, you can purchase the necessary pine boards, rope (for handles) and simple screws for less than $100. If you don't trust your own designs, invest in casket plans, which you can purchase online for about $30.00. To make the casket "pretty" you can always paint it (use non-toxic paints, please), allow loved ones to draw on it, or burnish it with linseed oil.

Purchase a Cremation Box – contact crematoria in your area and ask if they sell cremation boxes. These are usually sturdy cardboard or pressboard boxes that you can purchase for about $50.00. Additional benefits of using a cremation box as a casket are that a) you can decorate it, and b) it will decompose quickly.

Create your own Funeral Programs – with a little know-how and a simple program, such as Windows Publisher, you can design and print your loved one's funeral program with just a home computer and printer.

Hold Services in Private Places – hold the various services at home. Be it a visitation, a backyard funeral, or a memorial service, holding it at home is both intimate and affordable.

Hold Services in a Public Place – plan a memorial service in a public park or at the beach. Choose somewhere that was special to your loved one and ask everyone to gather there at a certain time on a specific day. If your loved one loved to fish, ask everyone to come with a fishing pole and go surf casting together. If she loved to hike, invite everyone on a memorial hike. At some point during the event, gather in circle and ask everyone to share one memory of their time with your loved one.

Transport the Body Yourself – unless you live in a state where only funeral directors or embalmers can transport a body, make your own transportation arrangements. This can mean borrowing a pickup truck or renting a van. Generally speaking, even if you do rent a van for a day, your costs will be much less than if you hire a funeral home for the service. Remember to contact your local registrar's office to ask about any transportation permits you may be required to purchase (this is usually quite inexpensive).

File you own Paperwork – unless local law mandates otherwise, file all the paperwork yourself. You will have to get signatures for the death certificate and pay any local fees, but you can save a great deal of money by accomplishing these simple tasks yourself. Contact the office that oversees funeral laws in your state (available in the <u>Resources section</u> at the back of this book) for more information.

Become a Member of a Memorial or Funeral Society – these are groups that offer members benefits, such as reduced fees for cremation or for work performed by certain funeral homes. These societies often require an up-front member fee (dues), but they can save a great deal of time and money. The societies work out member discounts for many of the services you will need. Of course, you may be limited to the funeral home(s) and/or cemeteries that have offered reduced pricing to members.

To give you a better idea of pricing, I've included the results from a 2009 survey (the latest available at the time of this writing) put out by the National Funeral Directors' Association. These prices are for an "average" adult funeral and do not include services and products such as submitting an obituary to the newspapers, flower arrangements, cemetery fees, marker fees, etc.

Non-declinable basic services fee	$1,817
Removal/transfer of remains to funeral home	$ 250
Embalming	$ 628
Other preparation of the body	$ 200
Use of facilities/staff for viewing	$ 395
Use of facilities/staff for funeral ceremony	$ 450
Use of a hearse	$ 275
Use of a service car/van	$ 125

Basic memorial printed package	<u>$ 125</u>
Subtotal without casket	***$4,265***
Metal casket (basic model)	<u>$2,295</u>
Average cost of funeral	**$6,560**
Vault	<u>$1,195</u>
Total cost of funeral with vault	**$7,755**

CARING FOR THE GRIEVING FAMILY

You may be a member of the grieving family, or one who cares for the family. Regardless, there is so much to be done when a person dies that the more who are able and available to help, the better.

Below, you will find arrangements that often need to be made when planning a funeral. For further help, please refer to the Checklist section in the back of the book.

Accommodations – In today's United States, where family members rarely live next door to one another, or even in the same town, accommodation plans have to be made for family and friends of the deceased. Hotels and motels are the easy, obvious answer, but they are not always practical. First of all, those travelling in from distant locations will usually be making last minute travel arrangements and these can be expensive. Secondly, depending upon where the funeral is going to be held, hotel accommodations might be too pricey for attendees, or may not even be available.

If you are making accommodation arrangements, you should consider asking local friends and family members if they have a guest room (or even a pullout sofa) where an out-of-towner or two can spend a couple of nights. Having this option available can sometimes make the difference between whether a friend or family member can afford to attend the funeral.

Once you have maxed out guest room accommodations, you should look at local hotels and motels. It is often a good idea to contact the reservations offices, to explain why you may need so many last-minute rooms, and to ask if the hotel can extend your group a courtesy discount. Having worked in the hospitality business for many years, I can assure you that hotels regularly extend this courtesy and you have only to ask. Once you have a list of hotels/motels where attendees can stay (hopefully with various price points), put together an email with the hotel names, addresses, reservations phone number and average prices, and send it out to attendees. To maximize exposure, ask them to forward the list to anyone you may have missed.

Being There - Those affected by the death of a loved one will experience a myriad of often-intense emotions. These can fluctuate wildly, from deep, dark lows, to hysterical exuberance (when recounting a favorite memory or event), and even to intense anger. Regardless of what a person is feeling at any given moment, what she often needs is simply to have a friend nearby to be with her, to listen to her, to hold her.

When Jahmila died, my cousin Teresa Barnett gave my sister the priceless gift of her presence. She spent the night with her, night after night. Teresa, whose four children and husband were swaying in a local hotel, went to Liz's house each night after dinner and slept beside her. When Liz invariably woke up crying or screaming, Teresa was there to hold her and listen to her.

To be sure, this meant that Tisa (our nickname for her) got little sleep and had to tend to her own family's needs on an abbreviated schedule during the daylight hours, but the gift she gave to my sister was incalculable. I firmly believe that without Tisa there to help Liz through those unending dark hours, she may not have made it.

You may not be able to spend night after night with a grieving family member. Even an hour now and again helps. If you can arrange a rotating schedule of caregivers, at least for the first week, do so. Know that some people are not comfortable with others doing so much for them. That's OK. If the grieving person does not want constant company, be sure to let him or her know that you are only a phone call away, and that you will welcome a call regardless of the hour.

Caring for Clothes – Growing up, I was a big fan of Ann Lander's advice column. Thirty some years later, I still remember one of the first columns I ever read. It was from a family member who wrote, not to ask for advice, but to share a story and to extend a thank you.

The writer wrote of the shock and pain of losing a loved one. During that awful time, however, something happened that, later, when she was able to process it, meant a great deal to her. It seems a neighbor, wanting to help, but not wanting to impose, came to the family's house soon after the death occurred and gathered up the family's shoes. That neighbor then took the shoes home and polished them before quietly returning them.

Some thirty years later, I am still struck by the beauty, generosity and grace of that simple gesture. When so many big and important decisions had to be made, the neighbor quietly attended to a simple task, one that was not absolutely necessary, and one that could easily have been overlooked, but one that took away just one more burden from the family.

Caring for the family's clothes is a beautiful, loving gesture. Children may not have formal clothes on hand (or may have grown out of them) and may need new ones, shoes may need to be polished, dresses and suits may need to be ironed or buttons may need to be sewn on. If you are in a position to do so, simply ask the family members what they plan to wear to the different services and take it upon yourself to make sure the clothes are clean and presentable. They may be overwhelmed at the moment, but one day the family members will remember that you gave them one less thing to worry about.

Childcare – When a family is dealing with loss, trying to figure out what that loss means and, at the same time trying to plan a funeral, childcare arrangements quickly move from necessary to overwhelming. In the first place, one or both of the parents may be struggling to handle his/her own emotions and they certainly don't want to terrify their children by falling apart in front of them. In the second place, if a parent is meeting with funeral homes and cemetery staff, it is unlikely that he/she wants to bring the children along to those heartbreaking meetings. Thirdly, the children themselves will be experiencing a range of emotions including loss, confusion, anger, fear, heartbreak, and sadness. Parents who are themselves vulnerable may not be able to best help their children.

Finally, children must be children. Their attention spans are often shorter than adults'. If they are not old enough to be a part of the decision making team, they may not understand why no one is paying attention to them. Further, they may only be able to understand what is going on in the abstract and so the high emotions of the moment may seem like so much drama.

Arranging childcare for the grieving family can feel like a miraculous gift to the parents whose attention is needed elsewhere and whose emotions are running amok. If the children are very young, taking them off for a play date for a couple of hours can give parents the chance to do what is needed and, possibly, to even take a much-needed nap. If the children are a bit older, taking them for a walk, for an ice cream, or even to the movies, can give them some space and time to begin to sort out their own thoughts and feelings.

Like adults, children may simply need someone to listen to them and to answer question so everything won't feel so overwhelming and scary. During that time, let the children set the pace and the topic of conversation. If they want to talk about their loved one, that's OK. Focus on the good memories. If they have questions, try to answer them in a positive, non-threatening way. If they want to avoid the topic all together, let them. Most importantly, if they want to laugh, let them. Laughter is, after all, highly therapeutic.

Remember, too, that childcare will be needed and appreciated long after all the friends and family members have gone home. Especially then. If it is at all possible for you to continue offering the family a few hours respite now and then, please do so. It will help both the parents and the children.

Cleaning House – Whether any of the services will be held in the family's home or not, house cleaning is certainly the last thing grieving people want to attend to. Yet, it still has to be done. Bathrooms need to be cleaned, windows to be washed, floors to be vacuumed and mopped.

If you can arrange a small group of friends to go to the family's house to clean it, or can afford to hire a service to do so, the gesture will be highly appreciated. If you can arrange for the outside of the house (garden, lawn, porch, etc.) to be tidied up as well, all the better.

Financial Assistance - Funerals are expensive. Fees for so called "traditional" funerals can easily exceed $10,000. Unfortunately, unlike other major life events (weddings, birthdays, anniversaries, vacations, etc.) death is not always budgeted and prepared for.

Added to the funeral costs is the fact that the death of a family member can severely impact the financial future of the surviving family members, especially if the decedent contributed to the family's earnings.

Many of us do not feel comfortable asking for financial assistance from friends and relatives. We'd prefer to add the mounting fees to our credit cards rather than feel the humility of asking for a hand out. And, because of that, it does not occur to our friends and family that we need financial help.

Ask yourself these questions: Knowing what you know about the grieving family, do you think they could easily write off $10,000 in unexpected bills? Was the person who died a breadwinner in the family? Are there children involved whose educations may now be at risk? Will the decedent's survivors be able to make up for the financial impact his/her death will have on the family?

You may not know the answers to these questions. Or, your answers may be entirely incorrect. The questions, however, are designed to help you realize how financially devastating a death in the family can be. Once you understand that, you can act.

How?

Ask yourself if you personally can afford to contribute to the family. Even if it is just $25, that is $25 less that they will have to come up with. Mention your concern to others who care about the family and who may be in a position to help financially. You can even set up a fund at a local bank where others can make contributions.

Remember, some families will be too proud to take an outright offering of money. If you think that may be the case, put the cash in an envelope and hand it to a family member. Tell that person an anonymous donor dropped it off. It is not important whether the family knows for certain that you made the donation. It is important, however, that they get the help they need.

Gift Management – Invariably, friends and business associates will send cards, flowers, food, and even gifts to the grieving family. While it is too much to expect them to write thank you cards at the time, at some point most will want to. This means that someone has to keep track of who sent what.

When my niece died, we set a basket by her front door. Every time a floral arrangement arrived or the grocery store where Jahmila worked sent over a platter of food, we dropped the card into the basket or jotted a note and placed it in the basket. My sister-in-law, who lives in the same town as my sister, did the same at her house and we had a third basket at the funeral home and church where services were held.

More than a month passed before my sister could bring herself to sit down and formally thank everyone who had been so kind but, when she did, she knew whom to thank for what. I highly recommend that you make similar arrangements.

Note Taking - I am the list maker and note taker in my family so this task inevitably fell to me – and was something at least that I felt I could handle. I took notes and, when necessary, made lists.

When Liz met with the funeral home, I was with her and wrote everything down. When we interviewed different churches about their availability and the services they could provide, I jotted it down.

I am a great note taker and list maker because I have learned over the years that I am highly distractible. I have also learned that my memory is not the best. Therefore, it is often easier to make a note of something than to trust myself to remember the details.

During my niece's funeral, I was much more distractible than usual and I really could not be counted on to remember anything. My sister was worse. My lists and notes, then, became something we could count on. When we couldn't remember if we'd given the church musical director the list of songs we'd like played, we consulted my notes. When we wondered if we'd contacted everyone who should be contacted, we checked my lists.

You yourself may be organizing a funeral and you may be both great under pressure and highly organized. If so, you might not need someone to keep on top of all the arrangements that have to be made and all the schedules that have to be set up. If you are helping a friend through this rough time, however, a great service you can offer is to follow your friend around with a notepad and to take notes.

Notices/Announcements – When a person dies, others must be notified. In the United States, it has been customary to place a death notice in the decedent's local newspaper. When the decedent had a history of living in another place, for instance, if he grew up in one town but relocated to another, a notice might have been placed in his hometown newspaper as well.

A death notice is not necessarily the same as an obituary and you should be aware of the difference between the two.

A death notice is a short statement, usually printed as a courtesy (free) by a newspaper that alerts the community that a death has occurred. Information included will often be the decedent's name, age, date of death and place and time of any funeral service(s).

An obituary reads more like a recap of the decedent's life. Besides the basics, an obituary will include information about the person's personal and professional accomplishments, his/her social and community activities, as well as a list of the decedent's closest survivors (spouse, children, parents, siblings).

Newspapers typically print obituaries of people they considered to have been significant, whether as a public figure or for special accomplishments. Depending upon the person's status, the obituary can run from a couple of paragraphs to full-page articles.

You may purchase newspaper space to run an obituary if you feel that is a desirable way to memorialize your loved one. Pricing varies from newspaper to newspaper and is largely dependent upon its length, whether you want it to be in black & white or color, and whether a photograph will be included.

Placing death notices in a newspaper is a lovely way to help the grieving family. It means one less chore they have to worry about.

Simply ask the family which papers they would like the notice to run in, research the paper's requirements and fees (if any), write up the basics and present it all to the family. Once you have their approval, make your call.

To find out more about requirements and pricing, simply go online and "Google" your favorite newspaper's name along with the words "obituary" or "obituary placement." Alternately, you can call the newspaper.

Funeral homes often offer the service of placing a death notice or obituary in the local paper – for a fee or included in a "package." Prior to accepting the service, ask yourself if it is really worth the money. In most instances, you will be writing the notice yourself, or providing the information that, because it is so limited, is akin to writing it. Further, is it really worth whatever the funeral home charges to make a phone call or go online? It is, of course, your call, but you should make sure you find value in the service. Otherwise, tell the funeral home you will take care of it yourself and ask them to remove the charge from your bill.

In today's digital world, newspapers are a bit passé. People are more likely to get their news online and from social media rather than reading about it in a newspaper. If you have accepted or offered to place notices/obituaries, then consider sending your announcements in emails, posting it on such social sites as Facebook, MySpace, and LinkedIn, and any other sites that you think the decedent's friends, family, professional colleagues and social circle will visit. Further, if the family has not already done so and would like you to do so, contact the decedent's school, place of work, clubs, etc. and ask them to spread the word.

Nourishment – Regardless of what is going on around them, the family has to eat. Not only that, but as more family and friends show up to pay their respects or to help out, those people have to eat as well.

One of the most thoughtful gifts you can extend to a grieving family is to drop off food and drink. This can be as simple as a casserole that can be refrigerated and warmed up at any time, to as extravagant as arranging for regular deliveries of sandwiches and fruit platters from a local deli or supermarket.

I will never forget my sister's good friends, Tammy Cook and Karen Kendall. The morning after Jahmila died, Tammy arrived at my sister's house with bags of sandwiches, condiments, sides, cases of drinks, disposable plates, cups and utensils, napkins, bags of ice and a number of coolers, much of it sent by Karen. She walked in, gave hugs all around, and then cleaned out Liz's refrigerator. Twenty minutes later, she was gone. Later that night, she quietly showed up, took away the trash, replenished the supplies and disappeared again.

Throughout that terrible week, at least once a day, I'd catch glimpses of Tammy restocking the fridge with food she and Karen supplied. She never called attention to herself. She never pointed out what she had done. She never conferred with the family. She simply saw a need and filled it.

Jahmila worked as a bagger at a local supermarket, Publix. The wonderful team of employees also saw to it that we never ran out of food or drinks. As I have mentioned, we have a large extended family that flew in from all points of the globe. Regardless of how many of us there were, we always had food and drink on hand.

You can certainly help the grieving family by providing food and drink. Or, if that is not your forte, you can coordinate with others so that nourishment is always on hand. This can mean organizing food for a vigil service, or setting up a longer-term schedule to provide hot meals for a family suddenly without one parent. It can even mean taking the kids out for fast food one evening to give them a moment to feel "normal" again.

Whatever you do, know that your efforts will be gratefully and eternally appreciated.

Pet care – Even when a death has occurred, pets need to be taken care of. Dogs need to be walked, cat litter needs to be changed, fish and birds need to be fed. You can help the grieving family through this time by caring for their pets. Your help can be as simple as making sure there is pet food on hand to setting up a regular dog-walking schedule until the family is able to resume those tasks themselves.

Print Services – Oddly, you may find that the family needs the services of a local print shop. We discovered this when we decided to print a funeral program for Jahmila's service.

My cousin Tisa and I were lucky enough to end up at the Wellington (FL) Staples where we met a woman named Karen Hausman. Karen was an angel who kindly attended to us for some five hours. She helped us to arrange (and rearrange) the program, to print 8 x 10 and 11 x 14 photos of Jahmila to display next to her casket, to order thank you cards.

Don't let me alarm you – five hours was excessive and, if you take on this task, it is more than likely you will need only a fraction of that time. Tisa and I had no idea what we wanted and we ended up designing everything on the spot. Karen was patient, professional and extremely helpful. Without her, we would have needed six hours. Minimum.

Spending time at a print shop is probably not what the grieving family wants to do. If you can take that task away from them, you will be providing them a great service.

Before going, make sure you know what the family wants. Make a mock-up of the service program, discuss lettering (fonts), paper quality and where they would like a photo to be included. Ask the family to provide you with several photos and to put them in order of desirability as their favorite photo may not fit into the available space, or may not be of high enough quality to print well.

For thank you cards, come up with something lovely but generic, maybe something on the order of, "Thank you so much for being with us in our time of need. Your love and concern will always be appreciated." And then leave room for a personal, handwritten message – "Thank you especially for the ___(fill in the blank)___."

Running Errands – There will be a million errands to run. Someone will have to pick up the Death Certificates when they are ready (original and copies that will be needed). Children may have to be picked up from school. A photo may have to be taken to the local newspaper. Medicine may need to be picked up. Making yourself available to run those errands is a priceless gift you can offer to a grieving family.

Transportation – Transportation will need to be arranged for friends and family who are travelling in for the services and someone (perhaps you?) should coordinate it all. This will mean getting ahold of all those expected to come who will not be renting their own cars, making note of their itineraries and where they will be staying, as well as coordinating pick up and drop off between hotels and the locations of the various services and events.

This is a huge job – especially if you do not know all the people with whom you will be in contact. To make your life easier, have the following supplies on hand:

- A cell phone – and charger. Make sure everyone has your number so they can call you if there are any changes to their travel plans,

- A notebook where you can list out everyone's itinerary, as well as details such as who will be picking them up and where they are to be taken,

- A phone list of everyone who will need transportation. Make sure that you tell them who will be picking them up as chances are good the two parties will not know one another. Also provide details about where the person will be picked up (at the gate, in the baggage area, outside the terminal, etc.),

- A phone list of the other team members helping with the arrangements. Plans will change. Things will go wrong. Expect that and be able to flow with the changes and to alert anyone else who may be affected by them,

- Tissues and bottled water. Invariably, someone will need one, the other, or both.

Long-term Care – Just because the funeral is over and the attendees have all gone home, does not mean that the family no longer needs assistance. In fact, without all the distraction, they may be in worse shape than ever. It is now that a true friend shines.

Look over the list above and ask yourself if the family will still be needing help in those areas. While they may no longer need a print shop, they certainly will appreciate the occasional warm meal. The kids will be grateful for some normal time away. The surviving spouse may be desperate for some quiet time. And the pets will still need to be cared for.

In addition to the above, thoughtful gestures include:

- Send the surviving spouse to a day spa for a massage, hair treatment or facial. She will likely not have been taking care of herself and this is a lovely way to remind her that she is important and should.

- If you can, arrange for the kids to attend a camp or after-school club. Give them the gift of a few hours of just being kids.

- Take the family or a family member out to dinner or to lunch.

- If there are repairs to be made to the family home, make them.

- Arrange for the lawn to be cut on a weekly basis for the coming months.

- Make a note in your agenda to follow up with weekly phone calls.

- Make an appointment for the head of the family with an accountant or financial planner. The family will need to understand the impact the death will have on its finances.

- Start and manage a college fund for the kids. Get the community involved. Arrange bake sales, fundraising events, donation drives, etc. Keep at it – this is a long-term investment of your time and love.

- Help the family to move. In truth, grief counselors recommend that no major decisions be made for at least a year after a family member dies, and this includes moving.

Realistically, the family may no longer be able to afford its current residence and the longer they remain there, the deeper the financial pit they will fall into. Be there for them. Help them to find an affordable home where they can live in a manner as consistent with their past as possible. When the time comes, help them to hold a garage sale, to prepare the new home, and to move in.

- Find local support groups for the various family members and take them there. Ask for recommendations from the kids' school guidance counselors for support groups for children, if any of the family members were/are in the military, research government agencies that provide support, and look to houses of worship and community services for guidance. Please see a list of national support organizations you can contact in the Resources section of this book.

PART III:
Tools to Help You Prepare

CHECKLISTS

My husband, Tim, has a running joke. He says I make lists of the lists I have to make. Like most jokes, this one is grounded in fact.

I am a prodigious list maker. It is the only way I can keep track of everything I have to do, as well as all the things I want to do. When it came to helping to plan a funeral and all the events and details surrounding it, my list-making capabilities disappeared. In fact, I was in such a daze that it did not occur to me to make a list.

Several months after my niece's death, I recognize how having a few helpful checklists could have streamlined things. Don't get me wrong. No list in the world could have made her death easier to bear. But, a few good lists could have ensured that we didn't repeat ourselves, or backtrack, or forget completely all the details that needed to be handled.

Recognizing that checklists could help others in need put me on the path to writing this book. After months of research and interviewing experts and reflecting on my own experiences through the deaths of my grandparents, my father and, most recently, my niece, I think I have narrowed the checklists down to the most helpful.

The next section of this book, then, is made up of checklists and worksheets. Here you will find the following:

Information You Will Need Worksheet & Checklist – throughout this process, you will need various pieces of information. This checklist allows you to compile that information so that you have it on hand and available whenever necessary.

End-of-Life Checklist – this is a list of all the documents you should begin to gather if your loved one is nearing death. Having them on hand now will save you a great deal of time and frustration later.

Contact Checklist – this is a list of immediate family, friends and business associates whom you will have to notify of your loved one's death or impending death.

Team Members Checklist – this allow you to designate different people to cover the many different chores that will have to be attended to. By assigning different tasks to different people, and keeping a list of who is supposed to do what, you will avoid a lot of frustration.

Organ and Tissue Donation Checklist – this provides considerations for you when thinking about organ and tissue donation. It also includes a list of questions you may want to discuss with the procurement agency.

Whole Body Donation Checklist – this is a list of questions to cover with a full body donation procurement agency.

Copies of Documents You Will Need to Acquire Soon after Death – these documents will be created when your loved one dies. You will need these to move past the death phase and to begin closing out your loved one's affairs.

Services Worksheet – use this worksheet to plan out the various services you will plan for your loved one.

Funeral Home Information Checklist – this is a list of documents you should bring with you when visiting any funeral home for quotations, etc.

Funeral Home Checklist – this is a list of documents the funeral homes should supply you with, as well as a list of questions/ considerations to review with the funeral home.

Funeral Home Comparison Sheet – this list allows you to compare, at a glance, the prices quoted by different funeral homes.

In-Ground Burial Questions for the Cemetery – this is a list of questions and considerations you should review with any cemetery you may be interested in.

Cemetery/Mausoleum Questionnaire – this allows you to compare the prices and services offered by different cemeteries.

Cemetery/Mausoleum Worksheet – keep a copy of cemetery and mausoleum negotiations here.

Burial in a National Cemetery Checklist – If you would like your loved one to be buried in a National Cemetery, use this checklist to gather the information you will need.

Cremation Worksheet – this is a list of questions/concerns you may want to cover if you are thinking about having your loved one cremated.

Burial at Sea Checklist – if burying your loved one at sea, this checklist will help you when making the arrangements.

Home Services Checklist & Worksheet – if you are planning to care for your loved one's body at home or to hold any services at home, you will certainly want to refer to this checklist and worksheet to make sure you cover all the basics.
Home Funeral or Memorial Service Worksheet – use this to plan an at-home funeral or memorial service.

Viewing/Visitation/Wake Worksheet & Checklist – use this to plan an at-home viewing, visitation or wake.

Memorial Service Worksheet – if you will be holding a memorial service, this checklist will help you to make sure all goes smoothly.

Graveside Service Checklist – if part of your funeral arrangements includes a graveside service, this list will help you to organize it.

Transportation & Accommodations Checklist – this list will help you to organize the transportation and accommodations of attendees coming in for the various services.

Gift List Worksheet & Checklist – you will be receiving gifts, in the forms of flowers, monetary donations, food, etc. This list will help you to keep track of who donates/gives what so that you can properly thank them at a later date.

Wrapping Up Your Loved One's Affairs Checklist – this list helps you to organize the many things you will have to do in order to wrap up your loved one's legal and financial affairs.

As every family is unique, every death and funeral is unique. There are details, I am sure, that these lists do not cover. Your state or county may have regulations not covered by any of these lists, or you might want to make arrangements that I have not foreseen. Regardless, though, I hope they provide a solid starting point for you, your family, and friends.

INFORMATION YOU WILL NEED WORKSHEET & CHECKLIST

As you work your way through funeral planning and beyond, you will need to have quite a bit of information on hand about your loved one. You will need this information and/or documents (all or part) in order to fill out the death certificate, to contact the social Security Administration, to apply for death benefits, to cancel or change bank account and credit card authorizations, to access bank boxes, and the list goes on. Taking time to gather this information once and then to keep it on hand will save you a great deal of time and aggravation.

Full legal name:_____

Also-known-as names: _____
(Include all legal names, such as maiden or by-marriage names, as well as nicknames he/she may have used)

Last legal address: _____
(Residential address)

Prior legal addresses: _____
(If decedent lived in the last address for less than three years)

P.O. Box (if applicable): _____

Gender: _____

Race: _____

If Spanish/Hispanic/Latino, of which origin? _____
(Mexican, Mexican-American, Chicano, Puerto Rican, Cuban, Other – specify)

Religion (if applicable): _____

Birth Date: _____

Place of Birth: _____

Date of Death: _____

Place of Death: _____

Citizenship: _____

Social Security Number and Name as it appears: _____

(Unfortunately, when people change their names through marriage, divorce, etc., they do not always notify the Social Security Administration of the change. Likewise, if someone has a hyphenated legal name but uses only one last name regularly, the S.S. card may be attached to the hyphenated name rather than the one he/she commonly uses. Make sure you know which name your loved one's Social Security Number is attached to.)

Driver's License Number: _____

Passport Number: _____

Enlistment date: _____

Highest rank achieved: _____

Discharge date: _____

Service number: _____

Type of discharge: _____
(Honorable, general, other than honorable, dishonorable or bad conduct)

Veteran's Discharge Number: _____

Father's legal name: _____

Father's place of birth: _____

Mother's legal name: _____

Mother's place of birth: _____

Spouse's legal name: _____

Next of kin, relationship & contact: _____

Name & contact information of authorized person pronouncing the death: _____

(If there is a problem with the death certificate, you may need to contact the medical representative who signed off on it)

Death Certificate - Local File number: _____

Death Certificate - State File Number: _____

Funeral Insurance Company, plan number & contact information (if applicable): _____

Method of disposition: _____

(Burial, cremation, entombment, donation, etc.)

Place of disposition: _____

(Cemetery, crematory, other location)

Date, time & contact information for final disposition:

(This could be a cemetery, private burial ground, boat and dock location if burial at sea, etc.)

Visitation location, date, time & contact information: __

_____

Funeral service location, date, time & contact information:

_____

Memorial service location, time, date, contact information:

_____

Funeral Facility (home) name, address & contact information (if applicable): _____

Attorney's name & contact information: _____

(This may be needed if there is a Will or Trust involved)

Executor's name & contact information: _____

Name of valid Trust & date (if applicable): _____

Trustee's name & contact information) :_____

Employer & contact information: _____

Occupation & Industry: _____

(This is information required by the U.S. Standard Death Certificate, though it will not appear on the final form: "Questions concerning occupation and industry must be completed for all decedents 14 years of age or older. This information is useful in studying deaths related to jobs and in identifying any new risks.")

Decedent's Usual Occupation: _____

(This is information required by the U.S. Standard Death Certificate, though it will not appear on the final form: "This is not necessarily the last occupation of the decedent. Never enter "retired". Give kind of work decedent did during most of his or her working life, such as claim adjuster, farmhand, coal miner, janitor, store manager, college professor, or civil engineer. If the decedent was a homemaker at the time of death but had worked outside the household during his or her working life, enter that occupation. If the decedent was a homemaker during most of his or her working life, and never worked outside the household, enter "homemaker". Enter "student" if the decedent was a student at the time of death and was never regularly employed or employed full time during his or her working life.")

Kind of Business/Industry: _____

(This is information required by the U.S. Standard Death Certificate, though it will not appear on the final form: "Kind of business to which occupation is related, such as insurance, farming, coal mining, hardware store, retail clothing, university, or government. DO NOT enter firm or organization names. If decedent was a homemaker, then enter either "own home" or "someone else's home" as appropriate. If decedent was a student, then enter type of school, such as high school or college.")

Highest Degree or Education evel Achieved: _____

(This is information required by the U.S. Standard Death Certificate, though it will not appear on the final form)

Bank Account(s): _____

Insurance Provider(s) and account number(s): _____

(This includes health as well as life insurance – anything that may have death benefits)

Investment institution(s) and account number(s): _____

If you can, have copies of the following documents on hand:

_____ A copy of the decedent's last known Will

_____ A copy of the decedent's last known Trust documents

_____ A certified copy of the decedent's birth certificate

(If you do not have this, contact the registrar's office in the town where he/she was born and ask how to acquire a copy)

_____ A death certificate (an original and at least 10 certified copies)

_____A certified copy of Letters Testamentary

_____ Marriage certificate(s)

_____ Divorce decree(s)

_____ Passport

_____ Citizenship papers

_____ Any children's birth certificates or adoption certificates

_____ Tax returns for at least the prior 2 years

_____ An up-to-date credit report on your loved one

_____ Insurance policies (life insurance, health insurance, anything that may have some   value)

_____ Military records (discharge or current)

_____ Bank records

_____ Deeds to property

_____ Property ownership papers (autos, boats, campers, etc. – if payments are still being made towards any property, you may need these to cancel or change them)

_____ Outstanding loan paperwork – bank loans, mortgages, auto loans, school loans,   etc. You will need access to any such paperwork in order to make any necessary changes or cancellations

_____ Pre-planning documents for funeral or cemetery arrangements

_____ Last Credit Card statements

END-OF-LIFE CHECKLIST

If your loved is in a hospital or other medical facility and is unable to make his/her treatment options known, you will want to take as many of these documents with you as possible. They will help establish that you can make decisions on his or her behalf.

_____Durable Power of Attorney for Health Care appointing you the Health Care Surrogate

_____Living Will indicating the care the person wishes to receive

_____Marriage certificate (if the patient is your spouse)

_____Birth certificate of your child if he/she is the patient

_____Your own legal identification (driver's license, passport, etc.) that establishes you as the appointed person in a Living Will, Durable Power of Attorney for Health Care, spouse, etc.

_____A medical history file for the patient, including contact information for any doctors the patient is/has been seeing, as well as a list of medications and the doses the patient takes

_____The patient's driver's license or other form indicating if he/she is an organ donor

_____A phone/address/email address book including contact information for legal representatives, employers, doctors, religious counsels, friends and family

CONTACT CHECKLIST

Use this chart to fill in the names and contact information of the people whom you will have to be in touch over the next few days. Make copies and pass this out to the people who will help you with all the arrangements.

	Name	Phone	Cell	Email
Spouse:				
Mother:				
Father:				
Step-Mother:				
Step-Father:				
Children:				
Siblings:				
Others Family:				
Doctor:				
Attorney:				
Friends:				
Employer:				
Other Contacts:				

TEAM MEMBER CHECKLIST

There is so much to be done when a person dies, so many people to notify, so many documents to locate and copy. To make this time easier and to keep on top of all that has to be accomplished in so short a time, I recommend that you use the following checklist to jot down the name of the person to whom the task has been delegated, and then to check it off once it has been accomplished.

_____ Gather contact info for family, friends and business colleagues:_____

(This person will go through the decedent's address books, email account, cell phone contacts, etc. to prepare a list of people whom should be contacted.)

_____ Notify family, friends and business associates: _____

(This person will make the initial notifications)

_____Meet with funeral home / crematorium personnel: _____

(These people will meet with/interview different funeral homes/ crematoria. At least one person should serve as note-taker)

_____ Meet with cemetery personnel: _____

(These people will meet with the staff of different cemeteries if burial in a cemetery is desired. At least one person should serve as note-taker)

_____ Meet with place of worship leaders: _____

(These people will meet with religious leaders to plan/discuss any religious services. At least one person should serve as note-taker)

_____ Order/Be in charge of flowers: _____

(It is more than likely that flowers will arrive from friends and family. Appoint someone to be in charge of making sure they are delivered to the different venues and who will keep track of who sent flowers so that you can send out thank you cards later)

_____ Coordinate disposition of flowers: _____

(If you would like the flowers to be delivered to a hospital, hospice program, etc. after the service(s) appoint someone to be in charge of this task):

_____ Design & print funeral program: _____

_____ Write and send out obituary: _____

_____ Place notice on various social media sites: _____

_____ Keep record of deliveries: _____

_____ Arrange food & drink: _____

(This can be one or more people. Food should be coordinated for the immediate family, as well as those who stay at the home of the decedent to help with planning. If food/drink is going to be served at any of the services, such as during a wake, then additional arrangements will have to be made)

_____ Arrange for cleaning: _____

(Visitors will stop by the decedent's house. Appoint someone to be in charge of cleaning)

_____ Arrange for childcare: _____

_____ Arrange for pet care: _____

_____ Contact creditors: _____

(Banks, credit card agencies, etc. will have to be notified and, possibly, new payments will have to be arranged)

_____Contact debtors: _____

(If money is owed to the decedent, for instance from a tenant, someone will have to notify debtors of new payment arrangements – consult decedent's attorney if a Will is in place, as that may specify to whom new payments are to be made)

_____ Contact Social Security Administration: _____

(If using a funeral home, this is a service they can provide. Notify the funeral director if you are going to do this yourself so that you won't be charged for the service)

_____ Contact Bank(s), Credit Unions, Insurance

Companies, etc.: _____

_____ Check Plans: _____

(This person will check all benefit plans, including casualty and life insurance, employment contracts – past and current, military benefits, bank and credit unions, social security, fraternal orders, trade unions, etc.

to determine if there are any income sources for the survivors)

_____ Notify Executor of the decedent's Will: _____

_____ Notify Trustee of decedent's Trust: _____

_____ Plan Wake/Viewing: _____

_____ Plan Funeral Service: _____

_____ Plan Memorial Service: _____

_____ Appoint and contact Pallbearers: _____

(These should be people who are healthy enough to lift and carry a casket. Those not healthy enough can be appointed as Honorary Pallbearers)

_____ Plan/Arrange Music: _____

(This person will choose background music, hymns, etc. to be played at the various services. If necessary, this person will make recordings – CDs – and will be in charge of delivering copies to the funeral home/ venues, etc.)

_____ Plan/Arrange Photo Memorial: _____

(This person will gather photos, create photo boards, etc.)

_____ Plan/Arrange Video Memorial: _____

(This person will create a video memorial to be played before or during any of the services. Some funeral homes can help with this by creating a video montage from photos)

_____ Choose a charity and gather contact information: _____

(If the family chooses "in lieu of flowers" this person will find out how donations can be made in the decedent's name and will inform all who need to know – such as those in charge of the funeral program, the obituary, etc.)

_____ Person in charge of Memory books, guest books, etc.:

(It is nice to have a memory book available at the various services where guests can write down their memories of the deceased. Having a guest book is also a nice touch if you plan to write thank you cards to those who attended)

_____ House-sitter: _____

(This person/people will ensure that someone remains at the decedent's home at all times to answer phones, receive deliveries, etc.)

_____ Coordinate transportation for those coming in from out of town: _____

_____ Coordinate accommodations for those coming in from
out of town: _____

_____ Contact Utility Companies: _____

(If the person was living alone, contact the utility companies to arrange
for service to be discontinued – but make sure to keep utilities
on until the decedent's affairs can be finalized. Inform utility companies
of new address to send bills to)

_____ Inform Post Office: _____

(If decedent's mail will be forwarded, this person will make those
arrangements)

_____ Write and send "Thank You" cards: _____

ORGAN AND TISSUE DONATION CHECKLIST

If your loved one died in a hospital or other medical facility, and he was signed up as an organ or tissue donor, chances are that you will be contacted soon after or just before death to coordinate the donation. If your loved one died at home (or is expected to die at home) or at another non-medical facility, you will want to contact an organ and tissue procurement agency as soon as possible. If your loved one has not indicated an agency to donate his or her organs and tissue to, you can contact the organ and tissue donation agencies listed in the Organ & Tissue Donation Resources section of this book. Below are a few of the details you will want to be aware of.

Procurement Agency: _____

Agency Contact: _____

Agency Contact Phone Number: _____

Pickup Time/Date: _____

Pickup Location: _____
    (This could be the hospital, your home, etc.)

Delivery Time/Date: _____

Delivery Location: _____
(This is where your loved one's body will be delivered after the donation. It could be back to the hospital/hospice center, to a funeral home, a crematorium, to your home if you are planning a home funeral, etc.)

Entity in Charge of Delivery: _____
(If your loved one's organs/tissues will be harvested at the hospital where he/she died, you may have to make separate arrangements with a funeral home to pick up and deliver your loved one's body to the funeral home afterward).

WHOLE BODY
DONATION CHECKLIST

If your loved one had already arranged to have her body donated, you will have to contact the procurement agency or facility with whom those arrangements were made as soon as possible after death. If your loved one died in a hospital or other medical facility, make sure you let the staff know of these arrangements so that your loved one's body will be kept cool.

If your loved one has not indicated an agency to donate his or her body to, you can contact the full body procurement agencies listed in the Whole Body Donation Resources section of this book, or your local medical schools. Below are a few of the details you will want to be aware of.

ProcurementAgency: _____
Agency Contact: _____
Agency Contact Phone Number: _____

Pickup Time/Date: _____
Pickup Location: _____
    (This could be the hospital, your home, etc.)
Will Remains be cremated? _____
Will the Cremated Remains be returned to you? _____
Expected Return Date: _____

Note that if you would like your loved one's cremated remains to be returned to you, you must make this clear to the procurement agency ahead of time (in most cases, cremation and delivery of remains will be paid for by the procurement agency, but be sure to ask about this).

DOCUMENTS YOU WILL NEED TO ACQUIRE SOON AFTER DEATH

_____ 8 – 10 Copies of the Death Certificate. You will need these to cancel credit cards, to have refunds issued, to cancel services, to deal with banks, etc.

_____ 8 – 10 Certified copies of the <u>Letters Testamentary</u> – an official document authorizing the executor to carry out the terms of a will (assuming, of course, you are the executor/executrix).

_____The Autopsy Reports (both preliminary and final). You will need these if there is any question of fault involved.

_____ Copies of any arrangement agreements that you enter into with a funeral home, crematory, cemetery, transportation service, etc. For your own protection, make sure that each product and service is individually listed out (in detail) along with its individual price.

SERVICES WORKSHEET

Use this worksheet to plan out the services you will hold for your loved one.

Viewing:

Location: _____

Date: _____

Time from: _____ to: _____

Wake/Vigil:

Location: _____

Date: _____

Time from: _____ to: _____

Funeral Service:

Location: _____

Date: _____

Time from: _____ to: _____

Graveside Service:

Location: _____

Date: _____

Time from: _____ to: _____

Final Disposition:

Location: _____

Date: _____

Time from: _____ to: _____

Memorial Service:

Location: _____

Date: _____

Time from: _____ to: _____

FUNERAL HOME INFORMATION CHECKLIST

If your loved one did not pre-pay for his funeral and you have decided to use the services of a funeral home, you will be arranging what is called an "at-need" funeral. Some of this information you can provide over the phone (if you are sure of which funeral home you will hire). The rest you will provide when you actually sit down with the funeral director to discuss the arrangements.

You will need to provide most of the information provided on the Information You Will Need Worksheet & Checklist. In addition to that, you may be asked for the following:

_____ The location of the decedent's body (hospital, nursing facility, residence, morgue, etc.).

_____ Your name, address and contact information.

_____ Your relationship to the decedent.

_____ A recent photograph of the deceased (the restorative artist will use this so make sure the photo is representative of how you would like your loved one to look – i.e. that the hairstyle is correct, etc.).

_____ Any pre-arranged funeral plan information, including the plan name and number.

_____ Pre-arrangement paperwork.

_____ Cemetery lot information (if you have a copy of the purchase paperwork, a deed, etc., take it with you to your appointment)

_____ The names and contact information of anyone who will be helping with the arrangements.

_____ Your budget – some funeral homes prefer that you simply add services as needed. This usually leads to a steeper bill than you originally planned. By providing a budget, as well as clear instructions that you do not want to go over-budget, the funeral home will be more conscientious about add-on services.

_____ The name and payment information of the person(s) who will be responsible for paying the bill.

_____ Weight and height of the decedent. This is important in determining casket size, whether the decedent can be cremated (some crematoria cannot handle a body over 300 pounds), the number of pall bearers required, etc.).

_____ Clothing you would like your loved one to wear during visitation, services, burial or cremation. This includes jewelry – BUT TAKE NOTE – most jewelry will be returned to you prior to cremation as metals, glass and some plastics can damage the retort.

_____ Contact information for any religious counselors or clergy who will be assisting in any of the services.

_____ The name, address and contact information for any place of worship (or other location) where services will be held.

Funeral Home Checklist

Remember, the Federal Trade Commission requires funeral homes to disclose their prices and services to all clients and potential clients, as well as any laws that require them to purchase any specific goods or services. Take this checklist with you when you meet with funeral homes, or refer to it when you make phone inquiries.

Going to a funeral home can be an especially painful and overwhelming time. You will be confronted with products and services that reinforce the fact that your loved one has died. And, you will have to make decisions. Not only that, but many of the products and services are extremely expensive.

At the moment, you may not care about expense. You may be so vulnerable and in so much emotional pain that you cannot imagine ever caring about finances again. But, I promise you, there will be a time when you will have to think about your finances and you will need to manage a budget. For that reason, you should bring someone with you to visit funeral homes. Choose a person whom you trust, who will take notes, and who can help you make intelligent decisions.

The funeral home must provide you with the following:

_____A copy of their General Price List (when you visit in person, or presented verbally if over the phone),

_____A copy of any separate price lists for caskets, vaults, cremation urns, etc.

_____A copy of any separate price lists for services offered (embalming, viewing rooms, video, sound, etc.).

To best understand and negotiate for the services you want, be sure to cover the following:

_____Mandatory fees – some funeral homes have "mandatory fees." Ask that these be explained in full, and that they be written down (if they are not already provided) with the fees itemized. If you are going to take care of some of the services provided in the funeral home's mandatory fee, insist that the fees be reduced for those services. For instance, if the funeral home includes notification of newspapers within its mandatory fees and this is something you want to do yourself, then make sure that the total charge is reduced by the item cost.

_____Packages – if the funeral home offers "packages" as opposed to à la carte (off the menu) services, ask that the package details be listed out in detail. For instance, if floral arrangements are included, make sure this appears as a line item and that the arrangements are described in full (i.e., type and number of flowers, whether a vase is needed, etc.). If you do not want that service, insist that the total package charge be reduced.

_____Embalming and other preparatory services – Some funeral homes automatically include embalming and other body preparation services in their packages. If those services are not wanted, or required, then insist that the charges be reduced.

_____If you are using the funeral home as a place to hold a viewing, then ask to see the room where it will be held, and make sure you are clear on the time it will be held and the length of time that will be allotted. Make sure to ask about "overtime" fees. For instance, if you rent the room for two hours, what happens if your guests do not all leave for two and a half hours? Will you be charged for the additional time, and at what rate?

_____If you rent a viewing casket, make sure you see the casket and approve it. This is often done when someone will be cremated. A more ornate casket will be used for the viewing than will be used for the actual cremation.

_____If you are going to provide a video and/or music to be played during the viewing, make sure you find out how the funeral home would like these supplied. For instance, their sound system may require that you supply a CD for audio and a DVD for video. Alternately, their system may be able to play directly off your laptop or tablet computer.

_____If there will be a viewing at the funeral home, discuss whether they will provide easels to hold framed photos and, if so, if there is a charge per easel.

_____If there will be a viewing at the funeral home, discuss whether they will provide easels and risers to display floral arrangements and, if so, if there is a charge per easel or riser.

_____If your loved one pre-paid for her funeral, review the details in depth so there will be no surprises. Insist that the home supply the goods and services your loved one contracted for, even if the purchase was made years earlier and the funeral home says that their fees have gone up since then. Also, make sure you see and approve the merchandise (casket, urn, etc.) ahead of time.

_____If your loved one pre-paid for a funeral, ask about any excess fees. If the funeral costs less than she paid, did she indicate to whom any excess fees should go (maybe to a charity or to the family)? If not, how will those overpayments be handled?

Do not leave the funeral home without a written, itemized list of all fees and services that were agreed upon. You can use this list to compare pricing with other funeral homes and to hold the funeral home you choose accountable.

Note: As noted earlier (but it bears repeating), funeral homes can help you to acquire copies of the death certificate. The funeral home or crematory may charge for this "service" and you should ask, up front, what the charge will be, and if the charge is per copy.

FUNERAL HOME
COMPARISON SHEET

Make copies of this worksheet to compare between funeral homes.

Name of funeral home: _____

Funeral Director: _____

Person in charge: _____

Person giving quote: _____

Date quote given: _____

Address: _____

Phone: _____

Fax: _____

eMail address: _____

Web link: _____

Simple Disposition of Remains:

Immediate Burial:

Casket: _____

Casket purchased from? _____

Casket price: _____

Burial location: _____

Cost of burial: _____

Staff fees: _____

Immediate Cremation:

Casket required? _____

Cremation container type: _____

Cremation box price: _____

Cremation cost: _____

Staff fees: _____

Full Body Donation:

Procurement Agency: _____

Procurement Contact: _____

Contact Info: _____

School or Medical Facility: _____

__Full Service Burial or Cremation:__

Basic service fee for funeral director: _____

Basic service fee for funeral home staff: _____

Pickup and transportation of the body: _____

Embalming fees: _____

Type (external, cavity and/or arterial): _____

Product Used: _____

Other Body Preparations: _____

Least Expensive Casket:

Casket description: _____

Casket model number: _____

Casket exterior dimensions: _____

Casket price: _____

Other casket costs (pillow, draping, etc.): _____

Outer Burial Container or Vault:

Container description: _____

Container interior dimensions: _____

Container price: _____

Visitation/Viewing:

Facility: _____

Capacity: _____

Date/Hours: _____

Facility price: _____

Staff price: _____

Additional fees (music, video, guestbook, tables, linen, easels, etc. – include quantity and description or model number): _____

Funeral or Memorial Service:

Venue: _____

Capacity: _____

Date/Hours: _____

Facility price: _____

Staff fees: _____

Additional fees (music, video, guestbook, tables, linen, easels, etc. – include quantity and description or model number): _____

Transportation of the body to/from Venue:

Hearse or vehicle: _____

Staff fees: _____

Graveside Service:

Cemetery or other Destination: _____

Staff fees (this is not for the cemetery staff): _____

Equipment needed (flower easels, etc.): _____

Transportation to Cemetery or other Destination:

Hearse or vehicle: _____

Other vehicles (for family members – include type and quantity): _____

Staff fees: _____

Other Services:

Forwarding to another funeral home: _____

Receiving from another funeral home: _____

Placing of Funeral Notices (include publication names, dates and prices): _____

Other fees: _____

In-Ground Burial Questions for the Cemetery

To make sure you fully understand the cemetery rules and regulations, be sure to ask the following questions when you meet with the sales person:

_____ Who owns the cemetery? (Is it a large company, such as Service Corporation International, or is a locally owned company?)

_____ Will I receive a deed to the plot?

_____ Are there any real estate fees associated with purchasing the plot?

_____ If the land is deeded, will I be assessed yearly property taxes?

_____ If so, what are they on average?

_____ Is there a maintenance fee?

_____ How much is it?

_____ What does it include?

_____ Is it a one-time perpetual care fee, or a yearly fee?

_____ If yearly, for how many years will it be charged?

_____ Will the maintenance fee ever go up?

_____ What happens if I can no longer pay the maintenance fee? What happens to my loved one's grave?

_____ Will you ever move my loved one's grave, and under what conditions?

_____ Do you bury in multiple-depth graves?

_____ What are the opening and closing fees?

_____ Are there any other plot preparation fees?

_____ If so, what are they and what do they cover?

_____ Do you have different burial fees on different days of the week?

_____ Are there material requirements for a casket, or may I supply a homemade casket or a shroud?

_____ Will the plot require a vault or casket liner?

_____ If so, can I purchase it elsewhere?

_____ What are the material and dimension requirements for a grave liner/vault?

_____ If I purchase it from you, what is its price?

_____ Are there delivery fees associated with purchasing the fee from you?

_____ Do you charge a receiving fee if I purchase it elsewhere?

_____ If I purchase it elsewhere, do you charge a fee to deliver it to the gravesite?

_____ Are there installation or placement fees for the grave liner or vault?

_____ If so, what are those fees?

_____ When will the liner/vault be installed?

_____ What style of grave marker do you allow?

_____ May I purchase a grave marker elsewhere?

_____ What is the price for purchasing a grave marker from you?

_____ Are there delivery fees associated with purchasing a grave marker from you?

_____ Are there installation fees for placing the grave marker on the site?

_____ If so, how much are they?

_____ Is a temporary marker required while waiting for the final grave marker to be inscribed and delivered?

_____ What is your policy on grave decoration (flowers, flags, etc.)?

_____ What are your days and hours of visitation?

_____ Is the cemetery closed on holidays? If so, which ones?

_____ Are there any other fees we haven't covered or any other information I should know about?

QUESTIONS FOR THE CEMETERY/MAUSOLEUM

To make sure you fully understand the cemetery rules and regulations, be sure to ask the following questions when you meet with the sales person:

_____ Who owns the cemetery? (Is it a large company, such as Service Corporation International or is a locally owned company?)

_____ What are the types of mausoleum crypts offered (indoor, garden or private)?

_____ What are the prices of each?

_____ Can I purchase two crypts at once (for my loved one and for myself)?

_____ Is there a discount when I purchase two now?

_____ Do you offer double crypts (one behind the other, or one on top of the other)?

_____ What is the location of my loved one's mausoleum crypt?

_____ Is there a maintenance fee?

_____ How much is it?

_____ What does it include?

_____ Is it a one-time perpetual care fee or a yearly fee?

_____ If yearly, for how many years will it be charged?

_____ Will the maintenance fee ever go up?

_____ What happens if I can no longer pay the maintenance fee? What happens to my loved one's crypt?

_____ Will you ever move my loved one's casket and under what conditions?

_____ What are the opening and closing (entombment) fees?

_____ Do you have different entombment fees on different days of the week?

_____ Are there any other preparation fees?

_____ If so, what are they and what do they cover?

_____ Do you allow sealed caskets?

_____ Do you require some sort of venting system/valve on the casket?

_____ Do you require caskets be made of a certain material, or do you accept homemade caskets or shrouds?

_____ What are the maximum outer dimensions my loved one's casket can be?

_____ What style of marker/plaque do you allow?

_____ May I purchase a marker/plaque elsewhere?

_____ What is the price for purchasing a marker/plaque from you?

_____ Are there delivery fees associated with purchasing a marker/plaque from you?

_____ Are there installation fees for placing the marker/plaque?

_____ If so, how much are they?

_____ Is a temporary marker required while waiting for the final marker/plaque to be inscribed and delivered?

_____ What is your policy on grave decoration (flowers, flags, etc.)?

_____ What are your hours of visitation?

_____ Is the mausoleum closed on holidays? If so, which ones?

_____ Are there any other fees we haven't covered or any other information I should know about?

CEMETERY/MAUSOLEUM WORKSHEET

Keep a record of the details of your cemetery negotiations here. Make sure you receive a final quotation in writing, including exact location of the plot you have decided upon. If you are purchasing a vault/liner from a company other than the cemetery, make sure its dimensions and material conform to cemetery standards. Regardless of where you purchase the vault/liner, make sure the casket's exterior dimensions will fit in the vault/liner.

Name of Cemetery: _____

Person in charge: _____

Person giving quote: _____

Date quote given: _____

Address: _____

Phone: _____

Fax: _____

eMail address: _____

Web link: _____

Casket Details

Casket:_____
(Include model number, color & description)

Casket purchased from? _____

Exterior dimensions: _____

Casket price: _____

Delivery fee: _____

Casket Total: _____

Vault/Liner Details

Vault/Liner: _____

(Description, material, etc.)

Vault/Liner purchased from? _____

Exterior dimensions: _____

Interior dimensions: _____

Vault/Liner price: _____

Delivery fee: _____

Installation fee: _____

Total Vault/Liner fees: _____

Plot Details

Burial location: _____

Plot Price: _____

One time maintenance fee: _____

Yearly maintenance fee: _____

Other plot fees: _____

Total plot fees: _____

Burial/Entombment Details

Opening & Closing fees: _____

Other Preparation fees: _____

Staff fees: Other burial/entombment fees: _____

Total burial/entombment fees: _____

<u>Copy each total below:</u>

Casket Total: _____

Total Vault/Liner fees: _____

Total plot fees: _____

Total burial/entombment fees: _____

Total Cemetery Fees: _____

BURIAL IN A NATIONAL CEMETERY CHECKLIST

In order to have your loved one buried in a National Cemetery, you will have to contact the National Cemetery Scheduling Office. They request that you fax your loved one's military discharge documents to the office prior to calling so that they can ascertain eligibility. Their fax number is: 1-866-900-6417

Please note that a "copy of an official military discharge document bearing an official seal or other supporting documentation is usually sufficient to determine eligibility for burial. The document must show release from service was under conditions other than dishonorable. Discharge documentation is not usually needed for scheduling when a Veteran or eligible dependent is already interred in a national cemetery."

Once eligibility has been established, you should call the office at 1-800-535-1117.

You will need to have the following information on hand:

_____ Cemetery of choice

_____ First or subsequent burial (Veteran or dependent already buried)

_____ If subsequent interment, who is already interred, section and site number (if known)?

_____ Decedent's full name, gender, SSN, date of death, date of birth and relationship (Veteran or dependent)

_____ Contact Info (funeral director's name as well as the name, address, and E-mail address of the funeral home)

_____ Next of kin information (name, relationship to deceased, SSN, phone number, address)

_____ Type of religious emblem for headstone (if known and desired)

_____ Did the decedent reside within 75 miles of requested cemetery?

_____ ZIP code of decedent at time of death

_____ County of decedent at time of death

_____ Type of burial (casket or cremation)

_____ Marital status of deceased (if Veteran is buried in a private cemetery but spouse will be buried in a National Cemetery, must provide documentation of marital status of spouse at time of death)

_____ Casket size/liner size/urn size/urn vault size

_____ Is surviving spouse a Veteran?

_____ Any disabled children for future interment (must provide name and date of birth). If requesting immediate interment (must provide marital status, doctor's statement stating type of illness, date of onset of illness and capability of self-support).

_____ Military Honors requested?

CREMATION WORKSHEET

Keep a record of the details of your negotiations with the crematorium of your choice here. Make sure you receive the final quotation in writing.

Name of Crematorium: _____

Person in charge: _____

Person giving quote: _____

Date quote given: _____

Address: _____

Phone: _____

Fax: _____

eMail address: _____

Web link: _____

<u>Cremation Container Details:</u>

Many crematoriums require a container, called a cremation container, which will be cremated along with the body. Make sure you inquire about this as some crematoriums allow the use of burial shrouds as an alternative to a casket. Also inquire about low-cost containers, which are often made of heavy-duty cardboard. If the crematorium does not offer low-cost containers, you are within your rights to purchase one online or from another funeral home.

Cremation container: _____

(Include model number, color & description)

Container purchased from? _____

Exterior dimensions: _____

(If you purchase the container from another source, make sure it fits within the retort)

Container price: _____

Delivery fee: _____

Container Total: _____

Urn Details:

You may purchase an urn from the crematorium, online, or from any place you want. If you would like the cremated remains to be placed inside the urn prior to pick-up, make sure you take the urn to the crematorium and discuss that option with staff. When choosing an urn, you must take into consideration the height and sex of your loved one at time of death. Larger, male bodies will need larger urns than smaller, female bodies. Discuss that detail with the urn salesman.

Urn: _____

(Include model number, color & description)

Urn purchased from? _____

Urn price: _____

Shipping/Delivery: _____

Total Urn Price: _____

Direct Cremation Details:

Use this worksheet if your loved one's body will be directly cremated upon arrival at the crematorium.

Pickup location: _____

Pickup date/time: _____

Cremation date/time: _____

Cremains available date/time: _____

Non-declinable basic service fee: _____

Pickup and delivery to crematorium: _____

Cremation container price: _____

Direct cremation fee: _____

Other fees: _____

Total Direct Cremation Fees: _____

Service with Cremation Details:

If you will be holding a service either prior to or after cremation at the crematorium, use this worksheet.

Pickup location: _____

Pickup date/time: _____

Will the body be embalmed? _____

Have other preparations been chosen? _____

Will a rental casket be required? _____

Service type: _____
(Viewing/Visitation/Funeral/Memorial)

Service date/time: _____

Capacity: _____

Non-declinable basic service fee: _____

Transportation to crematorium: _____

Facility fee (for the service): _____

Staff fee: _____

Embalming: _____

Other preparations of the body: _____

Rental casket: _____

Cremation container: _____

Cremation fee: _____

Urn price: _____

Other: _____

(music, video, guestbook, tables, linen, easels, etc.)

Total fees for Service with Cremation: _____

BURIAL AT SEA CHECKLIST

When contacting your regional Environmental Protection Agency office about a burial at sea, be sure to include the following:

_____ **Name of the Deceased:** _____

_____ **Date of Burial/Scatter:** _____

_____ **Type of Remains:** Cremated ( )   Non-Cremated ( )

_____ **Location of Burial/Scatter:**

_____ **Latitude:** _____

_____ **Longitude:** _____

_____ **Distance from shore:** _____

(minimum of 3 nautical miles)

_____ **Depth of water:** _____

(minimum of 600 or 1800 feet, depending on location)

_____ **Vessel Name:** _____

_____ **Vessel Point of Contact:**

_____ Name: _____

_____ Phone: _____

_____ **Port of Departure:** _____

_____ **For Non-Cremated Remains:**

_____ Did the remains appear to rapidly sink to the ocean floor?

Yes ( )   No ( )

_____ **Director or person(s) responsible for burial arrangements:**

_____ Name: _____

_____ Phone: _____

HOME SERVICES
CHECKLIST & WORKSHEET

Whether you keep your loved one's body at home for the Viewing or through the Home Funeral Service itself, you will have to keep the body clean and cool. In this section, you will find a list of supplies you should have on hand, as well as a section where you can fill in the names of those who will be in charge of the various tasks and service(s).

For more information regarding preparing a home funeral, refer to the chapter, "Steps for Arranging a Home Funeral."

Supplies you may need:

_____A table or bed to lay the body out on

_____A casket if you will lay the body out in one

_____Sheet(s) to lay the body on, roll the body and/or to cover dry ice packs

_____Blanket(s)

_____A small pillow to place behind her head

_____Q-tips to swab mouth

_____Cotton for packing orifices

_____Disposable gloves for placing of cotton

_____Soft cloths or sponges for cleansing the body

_____Vinegar

_____Mouthwash

_____Body Soap

_____Shampoo if washing her hair

_____Water in a basin

_____Towels

_____Scarf for tying her mouth closed

_____Hand towel to roll under her chin

_____Oil to rub on eyelids

_____Moisturizing lotion to keep skin from drying out

_____Lavender Essential Oil

_____Cedar Wood Chips (like those found in a pet store), saw dust or cat litter

_____Dry Ice (about 30 pounds per day for an average adult-sized body)

_____Leather gloves and apron to protect you when handling dry ice

_____An ice pick and/or hammer for breaking up ice

_____Pillow cases or towels to wrap dry ice in

_____A non-plastic container for storing extra dry ice (do not keep it in your freezer)

_____Scissors if it becomes necessary to cut off clothing

_____Plastic-lined diapers and/or mat for placing under the body

_____Makeup if you wish to touch up your loved one's face a bit

_____Scented candles or essential oil dispensers

_____Flowers

_____Mementoes from your loved one's life (awards, trophies, etc.)

_____Framed photos

_____Music

_____An air conditioner to keep the room cool

_____Chairs for visitors to sit in

_____A casket, burial shroud or other appropriate container

_____Vehicle for transporting the body – truck, van, SUV, station
      wagon, etc.

Caring for your loved one's body:

You will need at least four people to comfortably lift and move an average-sized adult body. These caregivers will cleanse and dress the body, groom your loved one's hair and nails, move her body from sick bed to its place for the service(s), which could be her freshly-changed bed or into a casket.

When you know who will help you to care for your loved one's body, refer the chapter, "Steps for Arranging a Home Funeral", for steps and instructions on doing so.

Use the Team Member Checklist to coordinate the many tasks.

Many of the tasks that will need to be taken care of, such as gathering photos, arranging for music, etc. have already been listed in the Team Member Checklist. Once you have appointed who will be in charge of which tasks, continue filling out the information below which is specific to designing home services.

Decide upon the services you will hold at home:

_____ **Viewing/Wake**   Date: _____   Time: _____

Viewing Location: _____

_____ **Funeral Service**   Date: _____   Time: _____

Funeral location: _____

_____ **Burial Service** Date: _____ Time: _____

Burial Location: _____

_____ **Memorial Service**   Date: _____   Time: _____

Memorial Location: _____

For a Viewing/Wake:

Estimated No. of Attendees: _____

No. of chairs needed: _____

Supplied by: _____

No. of tables needed: _____

Supplied by: _____

Will food be available? _____

Coordinated by: _____

Will drinks be available? _____

Coordinated by: _____

For a Funeral or Memorial Service:

Estimated No. of Attendees: _____

No. of chairs needed: _____

Supplied by: _____

No. of tables needed: _____

Supplied by: _____

Will food be available? _____

Coordinated by: _____

Will drinks be available? _____

Coordinated by: _____

For a Burial Service:

Burial Location: _____

Estimated No. of Attendees: _____

Transportation of the body: _____

Pall-bearers: _____

(Note: will these people be able to carry the body/casket to your chosen
   burial site? If not, will you have to arrange for a gurney, four-wheel drive
   vehicle, etc.?)

No. of chairs needed: _____

Supplied by: _____

Other supplies/equipment needed: _____

(shovels, straps for lowering the casket into the grave, tree/flowers to plant,
   etc.)

HOME FUNERAL OR MEMORIAL SERVICE WORKSHEET

Location/Venue: _____

Venue Contact: _____

Date: _____ Time from: _____ to: _____

Estimated No. of Attendees: _____

Service led by: _____

Reading(s) given by: _____

Eulogy given by: _____

Speaker(s): _____

Songs/Hymns: _____
(Print out copies if songs/hymns are not commonly known and hymnals are
    not available)

Music supplied by: _____

*Video supplied by: _____

Order of events: _____

No. of chairs needed: _____

Supplied by: _____

No. of tables needed: _____

Supplied by: _____

No. of floral arrangements: _____

Supplied by: _____

No. stands needed for flowers: _____

Supplied by: _____

No. framed photos: _____

Supplied by: _____

No. easels for photos: _____

Supplied by: _____

Transportation:

If you will be moving the body to a cemetery, crematorium or other location for final disposition, you will need to consider transportation. You can hire a funeral home to provide a hearse or, if you live in a state that allows it, you can apply for a transportation permit and then transport your loved one's body yourself.

Nourishment for Combined Services:

If you plan to combine services, such as a viewing followed by a home funeral service, then attendees will be at your home for a number of hours and you should consider whether you want to provide food and beverages.

You may want to include the following:

_____Guestbook and pen

_____Photo album

_____Photo Board

_____Funeral Program

_____Mementoes

_____Memory book and pen

*Video Memorial:

Because video requires special equipment, be sure you have

considered the following:

- If a video is going to be made for the event, who will make it?

- What format will video be supplied in?

- What equipment will be needed to play video?

- Who will supply the equipment?

VIEWING/VISITATION/WAKE WORKSHEET & CHECKLIST

Date: _____   Time from: _____ to: _____

Location: _____

_____Open Casket   _____Closed Casket

Equipment:

_____Tables

    Qty: _____   Rental (each): $_____   Total: $ _____

_____Skirts/cloths

    Qty: _____   Rental (each): $_____   Total: $ _____

_____Easels

    Qty: _____   Rental (each): $_____   Total: $ _____

_____Kneeler

    Qty: _____   Rental (each): $_____   Total: $ _____

_____Rental casket (if cremation)   Total: $ _____

_____Casket supplies (if rental)   Total: $ _____

    (i.e., pillows, padding, etc.)

_____Casket (if purchased)   Total: $ _____

_____Video Screen

Qty: _____   Rental (each): $_____   Total: $ _____

Format:_____

_____Monitor/TV

Qty: _____   Rental (each): $_____   Total: $ _____

Format: _____

_____ Audio Player

Qty: _____   Rental (each):$_____   Total: $ _____

Format (CD, MP3, etc.): _____

_____ Other   Total: $ _____

Personnel

_____ Funeral Director   Total: $ _____

_____ Staff

Number: _____   Fee (each): $_____   Total: $ _____

Supplies

_____ Guest Book/Pen

_____ Memory Book/Pen

_____ Photo(s) Album or Board

_____ Funeral/Burial Info

MEMORIAL SERVICE WORKSHEET

Memorial services are usually held after final disposition though, in the case of cremations, the cremated remains might be present during the service. You can plan a memorial service at any time, even months after the death of your loved one. Use this worksheet to help you to plan out the service.

Location/Venue: _____

Venue Contact: _____

Date: _____ Time from: _____ to: _____

Estimated No. of Attendees: _____

Service led by: _____

Reading(s) given by: _____

Eulogy given by: _____

Speaker(s): _____

Songs/Hymns: _____
(Print out copies if songs/hymns are not commonly known and hymnals are not available)

Music supplied by: _____

*Video supplied by: _____

Order of events: _____

No. of chairs needed: _____

Supplied by: _____

No. of tables needed: _____

Supplied by: _____

No. of floral arrangements: _____

Supplied by: _____

No. stands needed for flowers: _____

Supplied by: _____

No. framed photos: _____

Supplied by: _____

No. easels for photos: _____

Supplied by: _____

Nourishment:

Consider whether you will include food and beverages either before or after the service.

You may want to include the following:

_____Guestbook and pen

_____Photo album

_____Photo Board

_____Funeral Program

_____Mementoes

_____Memory book and pen

*Video Memorial:

Because video requires special equipment, be sure you have considered the following:

- If a video is going to be made for the event, who will make it?

- What format will video be supplied in?

- What equipment will be needed to play video?

- Who will supply the equipment?

GRAVESIDE SERVICE WORKSHEET

Generally, funeral services are held prior to final commitment (burial) and you would not then plan for readings, speakers, etc. graveside. However, more people are opting for burial outside of traditional cemeteries and may choose to combine the funeral service with the committal. Use all or part of this worksheet to help you to plan.

Location/Venue: _____

Venue Contact: _____

Date: _____ Time from: _____ to: _____

Estimated No. of Attendees: _____

Service led by: _____

Reading(s) given by: _____

Eulogy given by: _____

Speaker(s): _____

Songs/Hymns: _____
Supplied by: _____

*Video supplied by: _____

Order of events: _____

No. of chairs needed: _____

Supplied by: _____

No. of tables needed: _____

Supplied by: _____

No. of floral arrangements: _____

Supplied by: _____

No. stands needed for flowers: _____

Supplied by: _____

No. framed photos: _____

Supplied by: _____

No. easels for photos: _____

Supplied by: _____

Pallbearers: _____

Who will dig the grave? _____

Equipment (shovels, etc.) needed: _____

How will the casket be lowered? _____

Lowering equipment needed: _____

No. of chairs needed: _____

Supplied by: _____

Will a tent/awning be needed? _____

Supplied by: _____

No. of floral arrangements: _____

Supplied by: _____

No. stands needed for flowers: _____

Supplied by: _____

No. framed photos: _____

Supplied by: _____

No. easels for photos: _____

Supplied by: _____

TRANSPORTATION & ACCOMMODATIONS WORKSHEET

Use this sheet to keep track of visitors coming in from out of town and where they will stay. Have the names, phone numbers and average rates for at least two local hotels/motels available to share with visitors. Ideally, one or two people can pick up those who will not be renting a car and take them to their hotel or other lodging. Make sure those meeting visitors and the visitors share cell phone numbers in case any delays occur.

Hotel/Motel 1: _____

Phone: _____

Address: _____

Room rates: _____

Hotel/Motel 2: _____

Phone: _____

Address: _____

Room rates: _____

For each person being for whom transportation arrangements are being made, make sure you have the following:

Person being picked up: _____

Cell Phone #: _____

Arrival details: _____

Lodging details: _____

Person picking up: _____

His/Her cell phone: _____

GIFT LIST WORKSHEET & CHECKLIST

It is important to keep track of all gifts and donations so that thank you cards can be sent out at a later date.

When a "thank you" card is sent, check it off.

_____Donor: _____

Gift (flowers, childcare, etc.): _____

Address: _____

_____Donor: _____

Gift (flowers, childcare, etc.): _____

Address: _____

WRAPPING UP YOUR LOVED ONE'S AFFAIRS

Unfortunately, if your loved one died without leaving a Will, you may find yourself having to jump through some legal hoops in order to settle his/her estate. At that point, it is often a good idea to consult an attorney who regularly deals with inheritance law in the state where your loved one lived.

If your loved one did leave a Will that appoints you Executor/Executrix, you will want to take a certified copy of the death certificate and the valid Will to the local courthouse or city hall of the city/town where your loved one last lived and file a probate petition (a request that the court validates the Will).

Once the Will is validated, the court will issue you Letters Testamentary or Letters of Administration. These are legal documents that allow you to wind up your loved one's financial affairs. Like the death certificate, make sure you get multiple (at least 10) certified copies of the Letters Testamentary.

You must recognize that, if there is a Will (or Trust), you must carry out your loved one's wishes for distributing his/her estate. Unfortunately, while many of us make provisions for dividing our assets among our beneficiaries, we do not always include information about all our creditors, accounts, policies, etc. These will all have to be informed of your loved one's death, accounts will have to be cancelled, closed or changed, and provisions will have to be made for settling any outstanding claims.

Begin by making a list of all accounts, policies, plans, etc. that you know of. Next, go through your loved one's files to look for any that you may not be aware of. Make sure you order a current copy of your loved one's credit report from at least one of the three credit reporting agencies. That is because the agencies will tell you if there are any open accounts, even ones from many years ago, that have not been active in a while but which still must be cancelled.

List and contact all of the following (include company name & policy number).

Government Agencies:

_____ Social Security Administration

_____ Post Office

Credit Bureaus:

_____ Equifax

_____ Experian

_____ TransUnion

Legal:

_____ Attorney: _____

_____ Executor/Executrix: _____

_____ Trustee(s): _____

_____ Guardian ad Litem (if applicable): _____

_____ Parole Officer (if applicable): _____

_____ Other: _____

Insurance Policy Holders:

_____ Life: _____

_____ Homeowners: _____

_____ Renter's Insurance: _____

_____ Health: _____

_____ Major Medical: _____

_____ Dental: _____

_____ Vision: _____

_____ Disability: _____

_____ Auto: _____

_____ Other (boat, motorhome, etc.): _____

Investment Account Holders:

_____ IRA's: _____

_____ 401(k) plans: _____

_____ Pensions: _____

_____ Stock portfolios: _____

_____ Mutual funds: _____

_____ Other: _____

Bank Accounts:

_____ Accounts: _____

_____ Bank boxes: _____

_____ Certificates of Deposit: _____

_____ Money Market accounts: _____

Creditors:

_____ Mortgage Holder: _____

_____ Credit Card companies: _____

_____ Store credit cards: _____

_____ Auto loan holders: _____

_____ School loan holders: _____

_____ Other: _____

Employers or Clients:

_____ Employer: _____

_____ Clients (if self-employed): _____

Schools:

_____ School: _____

_____ School loan: _____

Utility Companies:

_____ Water: _____

_____ Electricity: _____

_____ Gas: _____

_____ Other: _____

Others:

_____ Landlords: _____

_____ Tenants: _____

_____ Housekeeper: _____

_____ Lawn Maintenance: _____

_____ Others: _____

PART IV:
Sample Forms

NON-DECLINABLE SERVICES DISCLOSURE

Under the Funeral Rule, funeral homes are allowed to include a non-declinable fee for "basic services." According the Bureau for Consumer Protection (an office of the Federal Trade Commission), this fee should include:

"services that are common to virtually all forms of disposition or arrangements that you offer, such as conducting the arrangements conference, securing the necessary permits, preparing the notices, sheltering of remains, and coordinating the arrangements with the cemetery, crematory, or other third parties. The basic services fee should not include charges related to other items that must be separately listed on the General Price List and that the customer may decline to purchase.

The basic services fee also may include overhead from various aspects of your business operation, such as the parking lot, reception and arrangements rooms, and other common areas. It also may include insurance, staff salaries, taxes, and fees that you must pay. Alternatively, instead of including all overhead in your basic services fee, you can spread the overhead charges across the various individual goods and services you offer. As a third alternative, you can combine the first two approaches: spread some portion of the overhead charges across the individual items, while including the remainder of such charges in your basic services fee."

The Funeral Rule dictates that no part of the other 15 funeral goods and services that are required to be listed can be included in the line item, "Basic Services of Funeral Director and Staff." For instance, it would be a violation for a funeral home to include any of the following arrangements in its non-declinable basic fee:

- Fees for transporting remains

- Fees for preparation of the body

- Fees for setting up and supervising the visitation service

The above-mentioned items must be separate, detailed, line items according to the Funeral Rule.

The National Funeral Directors Association recommends that funeral homes include generic disclosures for non-declinable service fees. It provides the following as an example:

"Our basic service charge includes, but is not limited to, staff to respond to initial request for service; arrangement conference with family or responsible party; preparation and filing of necessary certificates and permits; shelter of remains; placement of obituary notices; planning of funeral arrangements; and coordination of service with cemetery, crematory, vault companies and others as required."

"Also included in this charge are overhead expenses relative to our facility such as insurance, maintenance and utility expenses, secretarial and administrative costs, and equipment and inventory expenses."

If the fee is non-declinable, the Funeral Rule requires that the following disclosure be included with any price list:

"This fee for our basic services and overhead will be added to the total cost of the funeral arrangements you select. (This fee is already included in our charges for direct cremations, immediate burials and forwarding or receiving remains.)"

Funeral homes may decide to include their basic service fees in the price of a casket. If they do, they must include the following disclosure in their Casket Price List:

> "Please note that a fee of [specify dollar amount] for the use of our basic services and overhead is included in the price of our caskets. This same fee shall be added to the total cost of your funeral arrangements if you provide the casket. Our services include...[describe services]."

Sample Funeral Home Price Lists

The Federal Trade Commission provides the following four sample funeral home price lists. While funeral homes are required to provide you the following information per the Funeral Rule, the information may be arranged differently than supplied here.

Sample #1

ABC FUNERAL HOME
100 Main Street
Yourtown, USA 12345
(123) 456-7890

GENERAL PRICE LIST

These prices are effective as of [date].

The goods and services shown below are those we can provide to our customers. You may choose only the items you desire. However, any funeral arrangements you select will include a charge for our basic services and overhead. If legal or other requirements mean you must buy any items you did not specifically ask for, we will explain the reason in writing on the statement we provide describing the funeral goods and services you selected.

Basic Services of Funeral Director and Staff and Overhead $_____

Our services include: conducting the arrangements conference; planning the funeral; consulting with family and clergy; shelter of remains; preparing and filing of necessary notices; obtaining necessary authorizations and permits; coordinating with the cemetery, crematory, or other third parties. In addition, this fee includes a proportionate share of our basic overhead costs.

This fee for our basic services and overhead will be added to the total cost of the funeral arrangements you select. (This fee is already included in our charges for direct cremations, immediate burials, and forwarding or receiving remains.)

Embalming $_____

Except in certain special cases, embalming is not required by law. Embalming may be necessary, however, if you select certain funeral arrangements, such as a funeral with viewing. If you do not want embalming, you usually have the right to choose an arrangement that does not require you to pay for it, such as direct cremation or immediate burial.

Other Preparation of the Body $_____

[list individual services and prices]

Transfer of Remains to the Funeral Home(within __ mile radius)
$_____

Beyond this radius we charge __ per mile

Use of Facilities and Staff For Viewing at the Funeral Home

$_____

Use of Facilities and Staff For Funeral Ceremony at the Funeral Home $_____

Use of Facilities and Staff For Memorial Service at the Funeral Home $_____

Use of Equipment and Staff For Graveside Service

$_____

Hearse $_____ Limousine $_____

Caskets $_____ to $_____

A complete price list will be provided at the funeral home.

Outer Burial Containers $_____ to $_____

A complete price list will be provided at the funeral home.

Forwarding of Remains to Another Funeral Home $_____

Our charge includes: basic services of funeral director and staff; a proportionate share of overhead costs; removal of remains; embalming or other preparation of remains, if relevant; and local transportation.

Receiving Remains from Another Funeral Home $_____

Our charge includes: basic services of funeral director and staff; a proportionate share of overhead costs; care of remains; transportation of remains to funeral home and to cemetery or crematory.

Direct Cremation $_____ to $_____

Our charge for a direct cremation (without ceremony) includes: basic services of funeral director and staff; a proportionate share of overhead costs; removal of remains; transportation to crematory; necessary authorizations; and cremation if relevant.

If you want to arrange a direct cremation, you can use an alternative container. Alternative containers encase the body and can be made of materials like fiberboard or composition materials (with or without an outside covering). The containers we provide are a fiberboard container or an unfinished wood box.

A. Direct cremation with container provided by the purchaser $_____

B. Direct cremation with a fiberboard container $_____

C. Direct cremation with an unfinished wood box $_____

Immediate Burial $_____ to $_____

Our charge for an immediate burial (without ceremony) includes: basic services of funeral director and staff; a proportionate share of overhead costs; removal of remains; and local transportation to cemetery.

A. Immediate burial with casket provided by purchaser $_____

B. Immediate burial with alternative container [if offered] $_____

C. Immediate burial with cloth covered wood casket $_____

Sample #2

ABC FUNERAL HOME CASKET PRICE LIST

These prices are effective as of [date].

Alternative Containers:

1. Fiberboard Box $_____

2. Plywood Box $_____

3. Unfinished Pine Box $_____

Caskets:

1. Beige cloth-covered soft-wood with beige interior
   $_____

2. Oak stained soft-wood with pleated blue crepe interior $_____

3. Mahogany finished soft-wood with maroon crepe interior $_____

4. Solid White Pine with eggshell crepe interior $_____

5. Solid Mahogany with tufted rose tan velvet interior $_____

6. Hand finished solid Cherry with ivory velvet interior $_____

7. 18 gauge rose colored Steel w/ pleated maroon crepe interior

(available in a variety of interiors) $_____

8. 20 gauge bronze colored Steel with blue crepe interior $_____

9. Solid Bronze (16 gauge) with brushed finish white ivory velvet interior $_____

10. Solid Copper (32 oz.) with Sealer (Oval Glass) and medium bronze finish with rose tan velvet interior $_____

Sample #3

ABC FUNERAL HOME OUTER BURIAL CONTAINER PRICE LIST

These prices are effective as of [date].

In most areas of the country, state or local law does not require that you buy a container to surround the casket in the grave. However, many cemeteries require that you have such a container so that the grave will not sink in. Either a grave liner or a burial vault will satisfy these requirements.

1. Concrete Grave Liner $_____

2. Acme Reinforced Concrete Vault (lined) $_____

3. Acme Reinforced Concrete Vault (stainless steel lined) $_____

4. Acme Solid Copper Vault .$_____

5. Acme Steel Vault (12 gauge) . $_____

Sample #4

ABC FUNERAL HOME

STATEMENT OF FUNERAL GOODS
AND SERVICES SELECTED

Charges are only for those items that you selected or that are required. If we are required by law or by a cemetery or crematory to use any items, we will explain the reasons in writing below.

Deceased:

Purchaser:

Address:

Tel. No.:

Date of Death

Date of Arrangements

Basic Services of Funeral Director and Staff and Overhead $_____

Embalming $_____

If you selected a funeral that may require embalming, such as a funeral with viewing, you may have to pay for embalming. You do not have to pay for embalming you did not approve if you selected arrangements such as a direct cremation or immediate burial. If we charged for embalming, we will explain why below.

Other Preparation of the Body

1. Cosmetic Work for Viewing $_____

2. Washing and Disinfecting Unembalmed Remains $_____

Transfer of Remains to the Funeral Home $_____

Use of Facilities and Staff For Viewing	$_____
Use of Facilities and Staff For Funeral Ceremony	$_____
Use of Facilities and Staff for Memorial Service	$_____
Use of Equipment and Staff for Graveside Service	$_____
Hearse	$_____
Limousine	$_____
Casket	$_____
Outer Burial Container	$_____
Forwarding of Remains to Another Funeral Home	$_____
Receiving Remains from Another Funeral Home	$_____
Direct Cremation	$_____
Immediate Burial	$_____

CASH ADVANCE ITEMS

We charge you for our services in obtaining: [specify relevant cash advance items].

Cemetery charges	$_____
Crematory charges	$_____
Flowers .	$_____
Obituary notice	$_____
Death certificate	$_____
Music	$_____
Total Cash Advance Items	$_____
TOTAL COST OF ARRANGEMENTS	$_____

(including all services, merchandise, and cash advance items)

    If any legal, cemetery, or crematory requirement has required the purchase of any of the items listed above, we will explain the requirement below:

_____

Reason for Embalming: _____

SAMPLE EULOGY

Written by Sergio Mariaca for his niece, Jahmila Kyla Bertie-Mariaca.

"When you lose a child in this way, you question everything. You wonder if you can ever find peace and move on.

I have been thinking about Jahmila's life and have been questioning whether her 18 years were as full as possible. Wondering if we could have done anything more to have made that too-short time even more special.

I don't know, and I sincerely doubt I will ever be satisfied with the answer, if I ever do settle upon one. But this is what I am sure of: Jahmila was fully and completely loved. By her mother, her father, her sisters, her grandmother, and by all of her cousins, aunts and uncles. We are a close-knit, if far-flung, family. As a result of our mostly bi-annual reunions, our entire, extended family knew her well, and every single one of us understood just how special she was. Of all of us, Jahmila was the sweetest. Her heart was full of love for us, and, thankfully, I am sure that she knew just how important she was to our entire family.

Lizzie, I would give anything to take away your pain. I know how much you hurt because I witnessed, every single day, how committed you are to your daughters. Your love for each of them is without match. Your love for Jahmila was whole and complete, and there was really nothing more you could have done for her because, at all times, you did everything for her and gave everything you had of yourself to her. Jahmila never had to worry about anything because she had you to worry for her. She was blessed in having you as her mother.

Ilicia, Nicole, and Audrey, Jahmila could not have asked for a more loving, supportive and involved group of sisters. Individually, you are each strong and steady and true, but your greatest strength has always come from having each other. You are like the four points on a compass, the four seasons, and the four elements – uniquely precious, but only complete because of the other three.

Ilicia, your bond with Jahmila was the most special of all. The two of you have been like twins since the day you were born, and it was the rarest of moments when we'd see one of you without the other. Playing Taboo with the two of you was a wildly fun, but nevertheless fruitless, endeavor because, from the day you began to speak, the two of you could finish each other's sentences.

I had a very special relationship with Jahmila, as I do with each of my nieces. But, what we two shared was exceptional. The one thing I do with all whom I love is to play pranks, practical jokes and tease, tease, tease. I am ruthless in my pursuit of fun, and Jahmila was always my favorite target because she gave it right back to me.

Jahmie was extremely proud of her Latin heritage and the fact, as much as I hate saying it, that she was born in Puerto Rico where our family lived for many years. She knew I was born in Ohio and she would tease me about my poor luck. In return, I would tell her that one of our family secrets was that she was actually born in Kentucky, and that would drive her crazy. I am pretty sure that most of our exchanges ended with her making fun of me in some way for having been born in Ohio, and me saying how it wasn't as bad as being born in Kentucky.

Recently, I came up with a plan to drive her crazy at work. I started to drop in at Publix when I knew she wouldn't be around, to talk with her co-workers. I asked them to help me out by finding a moment to tell Jahmila, "Hey, I met your uncle. He is a really cool guy." I must have told 15 people, and I was sure they were on board with my plan. Every time I saw Jahmila after setting it up, or spoke with her, I waited for her to say something. But, she never did. After several weeks went by without her recognizing what a cool guy her co-workers thought I am, I couldn't stand it anymore. I gave in and asked her about it. At which point, she burst out laughing and told me what a dork I was.

Anyone else would have said something to me, if only to tell me how lame my plan had been, but Jahmie understood that by not saying anything, she was driving me crazy.

If Jahmila could be here, she would hug us and tell us all how much she loved us. She would thank us for being her family. She would also ask us find peace in our lives and to continue living. Let's try and find a way."

SAMPLE OBITUARY

Please note that while I've included spaces where you can insert education, cause of death and other factors, these are simply options. If you do not know when your loved one graduated, don't include that line. If you would rather not discuss cause of death, forego it.

You may include as little or as much information as you want. Generally, obituaries stick to the high points, such as degrees achieved, awards earned, honors bestowed, military details, career highlights, etc.

Name, of **Anytown**, died at **Place (at home, at General Hospital, etc.)** on **Date**. He was **Age.**

Name was born in **Another Town**, **State**, on **Date**, to **Father's Name** and **Mother's Name.** He graduated from **High School**, before going on to **College**. **Name** earned a degree in **Specialty** from **University** and a **Higher Degree** from **University**. He/She joined **Company** right out of school. **He/She** married **Spouse's Name** on **Date** at **Place**.

Name was honored with the **Award** for **His/Her** work on **Something** by **Organization** in **Year**. That achievement was considered essential to the furthering of **Industry**. Over the course of **his/her** career, **he/she** held a number of positions on various boards, organizations and industry alliances, including, **Name Them**.

(NOTE – in the biographical section above, you can include anything from sports highlights to community activities to social impacts made by your loved one. This is a highly personalized section).

Name is survived by **Next-of-Kin (spouse's name, children's names, parent's names, sibling's names, grandchildren's names)**. The funeral will be held at **Place** on **Date** at **Time**.

In lieu of flowers, the family has requested that donations be made in **Name's** name to his/her favorite charity, **Name of Charity**. **Contact information for Charity.**

SAMPLES OF MEMORIAL SCHOLARSHIPS

Below are examples of two memorial scholarship funds. The first, set up in my niece's name, is a specific scholarship within a larger non-profit organization (meaning that donations are tax deductible). To access that scholarship, donors simply click on the "Give Online Now" button and, when filling in their information, include "The Jahmila Kyla Bertie-Mariaca Scholarship Fund" on the line for "business name."

The second was set up through and administered by the Souhegan Scholarship Foundation, a 501(c)(3), which means that donations are tax deductible. The public is invited to donate online or to send a check to the scholarship foundation headquarters.

Visiting these sites may help you to figure out if and how you would like to set up a memorial scholarship (or other fund) in your loved one's name.

The Jahmila Kyla Bertie-Mariaca Scholarship Fund
CNMC Camps a.k.a. Brainy Camps Association
111 Michigan Avenue, NW
Washington, DC 20010
Phone: 877-260-2267
http://brainycamps.com/

The Kimberly L. Cates Memorial Scholarship Fund
Souhegan Scholarship Foundation
PO Box 451
Mont Vernon, NH 03057
http://www.kimcatesfund.org/index.htm

PART V:
Resources & References

RESOURCES

This section provides you with the resources you will need to begin planning a dignified and memorable goodbye for your loved one. You will find links to organizations that can help you with end-of-life planning, as well as government offices that can help you to locate necessary documents. The important things to note are that, a) this list is not exhaustive but is meant to help you get started, and, b) while I have looked into each of these links at the time of writing, I neither endorse them nor make any claim that the links are still valid at the time of your reading, and, c) you alone understand your needs and must perform your own due diligence.

I would greatly appreciate hearing from you if you can personally recommend any of the resources included here, or if you have found other resources that you think are of value to readers. Further, if you have a bad experience with any of the companies or organizations included here, please let me know. You can contact me by clicking on the "Contact Me" button that floats on the left side of your monitor at my site, www.KatherineMariaca.com.

FEDERAL GOVERNMENT RESOURCES

Federal Trade Commission (oversees the Funeral Rule)
600 Pennsylvania Avenue, NW
Washington, DC 20580
Phone: (202) 326-2222
www.ftc.gov

Department of Veterans Affairs
Phone: 1-800-827-1000
www.cem.va.gov

National Archives
(Contact the National Archives to request a copy of your loved one's military service discharge form. Service members or next of kin may request Form DD-214, others may request Form SF-180)
http://www.archives.gov/veterans/military-service-records/index.html

Medicare
Centers for Medicare & Medicaid Services
7500 Security Boulevard
Baltimore MD 21244-1850
Phone: 1-800-MEDICARE (1-800-633-43273)
http://www.medicare.gov/

Social Security Administration
Phone: 800-772-1213
www.ssa.gov

U.S. Department of Veterans Affairs National Cemetery Administration
Phone: 800-827-1000
www.cem.va.gov

Vital Statistics
(Copies of vital records, such as death certificates, are ordered by state – use the web address below to find your state's office)
http://www.cdc.gov/nchs/w2w.htm

U.S. Standard Death Certificate
(To download a copy of this form, please click on the link below)
http://www.cdc.gov/nchs/data/dvs/DEATH11-03final-ACC.pdf

FUNERAL LAW – STATE-BY-STATE

To learn more about the funeral laws in your state, please contact your state office.

While the great majority of these links are to state government sites, a few are links to membership funeral boards. Not all funeral boards are state-run. That is not to say that the information provided is not valuable. I point this out simply to alert you to the possibility that those boards' interests may be commercial.

Alabama Board of Funeral Service
P.O. Box 309522
Montgomery, AL 36130Physical Address:

Alabama State House
11 South Union Street, Suite 21
Montgomery, AL 36104
Phone: 334- 242-4049
Fax: 334-353-7988
http://www.fsb.alabama.gov/

Alaska Regulation of Morticians

P.O. Box 110806
Juneau, AK 99811-0806
Phone: 907-465-2691
Fax: 907- 465-2974
http://www.dced.state.ak.us/occ/pmor.htm

Arizona Board of Funeral Directors & Embalmers
1400 West Washington, Suite 230
Phoenix, AZ 85007
Phone: 602-542-3095
http://www.azfuneralboard.us/

Arkansas State Board of Embalmers & Funeral Directors
101 East Capitol, Suite 113
Little Rock, AR 72201
Phone: 501-682-0574
http://www.state.ar.us/fdemb/index.html

California Department of Consumer Affairs Cemetery & Funeral Bureau
1625 North Market Blvd., Suite S-208
Sacramento, CA 95834
Phone: 916-574-7870
http://www.cfb.ca.gov/

Colorado Office of Funeral Home and Crematory Registration
1560 Broadway, Suite 1350
Denver, CO 80202
Phone: 303-894-7800
http://www.dora.state.co.us/funeralhome-crematory/

State of Connecticut Office of the Attorney General
55 Elm Street
Hartford, CT 06106
Phone: 860-808-5318
http://www.ct.gov/ag/site/default.asp

State of Delaware Board of Funeral Services
Cannon Building, Suite 203
861 Silver Lake Blvd.
Dover, DE 19904
Phone: 302-744-4500
http://www.dpr.delaware.gov/boards/funeralservices/index.shtml

Florida Division of Funeral, Cemetery and Consumer Services
200 East Gaines Street
Tallahassee FL 32399
Phone: 850-413-3039
http://www.myfloridacfo.com/funeralcemetery/fc_contact.htm

Georgia Board of Funeral Services

237 Coliseum Drive
Macon, GA 31217-3858
Phone: 478-207-2440
http://sos.georgia.gov/plb/funeral/

Hawaii Cemetery and Pre-Need Funeral Authority
DCCA-PVL
Att: CEM
P.O. Box 3469
Honolulu, HI 96801
Phone: 808-586-2704
http://hawaii.gov/dcca/pvl/programs/cemetery

Idaho Board of Morticians
700 West State Street
Boise, ID 83702

Mailing address:

PO Box 83720
Boise, ID 83720-0063
Phone: 208-334-3233
Fax: 208-334-3945
http://ibol.idaho.gov/IBOL/BoardPage.aspx?Bureau=MOR

Illinois Cemetery Board Oversight
320 W. Washington
Springfield, IL 62786
Phone: 217-785-0800
Fax: 217-782-7645
http://www.idfpr.com/cemetery/cemeteryoversight.asp

Indiana State Board of Funeral & Cemetery Service
Indiana Professional Licensing Agency
State Board of Funeral and Cemetery Service
402 W. Washington Street, Room W072
Indianapolis, IN 46204
Phone: 317-234-3031
http://www.in.gov/pla/funeral.htm

Iowa Funeral Directors Association
1454 30th Street, Suite 204
West Des Moines, IA 50266
Phone: 515-270-0130
Toll Free: 800-982-6561
Fax: 515-270-1569
http://iafda.org/

Kansas State Board of Mortuary Arts
700 SW Jackson St., Suite 904

Topeka, Kansas 66603- 3733
Phone: 785-296-3980
http://www.kansas.gov/ksbma/

Kentucky Embalmers & Funeral Directors Laws

8412 Westport Road
Louisville, KY 40242
Phone: 502-426-4589
Fax: 502-426-4117
http://www.kbefd.ky.gov/bi.htm

Louisiana State Board of Embalmers and Funeral Directors

P.O. Box 8757
Metairie, LA 70011
Phone: 504- 838-5109
Toll Free: 888-508-9083
http://www.lsbefd.state.la.us/index.html

Maine Board of Funeral Service

35 State House Station
Augusta, ME 04333-0035
Phone: 207-624-8626
Fax: 207-624-8637
http://www.state.me.us/pfr/professionallicensing/professions/funeral/index.
htm

Maryland Board of Morticians and Funeral Directors

4201 Patterson Avenue
Baltimore, MD 21215
Phone: 410-767-6500
Toll Free: 877-463-3464
http://www.dhmh.state.md.us/bom/

Massachusetts Board of Registration of Funeral Directors and Embalmers

1000 Washington Street, Suite 710
Boston, Massachusetts 02118-6100
Phone: 617-727-1718
http://www.mass.gov/?pageID=ocaterminal&L=4&L0=Home&L1=Licensee
&L2=Division+of+Professional+Licensure+Boards&L3=Board+of+Registra
tion+of+Funeral+Directors+and+Embalmers&sid=Eoca&b=terminalcontent
&f=dpl_boards_em_about&csid=Eoca

Michigan State Board of Examiners in Mortuary Science

P. O. Box 30018
Lansing, MI 48909
Phone: 517-373-8376
Fax: 517-373-2162
http://www.michigan.gov/lara/0,1607,7-154-35299_35414_35464-114434--
,00.html

Minnesota Department of Health
Mortuary Science Section
85 East Seventh Place, Suite 220
P.O. Box 64882
St. Paul, MN 55164-0882
Phone: 651-201-3829
Toll free: 888-345-0823
TDD: 651-201-5797
http://www.health.state.mn.us/divs/hpsc/mortsci/mortsci.htm

Mississippi State Board of Funeral Services
3010 Lakeland Cove, Suite W
Flowood, MS 39232
Phone: 601-932-1973
http://www.msbfs.ms.gov/

Montana Funeral Directors Association
P.O. Box 4267
Helena, MT 59604-4267
Phone: 406-449-7244
http://www.mfda.net/consumer.html

Nebraska Department of Health and Human Services - Division of Public Health
Funeral Establishments
Nebraska State Office Building
301 Centennial Mall South
14th and M Streets
3rd Floor
Lincoln, Nebraska

Mailing address:

Licensure Unit
PO Box 94986
Lincoln, NE 68509-4986
Phone: 402-471-2115
http://www.hhs.state.ne.us/crl/mhcs/fun/funestab.htm#Contact

Nebraska State Funeral Board
PMB 186
4894 Lone Mountain Road
Las Vegas, NV 89130
Phone: 702-290-5366
http://www.leg.state.nv.us/NAC/NAC-642.html

New Hampshire Board of Registration of Funeral Directors and Embalmers
29 Hazen Drive
Concord, NH 03301
Phone: 603-271-4648

http://www.nh.gov/funeral/

New Jersey State Board of Mortuary Science
P.O. Box 45009
Newark, N.J. 07101
Phone: 973-504-6425
http://www.njconsumeraffairs.gov/mort/

New Mexico Board of Thanatopractice
Toney Anaya Building
2550 Cerrillos Road, Second Floor
Santa Fe, New Mexico 87505
Phone: 505-476-4970
http://www.rld.state.nm.us/thanatopractice/

New York Bureau of Funeral Directing
New York Department of Health
Hedley Park Place 433 River St., Suite 303
Troy, NY 12180-2250
Phone: 518-402-0785
http://www.health.state.ny.us/professionals/patients/patient_rights/funeral.
htm

North Carolina Board of Funeral Services
1033 Wade Avenue, Suite 108
Raleigh, North Carolina 27605
Phone: 919-733-9380
Fax: 919-733-8271
http://www.ncbfs.org/

North Dakota State Board of Funeral Service
P.O. Box 161
Rugby, ND 58368-0161
Phone: 701-776-6222
http://www.nd.gov/funeral/

Ohio Board of Embalmers and Funeral Directors
77 South High Street, 16th Floor
Columbus, Ohio 43215-6108
Phone: 614-466-4252
http://www.funeral.ohio.gov/

Oklahoma Funeral Board
4545 N. Lincoln Blvd., Suite 175
Oklahoma City, OK 73105
Phone: 405-522-1790
http://www.okfuneral.com/

Oregon Mortuary and Cemetery Board

800 NE Oregon Street # 430
Portland OR 97232-2195
Phone: 971-673-1500
http://www.oregon.gov/MortCem/contact_us.shtml

Pennsylvania State Board of Funeral Directors
P.O. Box 2649
Harrisburg, PA 17105-2649
Phone: 717-783-3397
http://www.dos.state.pa.us/portal/server.pt/community/state_board_of_
funeral_directors/1249633

South Carolina Board of Funeral Service
Synergy Business Park;
Kingstree Building
110 Centerview Drive
Columbia, S.C. 29210

Mailing address:

PO Box 11329
Columbia, S.C. 29211-1329
Phone: 803-896-4497
http://www.llr.state.sc.us/POL/Funeral/

South Dakota Board of Funeral Service
810 N. Main Street, Suite 298
Spearfish, SD 57783
Phone: 605-642-1006
http://doh.sd.gov/Boards/FuneralBoard/default.aspxx

Tennessee Board of Funeral Directors and Embalmers/Burial Services Sections
Davy Crockett Tower
500 James Robertson Pkwy
Nashville, TN 37243-1144
Phone: 615-741-5062
http://tn.gov/commerce/boards/funeral/index.shtml

Texas Funeral Service Commission
333 Guadalupe Street
Suite 2-110
Austin, Texas 78701

Mailing Address:

P.O. Box 12217
Austin, TX 78711
Phone: 512-936-2474
Toll free: 888-667-4881
http://www.tfsc.state.tx.us/

Utah Department of Commerce – Funeral Services
160 East 300 South
Salt Lake City, Utah 84111
Phone: 801-530-6628
Toll-Free in Utah: 866-275-3675
http://www.dopl.utah.gov/licensing/funeral_service.html

Vermont Board of Funeral Service
128 State Street
Montpelier, Vermont 05633-1101
Phone: 802-828-2363
http://vtprofessionals.org/opr1/funeral/

Virginia Board of Funeral Directors & Embalmers
Perimeter Center
9960 Mayland Drive, Suite 300
Henrico, VA 23233-1463
Phone: 804-367-4479
http://www.dhp.state.va.us/funeral/

Washington State Funeral & Cemetery Board
Department of Licensing
PO Box 9020
Olympia, WA 98507-9020
Phone: 360-664-1555
http://www.dol.wa.gov/business/funeralcemetery/fcboard.html

West Virginia Board of Funeral Service Examiners
179 Summers Street, Suite 305
Charleston, West Virginia 25301
Phone: 304-558-0302
http://www.wvfuneralboard.com/MainLinks/CONTACTUS/tabid/669/Default.aspx

Wyoming Funeral Directors Association
1800 Carey Ave, 4th Floor
Cheyenne, WY 82002
Phone: 307-777-3507
http://www.wyfda.org/index_consumer.html

In extreme cases where a funeral home or cemetery acted criminally, you may need to turn the matter over to your state's Attorney General. To find your states' Attorney General, please follow this link to The National Association of Attorneys General.

ORGAN & TISSUE DONATION RESOURCES

American Association of Tissue Banks
1320 Old Chain Bridge Road, Suite 450
McLean, VA 22101
Phone: 703-827-9582
www.aatb.org

Donate Life
(information on organ donation)
Phone: 804-377-3580
http://donatelife.net/understanding-donation/

OrganDonor.gov
(A division of the US Department of Health & Human Services)
http://www.organdonor.gov/default.asp

Transplant Recipients International Organization, Inc.
2100 M Street, NW, #170-353
Washington, DC 20037-1233
Phone: 800-TRIO-386
http://www.trioweb.org

United Network for Organ Sharing (UNOS)
Post Office Box 2484
Richmond, Virginia 23218
Phone: 804-782-4800
http://www.unos.org

Street & package delivery address:

700 North 4th Street
Richmond, Virginia 23219
Phone: 804-782-4800
http://www.unos.org

WHOLE BODY DONATION RESOURCES

Please make sure you ask about body use, if you are interested in whole body donation. One or more of these companies may "split" a body up among requesting schools/institutions.

Anatomy Gifts Registry
7522 Connelley Drive, Suite M
Hanover, MD 21076
Phone: 800-300-5433
http://www.anatomicgift.com

LifeLegacy Foundation
6825 East Outlook Drive
Tucson, Arizona 85756
Phone: 888-774-4438
http://www.lifelegacy.org/

Association of American Medical Colleges
2450 N Street, NW
Washington, DC 20037-1126
Phone: 202-828-0400
http://services.aamc.org/memberlistings/index.cfm?fuseaction=home.
search&search_type=MS

MedCure, Inc.
12013 NE Marx Street
Portland, OR 97220
Phone: 866-560-2525
http://medcure.org/

BioGift Anatomical and Surgical Education Center
17819 NE Riverside Parkway, Suite C
Portland, Oregon 97230 MAP
Phone: 503-670-1799
24 hour: 866-670-1799
http://www.biogift.org/index.html

Medical Education and Research Institute - MERI
44 South Cleveland Street
Memphis, TN 38104
Phone: 800-360-6374
http://www.meri.org

Genesis Donor Program
Medical Education & Research Institute
44 South Cleveland
Memphis, TN 38104
Phone: 877-288-4483
http://www.genesislegacy.org

Science Care – Arizona Headquarters
21410 N. 19th Avenue
Suite 126
Phoenix, AZ 85027
Phone: 800-417-3747
http://www.sciencecare.com/index.htm

Science Care of Colorado
19301 E. 23rd Ave.

Aurora, CO 80011
Phone: 866-887-0900
http://www.sciencecare.com/index.htm

The University of Florida State Anatomical Board maintains a list of Body Donation Programs in the United States. This site lists state-by-state medical schools and other organizations that accept full body donations. For more information, visit this site: http://www.med.ufl.edu/anatbd/usprograms.html

DEATH MIDWIFERY, FUNERAL SOCIETIES AND HOME BURIAL RESOURCES

Crossings: Caring for Our Own at Death
7108 Holly Avenue
Takoma Park, MD 20912
Phone: 301-523-3033

Final Passages
P.O. Box 1721
Sebastopol, CA 95473
Phone: 707-824-0268
http://www.finalpassages.org/

National Association of Chevra Kadisha
85-18 117th Street
Richmond Hill, New York 11418
Phone: 718-847-6280
http://www.nasck.org/index.html

Mormon Share
http://www.mormonshare.com/relief-society/lds-burial-help.php

FUNERAL INDUSTRY RESOURCES

Cremation Association of North America
Phone: 312-245-1077
www.CremationAssociation.org

Funeral Consumers Alliance
Phone: 800-765-0107
www.funerals.org

Conference of Funeral Service Examining Boards
15 Northeast 3rd Street
PO Box 497
Washington, Indiana 47501

Phone: 812-254-7887

Funeral Service Consumer Assistance Program
National Research and Information Center
2250 E. Devon Ave., Ste. 250
Des Plaines, IL 60018,
Phone: 800- 662-7666
http://www.funerals.org/

The Green Burial Council
550-D
St. Michaels Drive
Santa Fe, NM 87505
Phone: 888-966-3330
http://www.greenburialcouncil.org

International Order of the Golden Rule
3520 Executive Center Drive, Suite 300
Austin, TX 78731
Phone: 800-637-8030
http://www.ogr.org/

International Cemetery and Funeral Association
Phone: 800-645-7700
www.icfa.org

Jewish Funeral Directors of America, Inc.
250 West 57th Street, #2329
New York, NY
http://www.jfda.org/Home/tabid/38/Default.aspx

National Funeral Directors Association
13625 Bishop's Drive
Brookfield, WI 53005
Phone: 800-228-6332
www.nfda.org

National Funeral Directors & Morticians Association, Inc.
6290 Shannon Parkway
Union City, GA 30291
Phone: 800-434-0958
http://www.nfdma.com/index.html

MILITARY FUNERAL HONORS RESOURCES

Department of Defense
Directorate for Public Inquiry and Analysis

Room 3A750, The Pentagon
Washington, DC 20301-1400
www.militaryfuneralhonors.osd.mil

MILITARY BURIAL BENEFITS

U.S. Department of Veterans Affairs
Burial & Memorial Benefits
810 Vermont Avenue, NW
Washington, DC 20420
http://www.cem.va.gov/

NAVY BURIAL AT SEA RESOURCES

United States Navy Mortuary Affairs
U.S. Department of Veterans Affairs
810 Vermont Avenue, NW
Washington, DC 20420
Phone: 866-787-0081

San Diego, Calif.
Naval Medical Center
Decedent Affairs Code: BUB
34800 Bob Wilson Drive
San Diego, CA 92134-5000
Phone: 800-290-7410

Norfolk, Va.
Commander, Naval Medical Center
ATTN: Code 0210C
620 John Paul Jones Cir.
Portsmouth, VA 23708-5100
Phone: 757-953-2617\2618

Bremerton, Wash.
Commanding Officer
Naval Hospital Bremerton
Code: 015-BAS/HP01 Boone Road
Bremerton, WA 98312-1898
Phone: 360-475-4790/4543

Jacksonville, Fla.
Branch Medical Clinic
P. O. Box 280148
Naval Station
Mayport, FL 32228-0148

Phone: 904-270-4285

Honolulu, Hi.
Navy Liaison Unit
Tripler Army Medical Center
Tripler AMC, HI 96859-5000
Phone: 808-433-4709, 577-7590

COAST GUARD BURIAL AT SEA PROGRAM RESOURCES

Commanding Officer
USCG ISC (pw)
4000 Coast Guard Blvd.
Portsmouth, VA 23703-2199
Attn: CWO Van Clief

HOME FUNERAL RESOURCES

Crossings: Caring for Our Own at Death
7108 Holly Avenue
Takoma Park, MD 20912
Phone: 301-523-3033
http://www.crossings.net/

Final Passages
P.O. Box 1721
Sebastopol, CA 95473
Phone: 707-824-0268
http://www.finalpassages.org/

National Association of Chevra Kadisha
85-18 117th Street
Richmond Hill, New York 11418
Phone: 718-847-6280
http://www.nasck.org/index.html

Mormon Share
http://www.mormonshare.com/relief-society/lds-burial-help.php

HOMEMADE CASKET RESOURCES

Last Things: Alternatives at the End of Life
http://www.lastthings.net/coffins.html

DotCom Funerals

http://www.dotcomfunerals.com/do-it-yourself-coffin/diy-coffin

GREEN BURIAL RESOURCES

The Green Burial of Steve Sall
http://vimeo.com/groups/16610/videos/16916389

CBS News Video: Natural Undertaking
http://www.youtube.com/watch?v=ccN5pKaJa3U

Natural Burial Series – Terry Ward
http://www.youtube.com/watch?v=JPqmxE576Bw

Final Footprint
Phone: 650-726-5255
http://www.finalfootprint.com/index.html

The Green Burial Council
550-D
St. Michaels Drive
Santa Fe, NM 87505
Phone: 888-966-3330
http://www.greenburialcouncil.org/

The Champion Company – Enigma Eco-balming Products
P.O. Box 967
Springfield OH 45501
Phone: 800-328-0115
www.enigma-champion.com

All Natural Green Caskets
Nationwide Coverage
Multiple Locations
Phone: 855-740-8423
www.NaturalGreenCaskets.com

Concept Caskets, Inc.
2755 Principale
St-Edouard de Lotbinière Quebec G0S 1Y0
Phone: 800-463-9515
www.conceptcaskets.com

Artistic Urns, Inc.
1260 Rolling Green Drive
Acworth GA 30102
Phone: 770-591-1565
www.artisticwoodurns.com

Connecticut Casket Company
31 Moulton Court
Willimantic CT 06226

Phone: 877-706-5692
www.connecticutcasketcompany.com

Bamboo Caskets
317 Francois-Seguin
Boucherville Quebec J4B 1L6
Phone: 514-240-7115
www.bamboocaskets.com

Eternal Reefs
P.O. Box 2473
Decatur GA 30031
Phone: 404-875-1876
www.eternalreefs.com

Care Caskets
7118 Summerfield Rd.
Lambertville MI 48144
Phone: 877-568-6027
www.carecaskets.com

The Casket Makers
Lummi Reservation, WA
Phone: 360-758-2996
http://www.thecasketmakers.com/

Florence Casket Company
16 Bardwell St.
Florence MA 01062
Phone: 800-543-6929
www.florencecasket.com

Forlora, Inc.
1006 Sullivan Drive
White Bluff IN 37817
Phone: 615-797-2348
www.forloradesigns.com

Green Casket Company, LLC.
32 Walter Crawford Rd.
Candler, NC 28715
Phone: 828-301-3916
http://www.green-casket.com/index.php

Green Legacy Caskets
503 North Greene Rd.
Goshen IN 45626
Phone: 574-534-5216
www.greenlegacycaskets.com

Hainsworth USA LTD

2480 Route 97, Suite 7
Glenwood MD 21738
Phone: 866-763-0485
www.naturallegacy.com

In The Light Urns
40984 Grouse Drive
Three Rivers CA 92371
Phone: 800-757-3488
www.inthelighturns.com

Kent Casket Co.
545 Eighth Ave. Ste. 401
New York NY
Phone: 888-534-7239
www.kentcasket.com

Kinkaraco-Green Burial Products
126 Precita Ave.
San Francisco CA 94110
Phone: 415-874-9698
www.greenburialproducts.com

Limbo (eco-friendly urns)
33300 Egypt Lane
Suite B900
Magnolia, TX 77354
www.limbo-northamerica.com

Natural Burial Company
PO Box 11204Eugene, Oregon 97440
Phone: 503-493-9258
http://www.naturalburialcompany.com/

Nature's Casket
P.O. Box 3
Longmont CO 80502
Phone: 720-373-7613
www.naturescasket.com

Neptune Memorial Reefs
1250 South Pine Island Road Ste500
Plantation FL 33324
Phone: 888-716-7333
www.nmreef.com

New England Casket Company
1141 Bennington Street
East Boston MA 02128
Phone: 617-569-1510

www.newenglandcasket.com

Passages International, Inc.
6819 Cochiti Rd. SE
Albuquerque NM 87108
Phone: 888-480-6400
www.passagesinternational.com

Rustic River
257 SE Roberts
Gresham OR 97080
Phone: 503-618-8176
www.oregongreencaskets.com/green-caskets.html

Sustainable Funeral Products
P.O. Box 385
Sandy OR 97055
Phone: 503-893-8775
www.sustainablefuneralproducts.com

Victoriaville Funeral Supplies
P.O. Box 520
Victoriaville Quebec G6P 6T3
Phone: 819-752-3388
www.victoriavillegroup.com

GREEN CEMETERIES IN THE U.S.

People have different ideas of what "green" means. The cemeteries listed here call themselves "green" but they may or may not meet your own definition of green. Those certified as green by the Green Burial Council, with either one, two or three leaves, are marked with this symbol: ‌‌ʚ.

ʚ **Joshua Tree Memorial Park** – a hybrid burial ground in the high desert
60121 29 Palms Highway
Joshua Tree CA 92252
Phone: 760-366-9210
http://www.joshuatreememorialpark.com/index.php

Forever Fernwood – Funeral home, cemetery, and crematory with a green burial site
301 Tennessee Valley Road
Mill Valley, CA 94941
Phone: 415-383-7100
http://www.foreverfernwood.com/index.html

Glendale Memorial Nature Preserve – 350 acres located in Florida's Panhandle

region
297 Railroad Avenue
DeFuniak Springs, FL 32433
Phone: 850-859-2141
http://www.glendalenaturepreserve.org/index.htm

Eternal Rest Memories Park
2966 Belcher Road
Dunedin, Florida 34698
Phone: 727-733-2300
http://eternalrest.com

ଓ **Prairie Creek Conservation Cemetery** – 78 acre conservation burial
ground in north Florida
7204 SE County Road 234
Gainesville, FL 32641
Phone: 352-317-7307
www.conservationburialinc.org

ଓ **Honey Creek Woodlands Conservation Burial Grounds** – part of 2,00
acres owned by The Monastery of the Holy Spirit
2625 Highway 212 SW
Conyers, GA 30094
Phone: 770-483-7535
http://honeycreekwoodlands.com/

ଓ **Greenview at Roselawn Memorial Park** – hybrid burial ground (within a
traditional cemetery)
924 South 6th Street
Springfield IL 62703
Phone: 217-525-1661
www.roselawninfo.com

ଓ **Kessler Woods at Washington Park North Cemetery** – a hybrid burial
ground
2702 Kessler Blvd. West Drive
Indianapolis IN 46228
Phone: 317-259-1253
www.flanner-buchanan.com

Cedar Brook Burial Ground, Inc.
175 Boothby Road
P.O. Box 511
Limington, ME 04049-0511
207-637-2085
http://mainegreencemetery.com/

Mount Carmel Cemetery
138 Goodell Street
Wyandotte MI 48192
Phone: 734-285-1722
www.ste-wyan.org

ଓ **Ridgeview Memorial Gardens** – a hybrid burial ground (within a
traditional cemetery)
0-5151 8th Ave SW

Grandville MI 49418
Phone: 616-249-8439
http://ridgeviewmemorialgardens.com/GreenBurialOptions.aspx

ೞ **Steelmantown Cemetery**
101 Steelmantown Road
Steelmantown, N.J.
Phone: 609-628-2297
http://www.steelmantowncemetery.com/index.html

ೞ **Greensprings** – 93 acres of woodland in the Finger Lakes region of New York
PO Box 415
Irish Hill Road
Newfield, NY 14867
Phone: 607-564-7577
http://naturalburial.org/index.php

ೞ **White Haven Memorial Park** – a natural burial ground located in a wild-flower meadow
210 Marsh Road
Pittsford (Rochester) NY 14534
Phone: 585-586-5250
www.whitehavenmemorialpark.com

ೞ **The Garden of Renewal at Pine Forest Memorial Gardens** – a wooded hybrid burial ground
770 Stadium Dr.
Wake Forest NC 27587
919-556-6776
www.pineforestmemorial.com

ೞ **Green Hills Cemetery** – a hybrid burial ground
24 New Leicester Hwy
Asheville NC 28806
828-252-9831
www.greenhillscemeteryasheville.com

ೞ **Forest Lawn Memorial Park**
1498 Sand Hill Rd.
Candler NC 28715
828-667-8715
www.moorefh.net

ೞ **Foxfield Preserve Nature Cemetery** - a conservation burial ground
9878 Alabama Ave. S. W
P. O. Box 202
Wilmot, OH 44689
Phone: 330-763-1331
http://foxfieldpreserve.org/

ೞ **Estacada Cemetery District** – a hybrid burial ground
P.O. Box 1390

Estacada OR 97023
Phone: 503-730-0142

ଓ **Riverview Cemetery** – a hybrid burial ground (within a traditional cemetery)
8421 SW Macadam Ave.
Portland OR 97219
Phone: 503-246-6488
www.riverviewcemeteryfuneralhome.com

ଓ **Valley Memorial Park & Funeral Home** – a hybrid burial ground (within a traditional cemetery)
3809 SE Tualatin Valley Hwy
Hillsboro OR 97123
Phone: 503-648-5444
www.valleymemorialoregon.com

ଓ **Oakwood Cemetery**- a hybrid burial ground (within a traditional cemetery)
600 N. Oakland Ave.
Sharon PA 16146
724-346-4775

ଓ **Ramsey Creek Preserve** – the first conservation burial ground in the US
390 Cobb Bridge Road
Westminster SC 29693
Phone: 864-647-7798
http://www.memorialecosystems.com/Home/tabid/36/Default.aspx

ଓ **Greenhaven Preserve** – a natural burial ground
1701 Vanboklen Road
Eastover SC 29044
803-403-9561
www.greenhavenpreserve.com

ଓ **Mt. Pleasant Cemetery Association** – a hybrid burial ground
2001 E. 12th St.
Sioux Falls SD 57103
605-339-4760
www.mtpleasantsf.com

Ethician Family Cemetery
1401 19th Street
Huntsville, TX 77340
Phone: 936-581-4302
http://www.ethicianfamilycemetery.org/

ଓ **Our Lady of the Rosary** – a hybrid burial ground (within a traditional cemetery)
330 Berry lane
Georgetown TX 38626

512-863-8411
www.olotr.com

ଔ **Lakeview Cemetery** - a hybrid burial ground (within a traditional cemetery)
1640 East Lakeview Dr.
Bountiful UT 84010
801-298-1564
www.memorialutah.com

ଔ **Moles Greenacres Memorial Park** – a natural burial ground
5700 Northwest Dr.
Ferndale WA 98248
360-384-3401
www.molesfuneralhomes.com

ଔ **White Eagle Memorial Preserve** – 20 acres set within 1,300 acres of wilderness preserve
401 Ekone Rd.
Goldendale, WA 98620
Phone: 206-338-1041.
http://www.naturalburialground.com/default.htm

ଔ **Woodlawn Cemetery** – a hybrid burial ground (within a traditional cemetery)
7509 Riverview Rd.
Snohomish WA 98290
360-568-5560
www.woodlawncemeterysnohomish.com

PROMESSION RESOURCES

Promessa UK
Wellington House
East Road
Cambridge, England
CB1 1BH
Phone: +44 01223 389 005 *note, this is an international number
http://www.promessa.org.uk/index.php

ALKALINE HYDROLYSIS RESOURCES

Resomation LTD
583 Mosspark Boulevard
Glasgow, Scotland
G52 1SB

Phone: +44 (0) 141 882 3868
http://www.resomation.com/index.htm

Matthews International Cremation Division
2045 Sprint Blvd.
Apopka, FL 32703-7762
Toll-Free: 888-486-7713
Phone: 407-886-5533
http://www.matthewscremation.com/technology/bio-cremation.aspx

CRYONICS RESOURCES

Alcor Life Extension Foundation
7895 East Acoma Drive Suite 110
Scottsdale, Arizona 85260
Phone: 480-905-1906
http://www.alcor.org/index.html

American Cryonics Society
P.O. Box 1509.
Cupertino, CA 95015
Phone: 415-686-5292
http://americancryonics.org/links.html

The Cryonics Institute
24355 Sorrentino Court
Clinton Township, MI 48035
Phone: 586-791-5961
http://www.cryonics.org/

The Cryonics Society
http://www.cryonicssociety.org/index.html

PLASTINATION RESOURCES

Body Worlds: Institute for Plastination
http://www.bodyworlds.com/en/info/contact.html

The University of Arizona Plastination Science Laboratory
Joshua A. Lopez, LFP
Scientific Director
AHSC 3109
Box 245044
Tucson, AZ 85724
Phone: 520-626-6645
http://plastinate.arizona.edu/

University of Michigan
Office of Medical Education
3740 Medical Science II Building
Ann Arbor, MI 48109-5608
Phone: 734-615-2597
http://www.med.umich.edu/anatomy/plastinate/Contact_Us.html

MUMMIFICATION RESOURCES

ABC News
http://abcnews.go.com/US/story?id=6292080&page=1

CBS News
http://www.cbsnews.com/video/watch/?id=669346n

Edit International
http://www.editinternational.com/photos.php?id=47ddcf51d5a3e

Summum
707 Genesee Avenue
Salt Lake City, Utah 84104
http://www.summum.org/mummification/

BURIAL AT SEA RESOURCES

For more information about burial at sea, refer to the Code of Federal Regulations at http://www.epa.gov/region4/water/oceans/documents/burialcode.pdf

Region 1:
Connecticut, Maine, Massachusetts, New Hampshire, Rhode Island and Vermont

Ann Rodney (rodney.ann@epa.gov)
Burial at Sea Coordinator
US EPA Region 1
1 Congress St.
Boston, MA 02114-2023
Phone: (617) 918-1538

Region 2:
New Jersey, New York, Puerto Rico and U.S. Virgin Islands

Patricia Pechko (pechko.patricia@epa.gov)
Burial At Sea Coordinator
US EPA Region 2

290 Broadway
New York, NY 10007-1866
Phone: (212) 637-3796

Region 3:

District of Columbia, Delaware, Maryland, Pennsylvania, and Virginia

Renee Searfoss (searfoss.renee@epa.gov)
Burial At Sea Coordinator
EPA Region 3
1650 Arch Street
Philadelphia, PA 19103
Phone: (215) 814-2137

Region 4:

Alabama, Florida, Georgia, Kentucky, Mississippi, North Carolina, South
Carolina and Tennessee

Gary Collins (collins.garyw@epa.gov)
U.S. Environmental Protection Agency, Region 4
61 Forsyth Street Southwest
Atlanta, GA 30303
Phone: (404) 562-9395

Region 6:

Louisiana and Texas

Karen McCormick (mccormick.karen@epa.gov)
Burial At Sea Coordinator
US EPA Region 6
1445 Ross Avenue, Suite 1200
Dallas, TX 75202-2733
Phone: (214) 665-8365

Region 9:

California, Hawaii, American Samoa, Guam, Northern Marianas and Trust
Territories

Allan Ota (ota.allan@epa.gov)
Burial At Sea Coordinator
U.S. EPA Region 9
75 Hawthorne Street
San Francisco, CA 94105
Phone: (415) 972-3476

Region 10:

Chris Meade (meade.chris@epa.gov)
U.S. EPA Region 10
PO Box 20370
Juneau, AK 99802-0370

Phone: (907) 585-7622

Coastal Sunset Memorial Services
Captain Dennis Longaberger
125 Harbor Way, Ste. 13
Santa Barbara, CA 93109
Phone: 805-962-8222
http://www.coastalsunsetmemorial.com/index.html

New England Burial at Sea, LLC.
Captain Brad White
Phone: (617) 966.1986
http://www.newenglandburialsatsea.com/

SeaServices – Nationwide Maritime Funeral Providers
Phone: 888-551-1277
http://www.seaservices.com/index.html

MEMORIAL REEF RESOURCES

Neptune Society
1250 S. Pine Island Road, Suite 500
Plantation, FL 33324
Phone: 888-637-8863
http://www.neptunesociety.com

Eternal Reefs
P.O. BOX 2473
Decatur, GA. 30031
Phone: 888-423-7333
http://eternalreefs.com

Great Burial Reef (R)
4949 State Road 64 East, Suite 302
Bradenton, FL 34208
Phone: (941) 548-6123
http://www.greatburialreef.com/index.html

Poseidon's Garden
1616-102 W Cape Coral Pkwy
Suite #164
Cape Coral, FL 33991
Phone: 239-549-0000
http://www.poseidonsgarden.com/index.html

Mexico Beach Artificial Reef Association, Inc
PO Box 13006
Mexico Beach FL 32410
Phone: 615-479-4762

http://www.mbara.org/memorial-reef-program.cfm

Walter Marine (Reefmaker Artificial Reefs)
PO Box 998
22605 Andrews Lane
Orange Beach, AL 36561
Phone: 251-979-2200
http://www.reefmaker.net/

AIRPLANE SCATTERING RESOURCES

Final Flights®
Post Office Box 1912
Spring Valley, CA 91979
Phone: 888- 333-1165
http://www.finalflights.com/

Aerial Missions
Jim & Wendy Howard
10721 25th Ave. SW
Seattle, WA 98146
Phone: 206-409-0229
http://www.aerialmissions.com/

Homeward Bound
21355 East Fremont Place
Centennial, Co. 80016
http://ashscattering.org/Home/tabid/58/Default.aspx

Air Legacy, LLC
P.O. Box 1472
Englewood, CO 80150
Phone: 720-346-7581
http://www.airlegacy.com/home

CREMATION FIREWORKS RESOURCES

Angels Flight
Castaic, CA
818-934-0035
http://www.angels-flight.net/index.htm

Oceanic West, Inc.
P.O. Box 1310
Tiburon, CA 94920
Phone: 415-889-5023
https://oceanicwest.com/Home_Page.html

SPACEFLIGHT RESOURCES

Celestis – Memorial Spaceflights
2536 Amherst St,. Suite J
Houston, TX 77005
Phone: 866-776-2538
http://www.celestis.com/default.asp

HELIUM BALLOON SCATTERING RESOURCES

Eternal Ascent Society
8395 Yew Pine Court
Crystal River, FL 34428
Phone: 800-808-2082
http://www.eternalascent.com/index.html

MEMORIAL JEWELRY RESOURCES

LifeGem
836 Arlington Heights Rd. #311
Elk Grove Village, IL 60007
Phone: 866-543-3436
http://www.lifegem.com/

Memorial Gallery
P.O. Box 679
Gig Harbor, WA 98335
http://www.funeral-urn.com/index.aspx

Passages Int'l., Inc.
6819 Cochiti Rd. SE
Albuquerque, NM 87108
Phone: 505-830-2500
http://www.passagesinternational.com/

Perfect Memorials
PO Box 1037
Minnetonka, MN 55345-0037
http://www.perfectmemorials.com/

NON-TRADITIONAL BURIAL CONTAINER SUPPLIERS

Please note that this list is far from exhaustive. It does, however, introduce you to the sometimes bizarre world of non-traditional burial containers and may help you to find or design the perfect unique container for your loved one.

The Old Pine Box
PO Box 1713
Edgewood, NM 87015
Phone: 505-286-9410
http://www.theoldpinebox.com/index.html

Crazy Coffins
Crabtree Mill
Hempshill Lane
Bulwell, Nottingham, NG6 8PF
Phone: 0115 977 1571 *note: this is international
email: office@crazycoffins.co.uk
http://www.crazycoffins.co.uk/index.html

Trappist Caskets
16632 Monastery Road
Peosta, IA 52068
Phone: 888-433-6934
http://www.trappistcaskets.com/

Art Caskets
Phone: 877-278-2275
http://artcaskets.com/index.html

Sweet Earth Casket and Cradle Shop
1335 Third Street West
Kalispell, Montana 59901
Phone: 406-257-0092

Bert & Bud's Vintage Coffins
PO Box 995
Murray, KY 42071
Phone: 877-371-9279
http://www.vintagecoffins.com/index.html

Caskets by Design
M&T Construction
14339 Channel Rd
Caldwell, Idaho 83607
Phone: 208-455-6290
http://www.casketsbydesign.com/

A Fine Farewell (burial shrouds)
http://www.afinefarewell.com/index.html

Final Footprint

195 Airport Blvd.
Princeton by the Sea
CA 94019
Phone: 650-726-5255
http://www.finalfootprint.com/

FUNERAL/MEMORIAL PROGRAM SUPPLY COMPANIES

The Funeral Program Site
P.O. Box 270
Orinda, California 94563
Phone: 800-773-9026
http://www.funeralprogram-site.com/

Funeral Program Templates
http://funeralprogram-templates.com/index.html

Elegant Memorials
PO Box 38082
Charlotte, NC 28278
Phone: 888-295-1940
http://elegantmemorials.com/funeral-program-templates

Funeral Programs Online
5330 W Burleigh Street
Milwaukee, WI 53210
Phone: 866-216-9881
http://funeralprogramsonline.com/index.html

CREDIT REPORTING AGENCIES

You should report your loved one's death to the three credit reporting agencies as soon as possible. You can contact the agencies by phone. They will, however, want you to mail them a copy of your loved one's death certificate.

Equifax Information Services LLC
Office of Consumer Affairs
PO Box 150139
Atlanta, GA 30348
Phone: 800-525-6285
http://equifax.com

*Note: This is Equifax's fraud division phone number. This number should be able to direct you to the correct office to speak with.

Experian
> 475 Anton Blvd.
> Costa Mesa, CA 92626
> Phone: 714-830-7000
> https://www.experian.com/

TransUnion
> P.O. Box 6790
> Fullerton, CA 92834
> Phone: 800-493-2392
> http://www.transunion.com/

FINANCIAL SERVICES

You might find, after the death of a spouse or parent especially, that you need help organizing your loved one's finances. The National Foundation for Credit Counseling, a non-profit, is the nation's largest financial counseling organization. They may be able to offer assistance, or at least to tell you whom to contact.

National Foundation for Credit Counseling
> 2000 M Street, NW Suite 505
> Washington, DC 20036
> Phone: 202-677-4300
> http://www.nfcc.org/index.cfm

OTHER RESOURCES

AARP
> 601 E Street, NW
> Washington DC 20049
> Phone: 888-687-2277
> http://www.aarp.org/

Grief and loss resources
> www.aarp.org/griefandloss/

Association for Conflict Resolution (for mediation)
> 12100 Sunset Hills Rd., Suite #130
> Reston, VA 20190
> Phone: 703-234-4141
> Fax: 703-435-4390

www.acrnet.org

National Hospice & Palliative Care Organization (NHPCO)

1700 Diagonal Road, Suite 625
Alexandria, VA 22314
Phone: 703-837-1500
Phone: 800-658-8898
http://www.nho.org

Society for Critical Care Medicine

500 Midway Drive
Mount Prospect, Illinois 60056 USA
Phone: 847-827-6869
www.sccm.org

ONLINE TRIBUTE RESOURCES

Legacy.com

820 Davis Street
Suite 210
Evanston, IL 60201
http://www.legacy.com/NS/

Tributes, Inc.

280 Summer Street, Fourth Floor
Boston, MA 02210
http://www.tributes.com/

The MuchLoved Charitable Trust

PO Box 702
Amersham,
Buckinghamshire
HP6 9BW
http://www.muchloved.com/g_home.aspx

Remembered.com – Online Memorial Website

P.O. Box 900578
Sandy, Utah 84090
http://remembered.com/home

SUPPORT GROUPS & OTHER RESOURCES

AARP Grief & Loss - We are a nonprofit, nonpartisan organization that helps people 50 and over improve the quality of their lives. www.aarp.org/griefandloss/

Aging Parents and Elder Care – An organization dedicated to helping people overcome the challenges of elder care. http://www.aging-parents-and-elder-care.com/Pages/SupportGroup.html

Alive Alone - An organization that benefits bereaved parents by providing a self-help network and publications to promote communication and healing. www.alivealone.org

American Cancer Society - Programs and services to help people with cancer and their loved ones understand cancer, manage their lives through treatment and recovery, and find the emotional support they need. http://www.cancer.org/Treatment/SupportProgramsServices/index

American Pain Society - A multidisciplinary community that brings together a diverse group of scientists, clinicians and other professionals to increase the knowledge of pain and transform public policy and clinical practice to reduce pain-related suffering. http://www.ampainsoc.org/

Bereaved Parents USA - A national non-profit self-help group that offers support, understanding, compassion and hope especially to the newly bereaved, be they bereaved parents grandparents or siblings struggling to rebuild their lives after the death of their children, grandchildren or siblings. www.bereavedparentsusa.org/

Center for Loss & Life Transition – An organization that compassionately supports both mourners, by walking with them in their unique life journeys, and professional and lay caregivers, by serving as an educational resource and professional forum. www.centerforloss.com

CJ Foundation for SIDS (Sudden Infant Death Syndrome) - The largest non-government funder of programs meeting the needs of the SIDS community http://www.cjsids.org/

Fernside Online - A non-profit organization offering support and advocacy to grieving families who have experienced a death. www.fernside.org

Funeral Service Association of Canada - Provides programs and services to enhance and promote the value of the funeral profession in Canada. http://www.fsac.ca/

Gerontological Society of America - The oldest and largest interdisciplinary organization devoted to research, education, and practice in the field of aging. http://www.geron.org/

GriefShare - A friendly, caring group of people who will walk alongside you through one of life's most difficult experiences. You don't have to go through the grieving process alone. http://www.griefshare.org/

Growth House - Gives you free access to over 4,000 pages of high-quality education materials about end-of-life care, palliative medicine, and hospice care, including the full text of several books. www.growthhouse.org

GROWW – A non-profit online grief recovery resource. www.groww.org/

Innovations in End-of-Life Care – An online journal that features peer-reviewed promising practices in end-of-life care, useful tools, selected bibliographies, and other resources. http://www2.edc.org/lastacts/

Mayo Clinic Support & Bereavement Groups - Support groups are for people with a disease or the ill person's relatives who want to share their concerns with others and learn how to address disease-specific problems. Bereavement groups allow those who have lost a loved one to share their struggles with others who have experienced a similar loss. http://www.mayoclinic.org/support-groups/

National ALS Association - the only non-profit organization fighting Lou Gehrig's Disease on every front. http://www.alsa.org/

National Association for Home Care - The nation's largest trade association representing the interests and concerns of home care agencies, hospices, home care aide organizations, and medical equipment suppliers. http://www.nahc.org/

National Association of Social Workers - The largest membership organization of professional social workers in the world. NASW works to enhance the professional growth and development of its members, to create and maintain professional standards, and to advance sound social policies. http://www.naswdc.org/

National Catholic Ministry to the Bereaved (NCMB) - Ensures services and education which will respond to the needs of people throughout the grief process. http://www.griefwork.org/

National Hospice and Palliative Care Organization - The largest nonprofit membership organization representing hospice and palliative care programs and professionals in the United States. http://www.nhpco.org/templates/1/homepage.cfm

National SIDS and Infant Death Program Support Center - a national nonprofit health care organization, is dedicated to the prevention of sudden infant death and the promotion of infant health through an aggressive, comprehensive nationwide program http://www.sids.org

SHARE Pregnancy & and Infant Loss Support - Serves those whose lives are touched by the tragic death of a baby through early pregnancy loss, stillbirth, or in he first few months of life. http://www.nationalshare.org/

The Compassionate Friends - Assists families toward the positive resolution of grief following the death of a child of any age and to provide information to help others be supportive. http://www.compassionatefriends.org/home.aspx

UMASS Bereavement & Support Groups - Assists people with the loss and grief they experience after the passing of a loved one. http://www.umassmemorial.org/BereavementSupportGroup

WidowNet - the first online information and self-help resource for, and by, widows and widowers. http://www.widownet.org/index.shtml

Glossary of Terms

Administrator – When a person dies without leaving a Will, the court will appoint an Administrator to dispense with the decedent's estate.

Alkaline Hydrolysis – The use of lye, an alkali, and water to reduce a body to bone. Resomation LTD, a Scottish company, adapted the technique for the human death industry and partnered with Matthew International Cremation Division to bring it to the United States.

Apportionment – Dividing cremated remains into separate portions – possibly for disposition at different locations.

Apprentice – A person who learns the funeral business by working with a licensed Funeral Director or Embalmer.

Arrangement Conference – A meeting between funeral home staff and someone making funeral/disposition arrangements for a loved one.

Arrangement Room – A room commonly found in funeral homes where staff members meet with family members to discuss arrangements.

Ashes – A misnomer referring to the ash-like crushed bone remains left after cremation.

Aspirate – The process of removing gases and fluids from the abdominal cavity. Often performed with a trocar.

At-need Funeral – A funeral arranged when a person dies, as opposed to a pre-planned funeral.

Attorney in Fact - A person who is granted a Power of Attorney.

Authorized Representative – The person who has legal right to represent the decedent in making arrangements for final disposition and services.

Background Drapes – Drapes hung on a frame to add a "background" for a casket. Usually used during a viewing.

Beneficiary – The person (beneficiary) who benefits from a trust, will or insurance policy.

Bequest – A gift made to another via a Will. Can be property (real estate, paintings, books, etc.) or monetary.

Bereaved – Those grieving for a loved one.

Burial Certificate/ Permit – A permit issued by the local government allowing for a burial.

Burial Garments – Clothing made especially to dress the deceased. Some religions and societies mandate or recommend specific apparel.

Burial Insurance – An insurance policy that pays out in funeral expenses rather than in cash. Often taken out by a parent so that children will not have the burden of paying for a funeral.

Burial Shroud – A cloth wrap, winding sheet, drape or bag that is used to wrap a body for burial.

Burial Vault – Often made of reinforced concrete, this is installed around a casket so that the ground above it will not sink as it settles. Some burial vaults are sealed to offer "protection" from moisture.

Burial – The act of placing a body in the ground.

Calling hours – Hours when visitors may visit during a Wake or Viewing/ Visitation.

Canopy – A portable canvas awning or tent used to cover a gravesite during a burial or committal service.

Casket – A rectangular container used to house human remains.

Casket Liner – Like a burial vault, this is meant to keep the ground over a buried casket from settling or sinking. Unlike a vault, a liner does not fully surround the casket.

Casket Veil – A transparent veil that covers an open casket to keep insects off of the remains.

Catafalque – The platform or stand on which a casket rests during a funeral service.

Cemetery – Land specifically set aside for burial of the dead.

Cenotaph – A monument erected to honor a person or persons who have died (and whose remains are) elsewhere.

Chapel – A small, intimate place of worship. Funeral homes often have a room called a "chapel" where services can be held.

Church Truck – A collapsible catafalque (casket stand or platform) which may be on wheels.

Codicil – An amendment to a Will which makes a change to the original document.

Coffin – A container used to house remains. Unlike a casket, which is four sided, coffins are wedge-shaped six-sided containers.

Columbarium – A room, building or wall with niches meant to hold urns in which cremated remains have been placed.

Committal Service – The final part of a funeral service when the body or ashes are interred (buried, placed in a columbarium, etc.)

Conservancy Land – Green burial land that has been set aside by a Trust so that it will never be developed.

Contest – A legal challenge to a Will.

Coroner – A publicly appointed officer whose job it is to investigate all deaths that are of other-than-natural-cause.

Cortege – A funeral procession.

Cosmetology – The use of makeup (cosmetics) and restorative products to give the dead a "lifelike" appearance.

Cremains or Cremated Remains – the bone residue left after cremation. These are usually crushed to an ash-like powder.

Cremation – The use of high heat (1400 to 1800 degrees Fahrenheit) to reduce a body to bone.

Cremation Permit – A permit issued by the local government allowing cremation.

Crematory – A building that houses a specially-designed furnace (or retort) where bodies are cremated.

Cremulator - A mechanical device for crushing bone into an ash-like substance after cremation.

Cryonics – The process of deep-freezing a decedent in the hope that future medicine will be able to revive the person.

Crypt – A room or vault used as a burial place.

Death Certificate – A legal document issued by a coroner or other medical practitioner testifying to cause, date and place of death.

Death Midwife – A person trained to assist family members care for their own dead.

Death Notice – A short notice usually placed in a newspaper notifying the community that someone has died. Will often include information about any services to be held in that person's honor.

Deceased – A person who has died.

Decedent – A person who has died.

Derma Surgeon – A relatively new term used by some in the funeral industry to refer to the Elma

Direct Burial – A burial that occurs without any services preceding it.

Direct Cremation – A cremation that occurs without any services preceding it.

Direct Disposition – A term that refers to either direct burial or direct cremation.

Disinter – To dig up remains from a grave or tomb, to exhume.

Display Room – A room in a funeral home set aside for displaying caskets, urns, grave liners, burial garments, etc. that are available for purchase.

Disposition – In funeral terms, refers to the method a body is laid to rest, be it cremation, burial, etc.

Door Badge – A floral arrangement hung on the exterior door of a home to announce that a death has occurred.

Embalm – The process of preserving a body with the use of embalming fluids, usually a mixture that includes formaldehyde.

Embalmer – A trained and licensed individual who embalms (preserves) bodies through the replacement of blood with embalming fluid.

Embalming – The process of preserving a body with the use of embalming fluids, usually a mixture that includes formaldehyde.

Embalming Fluid – A combination of chemicals used to preserve a body.

Embalming Table – A specialty table, usually of stainless steel or metal with a porcelain top that holds a corpse through the embalming process. Usually contains a drain and splash guards.

Entombment – The process of placing a body in a tomb or grave.

Escheat – The law that returns property to the state when there are no heirs.

Estate Tax – A tax imposed upon heirs when property is transferred through an inheritance.

Eulogy – A laudatory speech or written tribute praising someone who has died.

Executor/Executrix – The person (male/female) appointed by a Will to administer an estate.

Exhume - To dig up remains from a grave or tomb, to disinter.

Family Car – The car, often a limousine or Town Car, used to carry the immediate family to a funeral service or burial.

Family Room – A room within a funeral home meant to give the family of the deceased privacy.

Final Disposition – The last process when laying a person to rest, be it by burial, cremation, etc.

Final Rites – Rites performed for a person in danger of dying, usually by a religious leader.

First Call – When a funeral director or embalmer is called to retrieve a body.

Flower Car – The car used to transport floral arrangements to/from the various funeral venues.

Flower Stands and Racks – Adjustable stands used to display floral arrangements during various funeral services.

Full Body Donation – The term used to indicate that a full body (as opposed to organ or tissue donation only) has been donated to science, to a medical facility, etc.

Funeral – A ceremony honoring a dead person. Usually prior to cremation or burial.

Funeral (or Burial) Society – Groups which aid members when a death occurs, either through caring for the body, or through the negotiation of lower funeral costs for members.

Funeral Arrangements – The services and products purchased from a funeral home, usually by next-of-kin. Also refers to the meeting between a funeral director and next-of-kin when the services and products are agreed upon and financial arrangements are made.

Funeral Coach – A special car, often a hearse, used to transport a casketed body.

Funeral Director – A licensed professional who oversees funeral arrangements, including preparation of the body for burial or cremation, and maintains a funeral home for those purposes.

Funeral Home – A place of business where funeral arrangements are made and bodies are prepared for final disposition.

Funeral Insurance/Burial Insurance – An insurance policy that pays out in funeral expenses rather than in cash. Often taken out by a parent so that children will not have the burden of paying for a funeral.

Funeral Procession – A formal escort of the body, usually in automobiles, beginning at the venue where a funeral service was held and ending at the place of final disposition.

Funeral Rule – A law, overseen by the Federal Trade Commission, that mandates how funeral homes must conduct business.

Funeral Service – A ceremony held in honor of a decedent, which can be either religious or secular.

Funeral Spray - A bouquet of flowers sent to the home of a decedent or to the funeral home as a tribute to the deceased.

Grave Liner - A box or receptacle made of reinforced concrete or other durable material into which the casket is placed to prevent the ground above it from sinking as the ground settles. States do not require one, though most cemeteries do.

Grave or Memorial Marker – Often made of stone or metal, this memorial is placed over a grave or outside a crypt or vault. It is inscribed with the name of the deceased, often includes birth and death dates, and sometimes an epithet.

Grave – In funeral terms, hole dug in the ground into which a person is buried.

Graveside Service – A final service held graveside right before a the casket or urn is placed in the ground.

Gravestone - Often made of stone or metal, this memorial is placed over a grave or outside a crypt or vault. It is inscribed with the name of the deceased, often includes birth and death dates, and sometimes an epithet.

Green Burial – A form of burial which attempts to do as little harm to the environment as possible. Bodies are not embalmed and burial containers are usually made of material that will easily biodegrade.

Green Burial Council – A nonprofit organization that encourages environmentally sustainable death care and the use of burial as a means of protecting natural areas.

Green Cemetery – A cemetery that is wholly or partially dedicated to green burial practices.

Headstone – Often made of stone or metal, this memorial is placed over a grave or outside a crypt or vault. It is inscribed with the name of the deceased, often includes birth and death dates, and sometimes an epithet.

Hearse – A special car, often a hearse, used to transport a casketed body.

Honorary Pallbearers – Friends or family of the deceased who escort the casket of the deceased but do not actually carry it.

In State – The tradition of laying out the body of the deceased for viewing prior to burial.

Inquest – Usually held before a jury, a formal investigation into cause of death.

Inter – To bury.

Interment – The act of burying.

Intestate – The term used when a person has died without leaving a legal Will.

Inurnment – The process of placing cremated remains in an urn.

Lead Car – The first car in a funeral procession.

Letters Testamentary/Letters of Administration – An official document authorizing the executor to carry out the terms of a will.

Liabilities – In the settling of an estate, these are outstanding debts.

Life Insurance Trust - An irrevocable, non-amendable trust which is both the owner and beneficiary of one or more life insurance policies. Upon the death of the insured, rather than paying out the proceeds, the Trustee invests the insurance proceeds and administers the trust for one or more beneficiaries.

Living Trust – A trust that is set up and administered during the grantor's lifetime.

Living Will – A legal, written document that details the type and circumstances of medical care that a person desires if he/she is no longer able to make his/her desires known.

Lowering Device – A mechanical devise placed over an open grave that lowers the casket into the grave.

Mausoleum – A wall, room or building which houses casketed remains.

Medical Examiner – A physician certified by the government to determine cause of death, especially when cause is not natural.

Memorial – Something, especially a structure, that reminds others of a specific person.

Memorial Reef – An artificial reef created by mixing the cremated remains of individuals with concrete and then placing the structure on the floor of the ocean.

Memorial Service – A service or ceremony held in honor of someone who has died. Can be held at any time after the death.

Minister's Room – A designated room in some funeral homes where clergy can robe or ready themselves prior to officiating at a service.

Monument – In funeral terms, a statue or structure placed over a grave in honor of the person buried there.

Morgue – A room which may be in a hospital or county medical examiner's office where bodies are kept until such a time as next of kin can be found or, if the death was suspicious, where they are examined in order to determine cause of death.

Mortician – Another name for Funeral Director or Embalmer. The term is rarely used nowadays.

Mortuary – Another name for funeral home. Like "mortician", the term is no longer in vogue.

Mortuary Science – The processes and practices of handling the bodies of the dead.

Mourner – An attendee at a funeral or other service held for one who has died.

Natural Burial – A burial that respects the environment. The body is not preserved with toxic chemicals and, if a burial container is used, it is made of biodegradable materials. Manmade grave markers are rarely used and, rather, indigenous plants are encouraged to cover the grave.

Niche – In a columbarium, an individual space to hold one urn.

Obituary – A short article, usually placed in a newspaper, that informs the community that a death has occurred and includes some of the highlights of the decedent's life. Usually includes information about the funeral services to be held.

Opening and Closing Fees – Fees charged by a cemetery to dig a grave and re-fill it after the casket has been placed inside. Can also be charged for opening and closing a mausoleum vault.

Organ/Tissue Donation – The act of donating certain organs and body tissues upon death, so that they can be implanted in a living person and thereby improve or extend that person's life.

Outer Burial Container – A grave liner or vault placed around or over a casket to keep the ground from sinking over time.

Pallbearers – Friends or family members of the deceased chosen to carry the casket into or out of the funeral service.

Perpetual Care Trust Funds – A trust fund set up by a cemetery (and paid into by those who purchase plots) to ensure long-term maintenance of a grave.

Plastination – The process of preserving organs or body through forced impregnation of plastics.

Plot – Burial ground.

Prearranged Funeral Trust or Funeral Trust – A trust fund set up to ensure that monies paid into it by people who want to pre-pay for their funerals are correctly managed.

Pre-need or Pre-planning – The arrangement of and payment for one's funeral prior to death.

Pre-need Funeral Insurance – An insurance policy one can take out that will make sure there are funds available to pay for a funeral.

Preparation Room – A room in a funeral home where bodies are prepared for funeral services and final disposition.

Pre-Planning or Pre-need – The practice of making funeral arrangements, including financial arrangements, while still alive.

Probate – Judicial certification or authentication of a Will.

Promession – An ecologically-conscious method for disposing of human remains by freeze drying.

Purge – Discharge of bodily fluids from a body upon and after death.

Registrar – A local government official who carries out a number of government services. Can issue transportation, burial and cremation permits.

Remains - The body of the deceased.

Repose – The act of resting or the state of being at rest. In the funeral industry, refers to the body of the deceased.

Reposing Room – A room in some funeral homes where the body lays at rest prior to a service.

Restoration – The term given to the repair and grooming of a body prior to a viewing.

Restorative Art – The practice of restoring, repairing and grooming a body.

Retort – The cremation chamber.

Rigor Mortis – A temporary rigidity that sets a number of hours after death.

Scattering – The act of tossing cremated remains.

Selection Room – A room in a funeral home where various funeral products are displayed.

Service Car – A utility vehicle used by funeral homes to transport flowers, chairs, etc. used in services.

Slumber Room – A room in some funeral homes where the body lays at rest prior to a service.

Testator – A person who has made a will or left a legacy.

Tomb – A grave, vault or chamber used to house the dead.

Tombstone – Often made of stone or metal, this memorial is placed over a grave or outside a crypt or vault. It is inscribed with the name of the deceased, often includes birth and death dates, and sometimes an epithet.

Trade Embalmer – A licensed embalmer who does not work for one specific funeral home but, rather, offers his/her services to a number of different funeral homes.

Transit Permit/ Transportation Permit – A permit offered by local government to allow for the transportation of a body.

Trocar – A large-bore needle-like tool used to puncture and aspirate internal organs.

Trust – A legal entity or fund that holds assets in reserve for a beneficiary.

Undertaker – An out-of-date term referring to a funeral director.

Urn – In funeral terms, a container for holding cremated remains.

Urn Garden – An outdoor facility meant to hold a number of urns.

Urn Placement – The permanent placement of an urn in a columbarium, a niche, the ground, or other location.

Vault – A sometimes-sealable container that fully surrounds a casket. Some cemeteries require one to prevent the ground above a casket from sinking as it settles (other cemeteries require only a grave liner). Some families purchase one because they believe it will help to "preserve" their loved one's body by preventing water from seeping inside.

Viatical – The purchase of an existing life insurance policy from a terminally ill person in exchange for cash.

Video Tribute – A video created to honor the deceased.

Viewing – An open-casket service during which visitors may elect to "view" the deceased for the last time.

Vigil – In the Roman Catholic religion, this is a service or viewing held the night before the actual funeral mass.

Visitation – Prior to final disposition, when friends and family members can spend time with their loved one's body for the last time.

Visitation Room – A room within a funeral home where family and friends can visit with their loved one's body.

Wake – A watch kept over the deceased which can last the entire night before final disposition.

Will – A legal document let by the deceased stating how he/she would like his/her estate dispersed.

BIBLIOGRAPHY

Baum, Rachel, R., ed. *Funeral and Memorial Service Readings, Poems and Tributes.* London: McFarland & Company, 1999.

Carlson, Lisa, *Caring for the Dead,* Hinesburg, VT: Upper Access Books, 1998.

Carnell, Geoffrey C. *The Complete Guide to Funeral Planning.* Guilford, CT: The Lyons Press, 2005.

Chamberlain, Andrew T., and Michael Parker Pearson. *Earthly Remains.* New York: Oxford University Press, 2001.

Cochrane, Don. S. *Simply Essential Funeral Planning Kit.* North Vancouver: International Self-Counsel Press Ltd., 2002.

Cromer, Michelle. *Exit Strategy.* London: Penguin Books Ltd., 2006.

Fitzpatrick, Jeanne and Eileen M. Fitzpatrick. *A Better Way of Dying.* London: Penguin Books, 2010.

Frontline: The Undertaking. PBS Home Video, Mead Street Films, 2007.

Harris, Mark. *Grave Matters.* New York: Scribner, 2007.

Henningfield, Diane Andrews. *At Issue: Disposal of the Dead.* Detroit: Greenhaven Press, 2009.

Jokinen, Tom. *Curtains: Adventures of an Undertaker-in-Training.* Cambridge: Da Capo Press, 2010.

Kaufman, Sharon R. *...And a Time to Die.* New York: Scribner, 2005.

Kiernan, Stephen P. *Last Rights.* New York: St. Martin's Press, 2006.

Miller, Clarence W. *The Funeral Book.* San Francisco: Robert D. Reed, Publishers, 1994.

Rosen, Fred. *Cremation in America.* Amherst, NY: Prometheus Books, 2004.

Shaw, Eva. *What to do When a Loved One Dies.* Irvine, CA: Dickens Press, 1994.

York, Sarah. *Remembering Well.* San Francisco: Jossey-Bass, Inc., 2000.

SPECIAL THANKS

This book took many, many months to research and write. Through it all, my husband Tim encouraged me to continue. He listened patiently, night-after-night, as I focused on death, and jumped in with thoughtful suggestions whenever I foundered. Strangely, a book about death brought us closer together. He is, as he has always been, my North Star, and I am eternally grateful we met.

I would also like to offer special thanks to the following people. They have freely shared their knowledge, answered my endless questions, provided resources and background information, and generally made this a better book.

Joe Sehee
> The Green Burial Council
> 550-D
> St. Michaels Drive
> Santa Fe, NM 87505
> Phone: 888-966-3330

David Cates
> The Kimberly L. Cates Scholarship Fund
> Souhegan Scholarship Foundation
> PO Box 451, Mont Vernon, New Hampshire 03057
> kimcatesfund@gmail.com

Shawn M. Smith, Funeral Director
> Connecticut Funeral Home
> 273 S. Elm Street
> Wallingford, CT 06492
> Phone: (203) 269-4630
> http://www.connecticutfuneralcare.com/index.html

Peter Mäsak
> Promessa Organic AB
> COO Peter Mäsak
> Lyr-Bö 102
> 474 96 Nösund
> www.promessa.se

Captain Dennis Longaberger
> Coastal Sunset Memorial Services
> 125 Harbor Way, Ste. 13
> Santa Barbara, CA 93109
> Phone: 805-962-8222
> http://www.coastalsunsetmemorial.com/index.html

Meredyth Mellor

Promessa UK Ltd
Wellington House
East Road
Cambridge CB1 1BH
www.promessa.org.uk

Chad Isenogle

Dalbert,Woodruff and Isenogle *Funeral Home*
2880 Boudinot Avenue
Cincinnati, OH 45238-2499
Phone: 513-922-1010
http://www.funeralplan2.com/dw&isenoglefuneralhome/

Jerrigrace Lyons, Executive Director

Final Passages Institute of Conscious Dying
Home Funeral & Green Burial Education
P O Box 1721, Sebastopol, CA 95473
707-824-0268
www.finalpassages.org

Lisa Dorsey

Sales Office Manager/Representative
The Champion Company
P.O. Box 967
Springfield OH 45501
Phone: 800-328-0115
http://www.enigma-champion.com/index.html

ABOUT THE AUTHOR

Katherine Mariaca-Sullivan is a trained hospice volunteer with the Visiting Nurses Association of Manchester, New Hampshire. She is an author and artist whose paintings have been shown in the United States, Puerto Rico and Mexico. Katherine taught writing at Hesser College in NH, but now focuses on her own books and art. She earned a Bachelor of Science in Psychology from Tufts University and a Master of Fine Arts in Creative Writing from Lesley University.

Katherine's books include "The Complication of Sisters", a collection of illustrated microstories on the theme of "sisterhood", in both full color and black and white editions, "Ruby Jane: Is She REALLY a Pain?", written with Heather Maurice-Stirnweis.

Katherine lives in New Hampshire with her husband, Tim Sullivan, her son, Derek Calzada, her step-children, Katie and Connor Sullivan, as well as two dogs and a cat who thinks he is a dog. To contact Katherine, please visit her website, www.KatherineMariaca.com and click on the "Contact Me" button that floats the left of the page.

To learn more about Katherine, please visit her websites:

http://www.KatherineMariaca.com

http://TheEssentialeBooker.com

and her online shops for books and artwork:

http://etsy.com/shop/KatherineMariacaArt

http://www.etsy.com/shop/MadaketLane

http://www.etsy.com/shop/TakenLiterally

<u>Also from Madaket Lane Publishers</u>

Madaket Lane Publishers, established in 2011, is a boutique publishing agency that is dedicated to publishing meaningful, quality books for children, young adults and adults. For copies of our books, signed and dedicated by our authors, please visit:

http://www.etsy.com/shop/MadaketLane

Printed in Great Britain
by Amazon